£ 30 -

£ 495

CW00550600

WILLIAM JAMES

The Arguments of the Philosophers

EDITOR: TED HONDERICH
Professor of Philosophy, University College, London

The purpose of this series is to provide a contemporary assessment and history of the entire course of philosophical thought. Each book constitutes a detailed, critical introduction to the work of a philosopher of major influence and significance.

Already published in the series

WILLIAM JAMES

Graham Bird

Department of Philosophy
Manchester University

Routledge & Kegan Paul
London and New York

First published in 1986 by
Routledge & Kegan Paul plc

11 New Fetter Lane, London EC4P 4EE

Published in the USA by
Routledge & Kegan Paul Inc.
in association with Methuen Inc.
29 West 35th Street, New York, NY 10001

Set in 10 on 12 pt Garamond
by Inforum Ltd, Portsmouth
and printed in Great Britain
by The Thetford Press Ltd
Thetford, Norfolk

© Graham Bird 1986

No part of this book may be reproduced in
any form without permission from the publisher
except for the quotation of brief passages
in criticism

Library of Congress Cataloging in Publication Data

Bird, Graham.

William James.
(The arguments of the philosophers)
Bibliography: p.
Includes index.
1. James, William, 1842–1910. I. Title. II. Series.
B945.J24B39   1986   191   86–6569

British Library CIP Data also available

ISBN 0–7100–9602–X

Contents

Preface

Books which deal with James's philosophy as a whole are not all that common. Perry's monumental two volume work is a valuable, near contemporary, record of James's ideas. Ayer's more recent book, *The Origins of Pragmatism*, is a tour de force which notes and examines many of James's central ideas with brilliant and astonishing brevity. I count myself fortunate in having had the advantage of reading Ayer's work; even more fortunate in finding that Ayer leaves some items out and that I disagree with him in interpreting others.

I have tried to give a comprehensive survey of James's philosophical ideas. In particular I have been guided by the thought that his pragmatism is not so vulnerable to immediate objections as is often supposed. Where possible I have tried to indicate lines of development in his ideas which have been pursued, and sometimes challenged, by later philosophers. Those more recent ideas have had, however, to take second place to the account of James's own thought, and I regret that I have not been able to pursue them further. Apart from the usually interesting detail of James's philosophy I commend him in two general ways: First because his pragmatic temper in philosophy is perennially worth a reminder, and second because his empiricism adds a welcome zest to the discussion of the traditional Locke, Berkeley, and Hume.

I acknowledge with gratitude the help of the British Academy in providing a grant to examine the James archive in the Houghton Library, Harvard, during three weeks in 1983. I am grateful to the Houghton Library and to Alexander James for permission to publish material from the James archive, and I acknowledge also the helpfulness of the librarians in the Houghton Library, and of Helmut Heckscher, during my brief visit. I am glad to have received comments, criticism, and encouragement from Christopher Hookway, Cindy and Graham Macdonald, Stephen Priest, and the editor of the series, Ted Honderich.

Manchester, October 1985

Motto

Il n'y a point de doute que l'homme ne soit tenu d'accepter, d'affirmer, et de croire la vérité qui lui apporte plus d'utilité, de commodité, de perfection en tant qu'il est homme, par laquelle il peut engendrer en soi du contentement, de la consolation, de l'espérance, de la confiance, de la sûreté et en éloigner le déplaisir et le désespoir, et par conséquent qu'il doit embrasser celle qui est plus aimable et plus désirable de sa nature, et en laquelle il y'a plus d'être et plus de bien, et nier et mécroire et repousser l'opposée à celle-la comme fausse et ennemie de son profit. Là où s'il fait au rebours il abuse contre soi-même de son entendement, il renverse entièrement la règle de la nature, il combat et soi-même et l'ordre universel des choses.

(There is no doubt that man is bound to accept, to affirm, and to believe that truth which brings him more benefit, convenience, and human perfection, and by which he can provide for himself contentment, consolation, hope, confidence, and certainty, and banish pain and despair; he must consequently embrace what is more likeable and more desirable in his nature, in which he finds more well-being, and deny, disbelieve, and reject the opposite as false and inimical to his own advantage. Were he to do the reverse he would misdirect his intelligence against himself, entirely subvert the rule of nature, and struggle against both himself and the universal order of things.)

(From Montaigne *L'Apologie de Raymond Sebond*. Quoted in James's unpublished manuscripts in the Houghton Library, Harvard B 4424.)

1

Introduction

William James was born in New York on January 11 1842, the first son of Mary and Henry James. His grandfather, also called William, had amassed a large fortune after emigrating from Ireland in the eighteenth century, and a portion of this wealth passed to Henry. After a rather unsettled youth and a period of training in theology Henry James devoted himself to writing on philosophical and theological topics. He became a disciple of Swedenborg and produced articles and pamphlets on the subject. His conversion to Swedenborgianism seems to have been triggered by a vivid hallucinatory experience, later diagnosed in Swedenborgian terms as a 'vastation'. This dramatic episode, and a subsequent period of serious depression, were later mirrored in some similar, equally dramatic, experiences of William James himself.[1] Although they did not result in William's conversion to Swedenborgian doctrines they nevertheless had a profound effect on his later life and thought. In a more indirect way this was true as well of Henry's influence on his son. William retained a deep and lifelong commitment to religious belief[2] which was manifested most publicly in his book *The Varieties of Religious Experience*. In that work there are clear echoes of Swedenborgian doctrine, and in William's later edition of a collection of his father's writings there is a recognition of his father's influence.

The James family was remarkable in many ways. It contained not only the novelist and playwright Henry junior, the second child, with whom William retained the strongest ties, but also a sister, Alice, and two younger brothers, Wilkinson and Robertson. The family travelled a good deal and the children quickly became familiar with Europe. Henry James's novels characteristically portray the contacts and interaction between wealthy Americans and European society at the turn of the century, and both older children must have experienced something of this at first hand. Both William and Henry spent long periods of their later lives in Europe, although only Henry made a permanent home there, eventually in Lamb

House, Rye. William, by contrast, felt and remained essentially American,[3] settled in Cambridge, near Boston, and kept a country retreat in the White Mountains at Chocorua in New Hampshire, where he died in 1910. William's familiarity with Europe and with European languages and culture enabled him to move with ease among the philosophers and psychologists of England, France, Germany, Belgium and Italy. One of James's biographers neatly captures this aspect of his life in writing:

> Il a pu passer en Amérique pour le plus cosmopolite, et en Europe pour le plus américain des philosophes.[4]

> (He was able to pass in America for the most cosmopolitan, and in Europe for the most American of philosophers.)

Before William James settled on a University career he spent a period studying art in Rhode Island, with the aim of deciding whether he should become an artist. His father seems to have been hostile to the idea of a permanent commitment to art but accepted the temporary experiment, and after a trial period William himself regarded his talent as insufficient for a career in art. He enrolled in the Lawrence Scientific School in 1861, and in the Harvard Medical School in 1863. Some facsimile versions of William's drawings and paintings can still be seen in the archives at Harvard's Houghton Library and most viewers would, I think, be surprised to find how talented he was. The quality of his work makes it natural to expect some regret on William's part at having to abandon an artistic career. It would be natural, too, to connect such regret with the unsettled period of emotional disturbance and physical ill-health which he began to suffer soon afterwards. Commentators, however, disagree on the importance of James's decision, and whatever regrets he may have felt he nevertheless embarked on an academic career which took him from medicine and physiology to psychology and philosophy.

Before he graduated from the medical school in 1869 he joined the Thayer expedition to Brazil with the noted American geologist Louis Agassiz. He was away from April 1865 to March 1866 and, particularly in the early period when he suffered a bad attack from a form of smallpox, plainly had serious regrets about his participation in the work. At the end of the period he expressed in his letters his great pleasure at the prospect of returning home, though a year later he again interrupted his work in Boston to spend a period in Europe. In part this was to study physiology in Germany, but in part it reflected a concern about ill-health. Perry records that 'He was now embarking upon a period of partial incapacity, physical suffering and depression, which lasted for nearly five years.'[5] This extended over the crisis period from 1869–1870, and began to be relieved only in the later 1870's after he had begun teaching at Harvard and had married Alice Gibbens in 1878.

In later life, in a letter to his colleague Hugo Münsterberg,[6] James recalled a conversation he had had in which a doctor had said that the recipe for a long and productive life was to be broken down in health before the age of thirty. James commented that this had been true of him, and implied that the doctor's hypothesis was confirmed by his own case. His health was evidently less than robust even before the crisis period. Perry reports that his physical frailty precluded the possibility of enlistment in the Civil War in 1861, though the two younger brothers both enlisted later. One commentator has argued,[7] in the light of the severity of James's medical symptoms, that he must have had a strong underlying personality to recover without extended medical treatment, but there is some evidence that he was for a time a patient at a mental hospital in Boston.[8] There can, in any case, be no doubt that his medical history qualifies James as one of those, like David Hume or Charles Darwin, for whom a period of serious ill-health in early life had a lasting effect on their life and work.

Between 1873 and 1876 James taught anatomy and physiology at Harvard. He began also to teach psychology there in 1875, and was made an assistant professor of psychology in 1876 and of philosophy in 1880. From the late 1870's he began to publish regular articles on psychology and cognition, many of which were later incorporated in his first major work *The Principles of Psychology*, published in 1890. It soon became accepted, and is still widely regarded, as one of the best psychological text books ever written. It made James's reputation both in America and Europe, but its publication also marked a transition in James's career from psychology to philosophy.

The transition was not all that decisively marked at the time. James already held a chair of philosophy. *The Principles* contains much that is recognisably philosophical, despite the fact that in it James draws a sharp line between psychological and metaphysical issues. In 1892 he published an abridged version in which he sought to exclude 'all the polemical and historical matter, all the metaphysical discussions and purely speculative passages'.[9] Thereafter, apart from his psychologist's interest in education, his published work became more and more philosophical.[10] It is likely that his own temperament, and some early influences, steered him in this direction. The crisis of 1869–70 had at its centre an intellectual and personal problem over free will and morality. Even at that early period James was reading much philosophy and later acknowledged the help he had received from the works of Charles Renouvier in resolving those problems.[11] But equally a certain impatience with experimental work in psychology, already evident in the *Principles*, and a physical incapacity for long periods of laboratory work also no doubt encouraged the transition. Though James regarded himself as one of the principal founders of experimental psychology in America, it was he who tempted Hugo Münsterberg to Harvard from Germany with the express aim of establishing an adequate experimental laboratory. James felt that he had neither enough capacity for, nor enough interest in, such experimental work to achieve that goal himself.

James was strongly influenced by his lifelong friend Charles Peirce, whose cause he persistently tried to promote at Harvard, though without much success. Peirce's best known articles on Pragmatism, 'The Fixation of Belief' and 'How To Make Our Ideas Clear', were published in the *Popular Science Monthly* in 1877 and 1878. In a footnote to the former Peirce indicates that their doctrines were already known to friends as 'Pragmatism', though he acknowledges that it was only later that 'the potent pen of Professor James brought their chief thesis to the attention of the philosophical world'.[12] James in turn frequently acknowledged his debt to Peirce, though his views by no means coincided exactly with those of his friend. In particular James was unsympathetic to the background of formal logic which Peirce exploited in his philosophical work. At the other extreme Peirce himself indicated certain metaphysical ideas, such as a belief in the absolute, which he held, but which he thought James could not accept. James was generally unhappy with the formal disciplines of logic and mathematics, and his mistrust of them forms part of an anti-intellectualism which runs through his work. Though there is no evidence to substantiate the idea it is easy to read the description in the *Principles* of the colleague who puts off the preparation of his lecture on formal logic as a description of himself.[13]

James's principal philosophy is published in a scattered and incomplete form. He himself complained, in a letter to Schiller, that his published work often arose from invitations to give popular lectures, so that his text presents an agreeable surface rather than hard or detailed argument.[14] This is true, as he indicated, of what is probably his best known philosophical work, the lectures on *Pragmatism* delivered at the Lowell Institute in 1906 and 1907. Some of his other major works, such as *The Will To Believe* (1897), *The Meaning of Truth* (1910), and *Essays in Radical Empiricism* (1912) consist of separate articles written over a long period. Though the publication dates broadly indicate the sequence of James's thoughts, particular essays are sometimes at odds with that sequence. One of the essays collected in *Essays in Radical Empiricism* was written before the title essay of *The Will To Believe*. The items collected in *The Meaning of Truth* generally comment on issues arising out of *Pragmatism*, but others address problems from James's radical empiricism. *Memories and Studies* (1911) is a miscellaneous collection of essays mainly concerned with people such as Agassiz, Myers, or Emerson, who influenced James, but it includes also an eye-witness account of the California earthquake in 1906 and an account of his interest in psychical research. *Collected Essays and Reviews* was edited by R.B. Perry and published in 1920. James published also his Hibbert lectures, *A Pluralistic Universe*, in 1909, a year before his death, and a projected introduction to philosophy, *Some Problems of Philosophy*, was published in 1911 in a version which he described as 'fragmentary and unrevised'.

James added a further dimension to his reputation with the delivery and publication in 1901–2 of the Edinburgh Gifford lectures, *The Varieties of Religious Experience*. In these lectures James came back to preoccupations with religion which had arisen in his relations with his father and in his earliest published philosophy in *The Will To Believe*. Though most of James's output is epistemological in character it would be misleading to allow that interest to eclipse his views on morality and religion. It was pointed out earlier that a problem about freedom and morality was a central issue in his 1869–70 crisis, and there is no doubt that he felt a strong personal need for both moral and religious beliefs. Though one part of his anti-intellectualism prevented him from ever subordinating those personal needs to intellectual arguments about morality or religion, he nevertheless constructed a philosophical account of these aspects of human life. His emphasis on the 'manly' virtues, on what he called the energetic and strenuous life, and on the doctrine of 'meliorism' which was designed to replace both pessimism and optimism, contrast interestingly with the morbidity and depression to which he had himself evidently been a prey. His views on religion, on morality, and on our beliefs about what might be called such 'non-cognitive' topics,[15] cannot be divorced from other aspects of his philosophy. This is true for at least two reasons. It is true, of course, simply because these views are a part of, and complete, James's overall philosophy. But it is also true because the notion of belief, which is at the centre of his non-cognitive interests, is also centrally involved in James's psychology and epistemology.

James's philosophical background, despite his initial commitment to psychology, is in part quite conventional. He was familiar with the standard figures of modern philosophy and held strong views about the traditional empiricists, about Kant, about Hegel and the post-Kantian idealists. Though he regarded himself as an empiricist he nevertheless thought that traditional empiricists had made a fundamental mistake. His own doctrine of 'radical empiricism' was designed in order to rectify that error. By contrast he had little sympathy with Hegel or with the later post-Kantian idealists in Germany or in Britain. Though he clearly re-tained a strong personal affection for his colleague at Harvard, Josiah Royce, he tended to see Bradley and Royce as the principal opponents to his own ideas.

Since James believed that neither the empiricists nor what he called the rationalists were wholly right, but that the former were closer to the truth than the latter, it would not be surprising to find James allying himself with the philosophy of Kant. But, though he treated Kant[16] with far more respect than Hegel[17] and even acknowledged the former's influence on his own philosophy, he did not approve of Kant either. Principally he was suspicious of the 'transcendentalism' in Kant and its later development in the nineteenth century idealist philosophers. This comes out most strongly in James's criticisms of Kant's and later philosophers' appeal to a supposed 'transcendental ego' in their accounts of the self. No doubt it was partly for this reason that James said that 'the right way with Kant is not so much *through* as *round* him'.[18] Yet there is more of an affinity here than James was inclined to admit. A French writer, Claparède, made a shrewd comment on this just after James's death when he said:

> Ce n'est que pour Kant que James a été quelque peu injuste. S'achoppant à la barbarie de son style, il n'a pas su retrouver dans le philosophe de Königsberg des idées et des aspirations bien conformes aux siennes. Car le pragmatisme et l'humanisme ne sont, à bien des égards, que du Kantisme refondu dans un creuset anglo-saxon.[19]

> (It is only to Kant that James was somewhat unfair. Stumbling over the barbarity of Kant's style he was unable to detect in the philosopher from Königsberg ideas and goals very similar to his own. For pragmatism and humanism are in many ways no more than Kantianism recast in an anglo-saxon mould.)

In other respects, however, the background to James's views is more difficult for us to recover. For one thing his initial interests were formally in psychology rather than in philosophy. It is true that he clearly recognised empiricists such as Locke, Hume, or Herbart as precursors of his own psychology. Equally we do not find it hard now to accept the powerful influence on James of contemporary Darwinism, though it is perhaps more difficult for us to appreciate the impact of Darwin's views at that time. But in any case James was prepared to be critical of Darwin himself, and was even more critical of popular philosophical extensions of evolutionary theory in such work as that of Spencer. In these respects James's psychological background and interests are not so foreign to those of present-day psychologists and philosophers.

Nevertheless James was involved with psychology in a crucial period of its development with which we have few contacts. Writers in psychology such as Stumpf or Wundt, Charcot or Janet, Ward or Myers are, perhaps unfairly, less well known now than in James's day. The issues of method which were alive to them, at a time when psychology was beginning to break away from philosophy, may not seem so to us now that the separation seems even more marked. Certainly during the heyday of later behaviourism those methodological issues were widely regarded as resolved. Watson, who paid a grudging respect to James, might have conceded that James's work pointed in the right direction, though it did not go nearly far enough. He spoke of James's views as if they were, even in his time, as out of date as a horse and carriage in the age of the car, and said: 'We have all been brought up on James, or possibly on an even worse diet, and it is hard to run counter to him.'[20] If later doubts about behaviourism have produced other models in psychology such as the computer models of artificial intelligence, these cannot take us back simply to the issues James faced in 1890. It remains to be seen whether his views nevertheless have some relevance to current ideas in philosophy or psychology.

The same general point can be made about the immediate background to James's philosophy. Many of the philosophers he admired, such as Renouvier, Bergson, or Shadworth Hodgson; many of the philosophers he opposed, such as Green, Royce, or even Bradley; and many of the philosophers who admired and followed him, such as Schiller, Papini, or even Dewey, are much less well known now. For a time pragmatism, the doctrine with which James was most closely associated, became an influential philosophy. Apart from its strict disciples, even philosophers critical of the doctrine, such as Russell, nevertheless acknowledged a debt to James.[21] They recognised pragmatism as one of the powerful forces attempting to break with an orthodox idealist metaphysical tradition, and accepted it as an ally. But there were other more powerful voices uttering, and extending the same message. Developments in logic, to which James was unsympathetic, produced movements such as logical atomism and logical positivism which seemed to provide a more solid foundation for their philosophical views.

Pragmatism in general, and James's writing in particular, have been influential in the later development of American philosophy. But even in that context their influence may seem to be overshadowed by the work of philosophers like C.I. Lewis, Carnap, or Quine who were more influenced by, and better equipped in, logic than James was. To some extent the apparent eclipse of pragmatism behind these later developments is a mark of its success. Many of the ideas central to, and sometimes originating in, pragmatism have passed into philosophical folk-lore. The notion of a cash-value for philosophical concepts, the method of exemplifying general philosophical claims in particular cases in order to examine them, distinctions between hard and soft determinism and knowledge by description and by acquaintance were all central features of James's philosophy even if he did not invent them. More importantly a certain general attitude of hostility to mystification in metaphysics which pragmatism shared with later movements like positivism has been widely accepted in philosophy and owes a large part of its origin to James. As in the case of his psychology the powerful doctrines which tended to eclipse James's philosophical ideas have now themselves moved to one side, and perhaps enable us to get a clearer view of James's overall position.

Since it is not the aim of this book to chronicle the period in which James developed his philosophy, or the subsequent periods in which it passed into philosophical folk-lore and became somewhat neglected, it is not necessary to fill out more of the background to James's views. In particular it is not my intention to deal more fully with the views of other pragmatist philosophers, or to make comparisons between James and Peirce or James and Dewey. The intention here is rather to present James's philosophical ideas and the arguments on which they rest. I therefore end this section by indicating the central features of James's philosophy on which I shall concentrate, and some of the connecting links between them.

James's philosophy is inevitably linked with the pragmatism which he made popular. It is, however, sometimes suggested that this association distorts James's own views,[22] though it is hard to see the ground for such a suggestion. It is, of course, true that pragmatist ideas were canvassed by Peirce well before James published his own philosophical works, and that James knew of and was influenced by those ideas. James's own book *Pragmatism* was not published until 1907, but even before that both in the *Principles* and *The Will To Believe* there are clear indications of a pragmatic view of both philosophical and psychological issues.[23] Though the term 'pragmatism' does not figure in the index to the *Principles* it is not hard to find arguments in that work which echo pragmatic methods. It would surely be wrong to think that James's pragmatism was simply a doctrine he held for a limited time around 1906. It is also true that James evidently toyed with some doctrines, such as panpsychism,[24] at various periods of his career, which sit awkwardly with the central doctrines of pragmatism itself. But I shall treat 'pragmatism' as a suitable general name for James's philosophical views.

It might be thought that James's association with pragmatism somehow distorts the interest he shows in what might be called the 'non-cognitive' areas of morality and religion. But it has already been suggested that James's pragmatism concerns essentially both cognitive and non-cognitive areas, both epistemology and moral or religious philosophy. Not only were the latter issues of a crucial personal importance in his own philo-sophical development, but, as I indicated, the central notion of belief precisely spans the gap between the two areas. It would not be too much to say that James's notion of belief, and the notion of truth that went with it, were designed in part to eliminate, or perhaps re-characterise, that sup-posed gap. To treat James's pragmatism as though it were exclusively epistemological in character would certainly be to distort James's philoso-phy, but it would be just as much a distortion of his pragmatism itself. So long as that pragmatism is understood, as it should be, in this inclusive way, there is no danger of the canvassed distortion.

The publication dates of James's major works may suggest a clear chronological progress in the development of his ideas, though I noted earlier how misleading this can be. Certainly the individual collections of essays contain items from different chronological periods. What is really more striking throughout James's writing is the strong continuity it displays from his early to his later work. The central issues in *The Will To Believe* antedate the publication of the *Principles*, but those issues are taken up again in the later *Pragmatism* and *The Varieties of Religious Experience*. James refers to his doctrine of 'radical empiricism' already in the preface to *The Will To Believe* though his *Essays in Radical Empiricism* were collected and published much later. Those later essays themselves take up issues with which James had been concerned both in *Pragmatism* and *The Meaning of Truth* and also in the earlier *Principles*.

It would, of course, be quite wrong to think that James never changed his mind, or that his thought did not develop. There are evident differences of view about the mind-body problem in the *Principles* and in the later elaboration of what has been called James's 'neutral monism'.[25] It has been suggested that his views on the self changed importantly from his early work to the later.[26] There is some evidence that James adhered to a doctrine of panpsychism in *A Pluralistic Universe*, though on other occasions he seems to reject such a doctrine. And Ayer[27] rightly notes an odd and apparently Platonistic view of concepts canvassed in the *Essays in Radical Empiricism*. But all these points of change seem quite minor against the major background of continuity in James's thought. Though I shall on occasion note such variations I shall, for the most part, treat James's philosophy as a coherent whole, rather than attempt a detailed chronological survey of his development.

On that basis the first item to consider must be James's pragmatism itself. James says that pragmatism is both a method and a theory of truth. Neither aspect has been regarded as well defined. The method, as the name 'pragmatism' seems to imply, appears to rest on no principled foundation, and this has been regarded by many as a handicap. This alone has encouraged later philosophers to prefer other doctrines, such as logical positivism, which offered a more explicit ideology. The theory of truth has also been extensively criticised. Here the central problem has been less the unclarity of the theory than its initial unplausibility, at least in some of the versions offered by James. When he claimed, for example, in a famous passage that 'The true . . . is only the expedient in our way of thinking, just as the right is only the expedient in the way of our behaving',[28] his view, like his equation of the true and the useful, seemed to many to be doubly objectionable. For not only did those critics believe that the truth was often, and correctly, to be contrasted with the expedient rather than identified with it, but they also disapproved even more strongly of the allegedly supporting equation of the expedient and the right.

James attempted to rebut these criticisms, especially in *The Meaning of Truth*, and generally took the view that these initial objections were simply shallow misunderstandings of his position. But he also came to recognise that he had not succeeded in making his theory quite clear, and he further admitted that the account had provided a sketch in need of further elaboration rather than a fully articulated theory. In the next two sections I shall deal with these two central aspects of James's pragmatism.

James recognised that his pragmatism fitted naturally into an empiricist tradition. It may therefore come as a surprise that even in his early *Principles*, and consistently in his later writing, he was highly critical of the traditional empiricists. Moreover, he makes it clear in *Pragmatism* that the two doctrines are strictly independent; that is, that it would at least be possible to be a pragmatist without being also an empiricist. James's 'radical empiricism' consequently takes his philosophy one step further and attempts to remedy defects which he claimed to find in the standard empiricist tradition. This further doctrine, however, presents a number of detailed puzzles, as well as one central problem. For it would be natural to think that any *radical* empiricism must be an extreme form of such a philosophy, though this plainly does not square with other views that James held. James famously distinguished, in *Pragmatism*, between what he called 'tough-minded' (empiricist) and 'tender-minded' (rationalist) philosophies.[29] It was evidently his intention to reconcile these temperamental tugs in opposite directions, but it is difficult to see how that intention is to be fulfilled if he is himself an extreme empiricist.

The problem, however, turns out to be illusory, because the supposition on which it rests is faulty. Perhaps James chose his title unwisely, but it is natural to resolve the apparent conflict by denying that 'radical' empiricism is an extreme form of the doctrine. Such a view is in any case borne out by the detail of James's own doctrine. If we regard the logical positivists as the natural successors to traditional empiricism, then James would certainly have wanted to classify them as 'tough-minded' along with other extreme empiricists whose views James wished to reject. There still remain problems about the attempted reconciliation of the two temperaments, but to recognise that 'radical' does not mean 'extreme' in this context is at least to remove one obstacle to that reconciliation.

That natural resolution of the general issue nevertheless rests on the specific form of James's empiricism and this will be considered in the next section. But that specific form has also strong links with James's views on psychology and his account of the mind-body problem. It would be inappropriate in this series to attend comprehensively to the rich and influential detail of James's psychology. Radical empiricism, however, has at its centre a doctrine of 'pure experience', sometimes called 'neutral monism', devised by James both as a general account of knowledge and as a philosophical resolution of the mind-body problem. The doctrine was acknowledged and partially endorsed in Russell's *Analysis of Mind* and deserves to be considered along with James's views about the science of psychology. In this way James's epistemology fits very closely into what we should now call his philosophical psychology. In the sections after the discussion of radical empiricism I shall therefore examine these issues in the philosophy of mind and look also at a selection of the specific topics in psychology to which James made a contribution. His account of the emotions, for example, associated with the Danish psychologist Lange, has attracted later philosophical and psychological comment.

Finally in the last section I gather a range of issues central to James's tender-minded rather than tough-minded attitude. It was indicated earlier that James's philosophy is essentially concerned not only with theory of knowledge but also with what might be called 'non-cognitive' attitudes, such as beliefs about morality and religion. This interest is, indeed, so important to James that there is even doubt about whether we should characterise such attitudes as 'non-cognitive' at all. For we shall find that James's theory of truth, and the pragmatism of which it forms an integral part, are designed to make room for such attitudes within a framework of truth. James, like Kant, wished to make room for faith, but, unlike Kant, he wanted to do this not by restricting but rather by extending knowledge or truth. This provides a further anxiety about James's account of truth, since there must be doubt about the soundness of any extension of truth beyond the bounds of ordinary cognitive or factual claims.

That anxiety is, of course, part of a more general question whether James can reconcile the opposed tough-minded and tender-minded temperaments in philosophy. That difficulty may provide another ground for thinking that James's pragmatism distorts his overall philosophy. For it may be thought that commentators faced with a choice between James's pragmatic epistemology and, say, his philosophy of religion tend to choose the former and to neglect the latter. In the face of such a decisive choice, of course, that outcome is perfectly possible, but I have suggested already that James's pragmatism itself already contains these potentially conflicting elements. If his overall philosophy turns out to be inconsistent in this way, then so will his pragmatism.

That threatened inconsistency remains to be demonstrated, and the demonstration will not be easy. For one thing the conflict is not simply between cognitive beliefs in science and affective beliefs in religion, but involves also the contrast between factual beliefs and beliefs about values. In its most general form, indeed, the conflict is wider still between what James calls our 'intellectual' and our 'passional' interests. When this wider range of beliefs is brought into view it becomes at least more plausible to see them as forming a continuous spectrum rather than as marking at some point a strict and impassable barrier. And this was in essence James's own view.

Another obstacle to the demonstration of an inconsistency in this area arises from the fact that James was himself well aware of the dangers in his own position. In his early paper 'The Will to Believe', which later gave its title to the collection of essays, James confronted the opposition in views ascribed to W.K. Clifford and sought to justify his own view against that opposition. He argues that in certain circumscribed contexts we are justified in holding beliefs without strict evidence for them. He believed this to be true not only of beliefs in religion but also of moral beliefs and of beliefs about inter-personal relationships. These views form a part of James's 'melioristic' moral philosophy, and are inevitably strongly linked to his views about free-will. His interest in, and discussion of, free-will go back not only to *Pragmatism* but also to the *Principles* and to his own earlier personal crisis. They provide another example of the strong continuity of thought throughout James's work.

That same continuity is shown in one further aspect of James's account of religious belief. From an early point in his career James had known of, and been interested in, what might be called abnormal extensions of consciousness. He was familiar with the case histories of the French psychologists Janet and Charcot, had reviewed work by Freud and Breuer, and generally approved of Myers's appeal to a 'subliminal' consciousness.[30] He even met Freud on one occasion in America.[31] He was himself actively involved in psychical research and was at least open to the idea that certain abnormal states might provide clues to the understanding of religious beliefs. This was, of course, a guiding principle in his examination of religious faith in *The Varieties of Religious Experience*. He was there at least willing to consider the claim that such states might reveal an underlying truth, a claim which he thought such experiences inevitably led their owners to make. Put in this rather bald way such views may sound extravagant and at odds with the generally down to earth attitudes of pragmatism. But it should be noted that James was also deeply sceptical of many claims made for psychical research. He believed that many of the fashionable mediums of his day were demonstrable frauds, though he admitted that one case, that of Mrs. Piper, eluded his scepticism.[32] On the other side, though, he was equally sceptical of a scientific establishment which dismissed all such cases out of hand in a way which he regarded as wholly unscientific.

This package of issues, relating to the general doctrine of meliorism, provides the final section of the book. It may seem that in putting it last I am already evincing an epistemological bias in presenting James's philosophy. But it may also be said in defence that this context provides the final, and crucial, test for the adequacy of that philosophy, and that to put it in the final position is to acknowledge its importance rather than to diminish it.

James has been appropriated for diverse schools of philosophy by various commentators. He has been associated with phenomenology, presented as a mainstream British empiricist, and claimed for Whitehead's 'process' philosophy.[33] Though I will sometimes offer comments on other interpretations of his views I have no wish to appropriate him to any particular ideology. James was not himself a pompous character[34] and would, I think, have been rather amused by these proprietary instincts. For the same general reason I shall avoid labelling his doctrines, since labels such as 'pragmatism' itself or 'coherence' are often misleading and uninformative rather than illuminating. My aim is rather to give an accurate account of his views and the grounds on which he held them. I shall also comment on and criticise some of these views, and link them with the ideas of other and later philosophers where these seem to conform to or usefully extend James's own position.

One final proviso might usefully be made. I have noted, as have other commentators, that there is a strong anti-intellectualist strain in James's thought. It appears informally in his attitude to logic, in his psychological methods, and in his view that ultimately philosophical disagreements reflect differences of temperament which are not susceptible of rational argument or decision. It appears, more formally, in the many disparaging comments he makes about metaphysics, about 'Erkenntnisstheorie',[35] and about the limitations of intellectual argument. More constructively it appears strongly in his view that on important matters our 'passional' interests have priority over our 'intellectual' arguments. One consequence of such views is that James is less alive to the philosophical demand for argument than philosophers commonly have been, or now are. Some of his beliefs just seemed to him to be unassailably true, and in need of no dialectical support. Others seemed to him to be empirical hypotheses for which argument was less relevant than factual evidence or just common sense. Such views were not simply the result of carelessness or insensitivity, but a consequence of his own deep suspicion of the dangers and errors of intellectualism itself.[36] Few would deny that such dangers and errors exist, but it is a further matter always to draw the line between what needs argument and what does not in the right place. In some cases it may be necessary to consider arguments in favour of James's views which he did not himself explicitly canvass. For the present it is worth noting that the anti-intellectualism which sometimes calls for this supplementation was not itself merely a prejudice on James's part but rather an integral part of his overall philosophy.

2

Pragmatic Method

In his lectures on *Pragmatism* James summarises his views in the following way: 'Such then would be the scope of pragmatism – first, a method; and second a genetic theory of what is meant by truth.'[1] The two aspects are connected in at least this way. The method is a means of settling disputes, and one philosophical dispute arises over the nature of truth. Later, in his Preface to *The Meaning of Truth*, he outlines the three central tenets of 'radical empiricism', of which at least the first has some relevance to James's pragmatic method. For the first item is the postulate 'that the only things that shall be debatable among philosophers shall be things definable in terms drawn from experience'. James later refers back to the idea of things of an 'inexperiencable nature' and says of them that while they may exist they form no part of the material for philosophical debate.[2] It is plain that his empiricism has strong links with his pragmatic method, though he himself regarded the two things as logically independent of each other. He says, for example,

> To avoid one misunderstanding at least let me say that there is no logical connection between pragmatism, as I understand it, and a doctrine I have recently set forth as 'radical empiricism'. The latter stands on its own feet. One may entirely reject it, and still be a pragmatist.[3]

He nevertheless allows that the pragmatist account of truth does offer support for radical empiricism when he says: 'Were this pragmatic contention admitted, one great point in the victory of radical empiricism would also be scored.'[4]

Pragmatism, then, is not equivalent to radical empiricism, and does not entail it, but at least part of pragmatism may lend support to the latter doctrine. I make these points here not to resolve the issues about the connections or disconnections between pragmatism and radical empiricism, but only to draw attention to the complex relationship in question.[5] Evidently radical empiricism is intended to add something to pragmatism rather than merely to repeat it. It is for this reason that I consider first James's pragmatic method, then his theory of truth, and then his empiricism.

James deploys a wide range of metaphors to outline his pragmatic method. In the story about Clerk Maxwell's childhood he talks of explaining the 'go' of things, that is, how they actually work. Elsewhere he speaks of 'putting concepts at work', of their 'cash-value', or of their 'fighting weight'. He also frequently adopts a terminology from his friend Shadworth Hodgson to ask of some puzzling item 'What is it "known-as"?'. These metaphors respond initially to two relatively uncontroversial ideas in philosophy. One is that since philosophers typically deal with a range of abstract and difficult concepts, it must be a part of their role to clear up the difficulties and obscurities in those ideas. Many traditional philosophers recognised this point and James endorses it in many ways. In one passage, for example, he enthusiastically claims a priority for Scottish and English philosophers in developing a 'critical' philosophy even before Kant.[6] More importantly he makes the point by referring to what he calls 'Peirce's Principle', taken from 'How To Make Our Ideas Clear'. 'To attain perfect clearness in our thoughts of an object, then, we need only consider what conceivable effects of a practical kind the object may involve . . .'[7]

Nothing is so far said of the *restriction* to philosophy to such a task of clarification. It is plainly possible to accept the general point but to insist nevertheless on other, more constructive, roles for philosophy. James explicitly treated the clarifying task of pragmatic method as a prelude to further work, when he said:

> But if you follow the pragmatic method you cannot look on any such
> word as closing your quest. You must bring out of each word its
> practical cash-value, set it at work within the stream of your
> experience. It appears less as a solution, then, than as a programme for
> more work . . .[8]

Such a view is reinforced by James's conception of philosophical claims as hypotheses. He says that in every genuine metaphysical dispute some practical issue, however remote or conjectural, is involved. In his earlier discussion of the 'freezing out' of what he calls 'ultra-rationalistic philosophy'[9] he likens this to the freezing out of the courtier type in republics. In such a circumstance, he claims: 'Science and metaphysics would come much nearer together, would in fact work absolutely hand in hand.'[10] It might be said that James's view is understandable in the light of his own work in projecting philosophical ideas onto a testable plane in psychology. There is plainly some truth in this, but James also envisaged a more general application for these ideas.

The second idea to which these metaphors respond is a more complex enlargement of the first. For it is at least a possibility that where concepts are blurred, obscure or confused, they may generate apparent hypotheses which, however, strictly cannot be put to any test, or cannot be put 'at work'. In such cases, there may then be no rational ground for accepting or rejecting such claims. James believed that it was typical of philosophical issues that they were liable to generate just such apparent, but spurious, hypotheses. He says at one point: 'The pragmatic method is primarily a method of settling metaphysical disputes that otherwise might be interminable.'[11] James does not mean by 'interminable' simply 'long lasting'. The notion of a 'terminus' arrived at in testing some claim has an almost technical significance in his later account of radical empiricism. Rather what he is drawing attention to is the existence of metaphysical disputes for which no terminus is possible. In such a case the supposed hypothesis has moved into the trans-empirical realm of inexperienceable things where, according to his postulate, there is no proper material for philosophical debate.

This second, extended, idea is close to two similar and influential philosophical doctrines. One, deriving partly from Kant, is the distinction between immanent and transcendent claims[12] or interpretations of claims. If we identify transcendent claims as those which are beyond any test or terminus, then James's view, like Kant's, rejects these as proper matters for dispute. Such claims, if they ever are to present genuine material, must be interpreted in some immanent way, that is, in some way related to experienceable phenomena. The other doctrine is associated with the logical positivists', or Hume's, further belief that such transcendent claims are simply meaningless. James's view, as I have so far outlined it, falls short of this positivist belief. It is one thing to reject transcendent, untestable, claims as futile and not worthy of serious attention, and quite another to reject them as strictly without meaning.

It would, however, be wrong to think that James made no connection between pragmatic method and meaning. His endorsement of Peirce's principle makes it clear that he accepted some such connection. In that same passage, moreover, he continues, 'Our conception of these effects . . . is then for us the whole of our conception of the object, so far as that conception has positive significance at all.'[13] Equally in using the method to establish the differences that would be made practically to anyone if a belief were true James clearly draws conclusions about the meaning of the belief. In particular, of two supposed alternatives, 'if no practical difference whatever can be traced, then the alternatives mean practically the same thing, and all dispute is idle.'[14]

On other occasions, however, the references to meaning are either less obvious or even absent. In *The Meaning of Truth*, for example, James writes

All that the pragmatic method implies is that truths should have practical consequences. In England the word ('pragmatism') has been used more broadly still to cover the notion that the truth of any statement *consists* in the consequences. . . . Here we get beyond affairs of method altogether; and since my pragmatism and this wider pragmatism are so different, I think that Mr. Schiller's proposal to call the wider pragmatism by the name of 'humanism' ought to be adopted. The narrower pragmatism may still be spoken of as the 'pragmatic method'.[15]

Here James seems to draw again a distinction between pragmatism's method and its theory of truth. What he says of the method here is rather carelessly formulated. We might wonder whether this is really *all* that the method implies, or indeed how we might stop truths from having practical consequences. But the method, so construed, seems to be differentiated from an account of truth, and to be still more remote from any theory of meaning.

James evidently envisages at least three connected uses for his pragmatic method. First it may help to clarify our concepts when they are obscure or ambiguous; second, it may enable us to differentiate or to identify hypotheses, according to whether we can find any conceivable difference in their consequences; and third, it may enable us to reject as spurious hypotheses which have no practical consequences for us. Although all three uses are different they nevertheless all have to do with the clarifying task of philosophy.

One thesis involved in James's account, and not totally trivial, may seem quite uncontroversial. It can scarcely be denied that philosophical concepts and claims tend to be obscure and in need of clarification. This is less a complaint against the subject than a recognition of the way in which philosophical problems typically arise from obscure or imprecise ideas in disciplines outside philosophy itself. It is scarcely more controversial to accept the extension of this thesis, that philosophers may formulate claims or apparent hypotheses which yield disputes of the kind James called 'interminable'. This may arise, for example, where two apparently rival hypotheses cannot strictly be distinguished, although the proponents of each view confusedly suppose that we have to choose between them. It may also arise where the hypothesis is so formulated that no test or terminus for it can be conceived. The extent to which such general claims are now uncontroversial is some measure of the success of pragmatism itself.

Nevertheless there may still be philosophers who even now would wish to reject such injunctions and the practice which those pragmatic claims express. I do not mean here to refer to philosophers who might wish to query the exact formulation of those claims, or who might raise questions about their strict justification. It would after all be quite possible to accept these pragmatic views even though their exact formulation and justification remained questionable. Rather I mean to refer to anyone who wished to reject, or simply disregard, the whole spirit of James's enterprise at this point, and who consequently thought that philosophy had as a part of its task the formulation of transcendent claims and the prosecution of interminable disputes. To such a person James has nothing more to say. He took the view that ultimately philosophical positions are determined by temperament and not by rational argument or logic. This is, indeed, the point of his well-known contrast between the tough-minded, Rocky Mountain, temperament in philosophy and its tender-minded, Bostonian, counterpart. The point is nicely put in *The Meaning of Truth* where James talks of scepticism as a 'permanent torpor of the will' and says of it 'You can no more kill it off by logic than you can kill off obstinacy or practical joking.'[16] Such a view reflects part of James's anti-intellectualism. But he would, rightly, have seen those who rejected the uncontroversial claims of pragmatic method not as anti-intellectualists but as irrationalists. It was no part of James's philosophy to confuse these or to allow his own anti-intellectualism to go to the lengths of such irrationalism.

This issue is connected with other corollaries of James's pragmatic method. James himself emphasises that the method does not determine any definite answers to philosophical problems; rather it offers a technique for locating those answers whatever they may turn out to be. It places constraints on philosophical enquiry but does not anticipate its outcome. The method is not a substantive doctrine but rather an injunction with which substantive doctrines in philosophy and elsewhere should be measured. It would be natural to link such a view with two connected ideas in philosophy, namely those of anti-foundationalism and holism.[17] Both ideas can be found in James's philosophy.

'Foundationalism' is the (ugly) name for the view that if knowledge is to be adequately justified and understood, then some fundamental basis for that knowledge must be identified. The thought requires both that all genuine knowledge must rest upon that specific identifiable foundation, and that the foundation itself must be demonstrably secure. Only in this way, it is supposed, can our knowledge be adequately defended against scepticism. The standards of security, however, and the models for the constructive process, differ from one adherent of the doctrine to another. In traditional philosophy, typically, the former is to be identified in some proposition, or set of propositions, which cannot be doubted and the latter is to be identified through some deductive model. When James suggests that there is no final answer to scepticism, and gives priority to his method rather than to any fundamental belief, he indicates a preference for the rejection of such foundationalist models. The idea that there are certain propositions whose status is so secure, and whose power is so great, that they can serve as such foundations is quite foreign to James's philosophy. Such a view can be seen plainly enough in his radical empiricism, but James also links it with what he calls 'humanism' in *The Meaning of Truth*, where he says

> The essential service of humanism . . . is to have seen that though one part of experience may lean on another part to make it what it is . . . experience as a whole is self-containing and leans on nothing.[18]

James advocates this view on the grounds of its 'matchless economy' in eliminating such metaphysical mysteries as the notion of a trans-empirical reality to be found in Royce's or Bradley's conception of the 'absolute'. James's own position is one in which each part of our experience is held in place by other parts, but in which no radical preference is given to any one part over all the others. James illustrates this sometimes with the natural holistic images of the stones in an arch which hold each other in place, or of the pieces of a mosaic all of which make a comparable contribution to the final pattern.[19] Though this feature of James's thought is perhaps more naturally associated with his empiricism than his pragmatism, nevertheless his conception of pragmatic method undoubtedly points in this holistic direction.

It is easy to map such ideas onto the metaphors which James uses to describe pragmatic method. The idea of a 'cash-value' is that of the real immanent purchasing power of conceptual coin; the 'fighting weight' of some conception is its stripped-down form with no redundant fat and no concealing clothing. To see concepts 'at work', or to find the 'go' of them, is to present them fulfilling their genuine roles, so that we are not deluded into attaching to them a significance which those roles cannot sustain. We may, in philosophy and elsewhere, mistake the role which some part of our experience plays, and in the extreme case we may invest it with a significance which it strictly could not have.

This is to represent concepts, or the hypotheses in which they figure, as items with an essential functional role in some theory or system of belief. James frequently uses the technique, in his own analysis of specific concepts, of presenting them not as related directly to any object in our experience but rather as fulfilling a functional role with respect to other items in that experience. The best known example of this is his claim that 'consciousness' is not the name of an entity but of a function.[20] In general James draws a distinction between what he calls 'entitative' and 'functional' concepts,[21] and he plainly believes, as in the case of 'consciousness' itself, that philosophers and psychologists have committed mistakes through failing to appreciate this distinction. He thought, for example, that the Kant-style appeal to a 'transcendental ego' was an erroneous response to the bogus quest for the entity which 'consciousness' named. In an extended way James also thinks of concepts and hypotheses generally as having a distinctive role in facilitating the operation of the system to which they belong. His central idea of analysing such concepts is that of clarifying and displaying that distinctive role. To be clear about such items is to be clear about the operation of the system and the role or roles they play in it.

This preliminary general account of James's pragmatic method suffers from that absence of specific examples which the method officially deplores. James, himself, throughout his writings, offers many such illustrations of his method at work. Though the main source of such examples comes from *Pragmatism* itself, others are to be found both in his later writing on radical empiricism and even in his earlier work on psychology in the *Principles*. What James there called the 'psychologists' fallacy'[22] can be seen as a pervasive application of his method to psychological topics. In *Pragmatism* James deals with a variety of specific cases. He has initially two illustrations designed to introduce his views, the 'squirrel' and 'yeast' cases, and then a discussion of the method's application to traditional philosophical problems such as those of free-will, design, and religious belief, monism and pluralism, and substance. It would not be sensible to consider all of these, and I shall outline the two introductory examples and then look more closely at James's account of substance.

1 The introductory cases

In what is probably the best known of James's specific examples of the method he relates a story of a quarrel over the description of a man chasing a squirrel on a tree-trunk. As the man runs round the tree, so the squirrel runs round the trunk with its belly always turned towards the man. The controversy arose because some participants thought that the man went round the squirrel while others vehemently denied this. James was brought in to arbitrate and resolved the issue by distinguishing 'what you *practically mean* by "going round" the squirrel'. In one way the man 'goes round' the squirrel by passing successively from the north to the east to the south and to the west of the animal and the tree. In another way, since the squirrel does not itself remain in one posture, the man does not successively pass from a position in front of the squirrel to its right, back, and left. James thought, and it seems that eventually the disputants agreed, that both parties are 'right and wrong according as you conceive the verb "to go round" in one practical fashion or another'.[23]

James himself described the example as trivial, and yet it plainly has some value. Disputes, however pointless, may become heated and interminable precisely through a failure on the part of the disputants to recognise practical ambiguities in the very terms of the dispute. In such a case the recognition of those unclarities is at least a first step towards resolving the dispute. The same message arises from James's second introductory example, in which he quotes a chemical text from Ostwald[24] about the action of yeast. Here the suggestion is that two apparently rival explanations of the phenomenon cannot be distinguished. The claim is that it is as if one explanation invoked a reference to an 'elf' and the other to a 'brownie' in explaining the phenomenon. According to Ostwald, and James, there is in such a case no practical difference to be found in the two offered explanations, so that the apparent conflict between them is illusory.

Once again the very terms of the dispute are shown to be unclear. Once they have been clarified, then the suggestion is that the dispute itself is shown to be futile and unnecessary. There is, though, an evident difference between the two introductory cases. It is not just that in the first case the dispute involved one term with two distinguishable practical meanings, while in the second it involved two terms whose meanings could not be distinguished. It is also that in the second case we might regard the explanation offered by either term as empty if we believe that elves and brownies do not exist. We might say that this example carries two messages: First that the two purported explanations are practically indistinguishable, and second that they are both empty. The first message corresponds to that use of the method in which hypotheses are shown to be identical because their practical consequences are indistinguishable; the second corresponds to the use in which a hypothesis is shown to go beyond the bounds of the experiencable. Some doubt remains, therefore, about the relation between the two messages. It would not be possible to infer the second directly from the first, for we might have indistinguishable hypotheses which were not empty where, for example, the different terms named the same existent. But it might be possible to infer the first from the second on the ground that all empty hypotheses are, from their explanatory point of view, indistinguishable.

Perhaps this is to press the example further than it warrants, but there remains an anxiety about both cases. Few readers will fail to acknowledge an intuitive value in James's initial examples. It would be unfair to complain that they have no great philosophical significance, since he goes on to give extensive illustrations of the method from traditional philosophy. Yet it may be asked whether the cases make it clear when we are entitled to speak of terms or hypotheses with the same or different meaning. The general question obviously arises from the doubt already expressed over the second case, whether the emptiness of two terms entails that they are indistinguishable in meaning. But the same general problem arises in the first example as well. For, although we might be ready to admit the intuitive plausibility of James's account, we might also seek a more explicit justification for the conclusion that the key term has at least two separate meanings. The suggestion is that such a justification would be provided by a less intuitive, more articulate, theory of meaning.

James, as we have seen, gestures towards this need. In endorsing Peirce's principle he evidently takes a first step towards some general account of meaning. But a question arises about the extent of that underlying account, and it has been suggested that there really is no such underlying account to provide the needed support.[25] Two initial comments might be made at this stage. First James signals some provisos to be made to his view. Sometimes he speaks of pragmatic method without appealing to the notion of meaning at all. Even where the idea of meaning is present James sometimes qualifies it by talking not simply of 'meaning' but rather of 'practical meaning' or 'interpretation'.[26] Where the notion of meaning is undeniably present James evidently relies on Peirce's principle, but that principle indicates more the recognised need to move towards some theory than the nature of such a theory.

Second, however, it is important to ask how vital such a need is, and to indicate one limitation on such a need which James would rightly have stressed. For it does not follow from our lack of an adequate theory that the corresponding practice is itself defective. Indeed in some cases we might be so persuaded of the benefits of the practice that we could not envisage accepting a theory which did not endorse them. In such a case the practice itself would provide criteria by which we determined the adequacy of the corresponding theory. Such a position is widely thought to arise, for example, in the relation between a linguistic theory and our speech habits, but it naturally arises in other contexts, too.[27] We would not want, for example, to reject the practice of prescribing a drug known to relieve some medical condition simply on the ground that we had so far no adequate theory to explain its beneficial action. Clearly in all such cases the existence of a satisfactory theory may help to support our intuitive acceptance of the practice. But the absence of such a theory, though a loss, is not a decisive objection to that intuitive acceptance. In other contexts James expresses his suspicion of an intellectual tendency to exaggerate the importance of theory. To believe that the absence of an adequate theory of meaning is enough to destroy James's pragmatic method would be a good example of such an error.

2 Substance and materialism

In *Pragmatism* James goes on to discuss pragmatic method's application to some philosophical issues. These include a traditional conflict between monism and pluralism and the problem of substance. James's treatment of the latter is unusual and I shall concentrate on it. First James carefully separates a number of different questions which have been at issue in the traditional debates over the notion of substance. He notes summarily the following four problems:

(1) The question whether, distinguishing between substance and attributes, the notion of a substance is needed to support or explain the cohesion of attributes in our experience.

(2) The question whether, distinguishing between material substance and sensations, the notion of a material substance unapproachable by us is nevertheless needed to support and explain those sensations.

(3) The question whether, distinguishing between a substantial soul and the stream of our experience, the former is something additional to our consciousness or is merely a name for verifiable cohesions in our inner experience.

(4) The question whether we should accept materialism or spiritualism. Materialism is represented as a doctrine claiming that the laws of physical nature exclusively govern the universe, so that even our minds operate through the 'blind' laws of physics. Spiritualism claims by contrast that minds not only witness and record phenomena, but also run and operate them, at least in some cases.

These initial moves indicate a generally uncontroversial aspect of pragmatic method in which it brings out the complexities and ambiguities attending traditional philosophical debates. *The* problem of substance is here represented as at least four distinguishable problems which may be connected but may also need to be treated separately. This technique is even more forcibly illustrated in James's discussion of monism and pluralism where his resolution of *the* issue consists primarily of distinguishing at least eight different respects in which we might ask whether the universe is 'one' or 'many'. James's sensitivity to these complexities, and his insistence that a failure to note them is bound to lead to confusions, is very like Moore's later treatment of traditional philosophical problems.[28] In Moore's discussion of the problem of the 'external' world, for example, it is made plain that even so innocuous a term as 'external' has not been properly clarified in the traditional debates. Moore's own method echoes James's conviction that such a lack of clarity inevitably confuses the search for an adequate solution to the problems.

In the case of a term like 'substance' James's message should seem even more plausible. For not only is it a term of art less obviously linked to common usage than such a term as 'external', but it has notoriously been the subject of much confusion in the history of philosophy. James implies as much in his comments on the debate between Locke and Berkeley, since the suggestion is that at various stages in that debate no clear distinctions have been drawn between the problems (1)–(4). It is, indeed, true of Berkeley that his arguments against Locke sometimes fail to discriminate between issues (1) and (2), though James generally indicates a preference for the Berkeleyan position in the distinguished issues. Though James does not discuss (1)–(3) extensively Berkeley is represented as a pragmatist in his rejection of an 'inexperiencable' material substance. In this way Berkeley is presented, charitably but not unplausibly, not as rejecting any common sense beliefs about objects but as denying only an unpragmatic appeal to a supposed inexperiencable reality.

23

It is to James's credit that he so clearly records these distinctions, but two limitations in this part of his discussion deserve to be noted. First James's own position on these issues remains ambiguous. He might be canvassing only a weak pragmatist conclusion in which certain clear transcendent appeals are rejected; or he might wish to go further to hold that some of these ideas of substance can be reduced to the ideas with which the notion of substance is contrasted. In relation to (1), for example, James could take the weak view that a notion of substance totally divorced from attributes, what is sometimes called a 'bare' substance, is to be rejected; or he could take the stronger view that the notion of substance simply reduces to the idea of sets of attributes.

The two theses are distinguishable. For I might take the view that the notion of a substance without attributes is absurd or empty without however wishing to claim that the notion of a substance can be eliminated in favour of the notion of an attribute. If, for example, the latter claim entailed an exclusive priority given to the notion of an attribute over that of a substance, then the former claim is compatible with a rejection of that exclusive priority. For the former claim might be held together with the plausible belief that just as it is impossible to have substances without attributes, so it is equally impossible to have attributes without substances.

Second, however, James's main interest in the four distinguished issues lies not in the first three but in the fourth. His brief comments on the complexities of (1)–(3) are only a preparation for his central account of (4), which he considers at length. In that account he distinguishes between the world's past and its future and claims that it makes no difference with respect to the past whether one accepts materialism or spiritualism. Later James added a proviso to this view in his comment on the 'robot sweetheart',[29] but that does not significantly affect his argument. For he believes that a difference between the two hypotheses arises with respect to the future. The materialist hypothesis carries a message of pessimistic hopelessness in the ultimate loss of everything of human value. James speaks, with Balfour, in poetic tones of the 'disconsolateness of its practical results', and complains of it that it is not 'a permanent warrant for our more ideal interests, not a fulfiller of our remotest hopes'. The notion of God, on the other hand 'guarantees an ideal order that shall be permanently preserved'.[30]

For James each of the rival hypotheses is an adequate explanation of the past. The two theories are empirically equivalent with respect to those past occurrences. With respect to their explanatory adequacy in the future James admits that we cannot legislate for this in advance. 'The truth of "God" has to run the gauntlet of all our other truths' so that 'our final opinion about God can be settled only after all the truths have straightened themselves out together'. But, James adds, 'let us hope that they shall find a modus vivendi'. Construed, then, as a choice between alternative cognitive hypotheses there is so far no ground for any preference; but the promise, or hope, present in one hypothesis but absent from the other entitles us 'to enjoy our God in advance of all that labour'. The spiritualist alternative is, as James says, a doctrine of *promise*, just as the doctrine of free-will 'has no meaning unless it be a doctrine of relief'.

What is immediately obvious and striking in this discussion is the move from issues of epistemology or logic to questions of value. James is, of course, reinforcing his earlier conviction that traditional treatments of (1)–(4) tend to run these issues together. James, by contrast, highlights the fourth issue by postulating the empirical equivalence of the two hypotheses. Once that is done the issue between them is no longer 'cognitive' so much as 'affective', so that what determines our acceptance or rejection of either hypothesis has to do with the emotional attitudes of hope or despair which James associates with them. But although James wishes to distinguish these considerations he also wishes to assimilate them in various ways. For he suggests not only that the cognitive and affective considerations legitimately determine the acceptance and truth of either belief, but also that the affective considerations may determine their meaning. In this way James's discussion refers to his theory of truth and his account of the ethics of belief in *The Will To Believe*, and these will be discussed later.[31] But a number of potential problems for these doctrines arise directly from his account of materialism and spiritualism.

There is, for example, some ambiguity in the spiritualist hypothesis. Although James expresses it in terms ultimately of a belief in God, the issue of the universal application of physical laws might be thought to arise independently of that belief. For the issue between the two hypotheses might be put in terms of the adequacy of a physical explanation for human consciousness. A cognitive dimension to the dispute still exists in this way, but even if it turned out that there was no complete physical explanation of human consciousness it would by no means follow that an ideal order of human value would be permanently preserved through God. All that could be said in such a case is that this might be regarded as at least offering the possibility of a future for those human values. But even if physical laws alone do govern human consciousness it is not obvious that this strictly excludes every conception of God. James perhaps assumes this because, as we shall see later, he believes that determinism is incompatible with free choice.

More problematic anxieties arise from James's view that the affective considerations determine the grounds for accepting, and even the meaning of, the hypotheses. The former issue of the legitimacy of accepting hypotheses on non-cognitive grounds has to be considered later in connection with James's thesis in 'The Will To Believe'; but the latter issue about the determination of meaning yields an obvious objection to James's view. For it might be said that the question of the 'promise', 'hope', or 'despair' attaching to the hypotheses *cannot* be part of their meaning. One, relatively weak, ground for this would point to the variability of people's reactions to such hypotheses. James himself recognises that someone might, sincerely, find more pleasure from the materialist hypothesis, or alternatively might find no clear difference in their reactions to the hypotheses. He says of such a view that it is a refuge for a shallow mind, and he has at least a clear line of defence against such a point. Other things being equal it does require some artificiality to prefer a universe without human values and achievements to one which has these. James, of course, is not here contrasting human values with others which might be superior but with a situation in which no values exist at all.

A better ground for the objection would build upon this variability of response to ask how the meaning of such hypotheses might accommodate such responses. There is an intuitive sense in which what such hypotheses mean to, or for, some individual might include their emotional reactions. In that way the supposition that Jones has won a prize of, say, £5,000 would be expected to elicit quite different responses from Jones if he is a millionaire or if he is a pauper. The news, and even such an imagined outcome, would mean something different to him in these situations. But, it will be said, the strict or literal meaning of the sentence 'You have won £5,000' does not vary from one reaction to the other. On the contrary, it might be said, the intelligibility of the emotional reactions to such an announcement itself depends upon a prior determination of the strict meaning of that announcement. But in that case the emotional reactions cannot themselves be part of the literal meaning.

These considerations produce two related difficulties for James, though both have to do with his account of meaning. On one side there is the question of the relation between individuals' responses to language and the language itself. On the other there is the question of the relation of strict or literal meaning to emotional meaning; between the literal meaning of some sentence and what the utterance of that sentence might mean to some audience. Both are serious difficulties, but it is the second which seems to present a distinctive objection to James's application of pragmatic method in this case.

For the first difficulty is by no means peculiar to James. It arises for any account of meaning in the following way. We commonly distinguish between the meaning of expressions in a language and individuals' grasp of those meanings. We also naturally think that the former is in some way dependent upon the latter, and even may be somehow constructed out of the latter. For it seems absurd to suppose that expressions of a language have their meaning quite independently of the speech habits of the language users. Any adequate account of the meaning of expressions of a natural language would have to explain these different requirements, and since James's time this problem has attracted much attention. If this were

James's only problem in this context, then it could be said that he has identified a serious general difficulty in the philosophy of language but not one to which he is especially vulnerable.

The second difficulty, however, seems more serious for James. It is intuitively clear that our emotional reactions to hypotheses may already depend on our prior understanding of those hypotheses. In order that someone may consider their emotional reaction to materialism, for example, it seems required that they should understand what it is that they are reacting to. That understanding seems, in turn, to define a notion of the strict or literal meaning which either excludes or can be separated from any emotional response. In Fregean terms it is as if James here blurs the distinction between 'sense' and 'tone'; as if he is returning to a psychologism in meaning which Frege rejected. It is important to recall, however, that even if James is wrong in these claims he can still fall back to the claim that we are at least justified in accepting or rejecting such hypotheses for 'affective' rather than strictly 'cognitive' reasons. It is important also to recognise a further ambiguity in James's account. He could be claiming, strongly, that such emotional responses always are part of the meaning of the associated hypotheses; or he could be claiming only that it is at least possible in some cases for such emotional reactions to be included in their meanings.

3 The method's roles

It was suggested earlier that James's pragmatic method had three explicit uses; to clarify unclear or ambiguous concepts, to reject transcendent claims, and to identify or differentiate hypotheses. It was further suggested that these tasks of clarification might rest on different supports and respond to distinct motivations, some of which seem uncontroversial while others seem questionable. In this section I want to look over these different accounts from the weakest and less controversial to the strongest. The principal determinant of the strength of the account has to do with its commitment to meaning. In the weakest accounts what is stressed is simply the clarificatory value of examining specific cases in philosophy; in the intermediate cases what is stressed is something less than a full-scale appeal to a theory of meaning; while in the strongest what is stressed is a full-scale account or even theory of meaning. The intermediate cases will cover, for example, the suggestions that pragmatic method might offer a criterion for sameness or difference of meaning, even though it did not provide a full theory of meaning; or that it might provide an account of pragmatic or speaker meaning which also fell short of a theory of conventional meaning.

The least vulnerable aspect of the method is simply its appeal to specific examples in philosophy. It has been suggested already that even such a weak account has genuine merits partly but not only because of the nature of philosophy itself. There can be little doubt, for example, that the injunction to spell a philosophical thesis out in terms of specific cases may well throw light on the inadequacies of the thesis itself. Such a method may reveal limitations in the scope of some plausible general thesis by encouraging the search for counter-examples. Treated in this way the method has a formal analogue in the search for counter-examples to some claimed tautology in logic. James might not have welcomed such a parallel between philosophical argument and formal logic, but it is implicit in the account of pragmatic method. So understood the method has also close affinities with the later Wittgenstein's plea for the examination of 'intermediate' cases in philosophy in order to restrain what he called the 'craving for generality'.[32] It is probably unnecessary nowadays to insist on the merits of such prophylaxis. Perhaps the greater danger is not that such injunctions go unrecognised, but that their recognition is so widespread they may no longer be properly appreciated. James, like Wittgenstein, would have wanted to underline the value of such techniques in philosophy as heavily as possible.

In one respect, however, James and Wittgenstein disagree. While Wittgenstein saw the role of philosophy as exclusively therapeutic, James, like Russell and Austin, saw it rather as preparatory.[33] The clarification of philosophical theses for James was a prophylactic against the failure to formulate those theses in a testable form. In James's ideal pragmatic republic science and metaphysics overlap and the central aim for philosophy should be to push its hypotheses towards that area of overlap. Ultimately, no doubt, the fate of such philosophical views is to be handed over to the practitioners of some non-philosophical discipline. The philosopher of merit was simply one who handed his hypothesis over in good testable shape. Certainly James did not believe that pragmatic method was exclusively a specific for philosophers and their ailments. What he called the 'psychologists' fallacy' was a comparable failing in a non-philosophical discipline. But it seems that he thought such a specific especially necessary in the area of overlap between philosophic and non-philosophic disciplines.

In the intermediate range of characterisations of pragmatic method what is stressed is some reference to meaning which falls short of a full-scale theory of meaning. The weakest and the intermediate characterisations, of course, overlap. We may intuitively use the specific examples in the weakest use of the method to mark ambiguities in some philosophical thesis, or to define loosely some classification for those examples. But the intermediate accounts might also make a more explicit appeal to meaning, either suggesting a criterion for meaninglessness, or for differentiating between the meanings of hypotheses, or alternatively using it to indicate what some individual or group mean by some expression, even if this differs from the conventional meaning assigned to that expression in a language. In any of these ways the claims of the method would fall short of a full-scale theory of conventional meaning, though no doubt such limited claims could usefully depend on the support of some such theory.

What I have called the 'intermediate' account of pragmatic method is not totally unmarked in James's discussion. He appeals sometimes to 'practical' meaning or to the 'interpretation' of some expression, where these might be construed as falling short of the ascription of conventional meaning. James also says that practical meaning is all there is, as if he drew no explicit distinction between conventional and pragmatic meaning. This could be taken to mean not that the two items are simply identical but rather that the former rests somehow upon the latter. Then conventional meaning might be represented, as in Grice's theory,[34] as a development or construct out of pragmatic meaning. James's practice, moreover, indicates clearly that he is generally more interested in what some person or group, often philosophers, meant by some term than in providing a dictionary definition of that term. This is so for his discussion of monism and pluralism and of substance as well as of the disagreement over the squirrel. It seems entirely plausible in such cases to represent the clarification of pragmatic meaning as a contribution towards an ultimate definition of some expression, but not necessarily identical with it. Beyond that the uses of the method to differentiate hypotheses or to indicate their untestability rest on a natural intuitive criterion of meaning. One natural way to distinguish hypotheses is simply to show that their application is different; and one natural way to indicate the untestability of some hypothesis is to challenge its advocate to illustrate an appropriate test. It is true that a failure to meet such challenges does not establish either of the claims. For it may be that though there is a difference between two hypotheses we cannot locate it, or that although there is a possible test we are unable to formulate it. But at the pragmatic level of the intermediate cases these limited conclusions are all that the method provides. We may conclude that at least we have no reason to think the two hypotheses distinct, if we are unable to find any difference in their application; or that Jones, who advocates hypothesis H, has no ground for thinking that H is testable if he is unable to formulate any such test.

In some of these intermediate uses of the method James gets close to another aspect of Wittgenstein's therapy. To ask for the practical meaning of some expression is to ask for its use. To ask what Jones means by hypothesis H is to ask how he envisages its use. That similarity is supported by James's other more general terminology of 'function'. The suggestion is that James regarded the meaning of expressions as determined by their function within some system of belief, and although the terminology is imprecise such an account is like Wittgenstein's view that at least 'for a large class of cases the meaning of a word is its use in the language'.[35] It is true that Wittgenstein's slogan seems to talk more of an expression's use in a language than of a person's use of some expression, while James's account does not make any such distinction. But that unclarity is of less significance than the unclarity in both slogans over the words 'use' and 'function'. It has commonly been regarded as an objection to Wittgenstein's account that the term 'use' is so ill-defined, and the same is patently true of James's term 'function' at this stage. It is sometimes said of Wittgenstein that he would have regarded the attempt to clarify his term 'use' in order to develop a theory of meaning as misconceived, because he evidently did not think it appropriate for philosophers to develop theories. Whether Wittgenstein is right or wrong on such a matter, however, it is plain that James could not take such a view. If the notion of an expression's function is both fruitful in this context and unclear then the evident task for James must be to clarify it. The attempt to provide such clarification leads us towards the third and most vulnerable characterisation of the method.

James's only formal attempt to provide such clarification is his endorsement of Peirce's principle. In that account the clarification of our thoughts rests upon the effects of a practical kind we conceive some object to involve, so that our conception of those effects is for us the whole of our conception of that object. At least four objections might be directly raised against such a principle.

(1) It may be said that James's term 'object' is too restricted in its suggestion that we are dealing only with the meanings of individual terms, or concepts, rather than with whole sentences, or propositions.

(2) It may be objected that James's appeal to causal connections is quite out of place in an account of meaning.

(3) It may seem objectionable that the principle places no restriction on the range of causal connections used in determining meaning.

(4) It may be said simply that the formula is too imprecise to indicate a theory of meaning.

Of these the fourth objection can scarcely be denied. The most that might be expected is that if the formula can survive the remaining objections it may do so in a form which partially remedies that imprecision.

None of the first three objections is at all decisive. Although it is true that the principle, as it stands, says nothing explicitly about what is to count as an object James himself in other places draws a very clear distinction between individual concepts, or sub-propositional constituents, and whole propositions themselves. In the *Principles* he wrote:

> Thus if anyone asks what is the mind's object when you say 'Columbus discovered America in 1492' most people will reply 'Columbus', or 'America', or at most 'the discovery of America'. They will name a substantive kernel or nucleus of the consciousness and say that the thought is 'about' that – as indeed it is – and they will call that your thought's object. Really that is usually only the grammatical object, or

more likely the grammatical subject, of your sentence. . . . But the *Object* of your thought is really its entire content or deliverance, neither more nor less. It is a vicious use of speech to take out a substantive kernel from its content and call that its object.[36]

In this passage James evidently runs together a discussion of linguistic objects, such as sentences, and objects of consciousness, such as thoughts. It is nevertheless clear that the general term 'object' in Peirce's principle must have been intended to cover what James here calls the whole content of a thought.

The second objection rests on a simple distinction between causal relations and meaning relations, but it applies only dubiously to Peirce's principle. If we consider a mass term, such as 'gold', we ordinarily draw a distinction between what the term means and the causal properties of the material. We do not suppose, for example, that we can discover the latter merely from an attentive consideration of the former. Even if we admit that known causal properties may come to be included among the defining characteristics of the material, we do not suppose that all of the former might be included in the meaning of the term. These natural intuitive claims, however, cannot directly form an objection to the principle. For in that formula what determines the meaning of some 'object' is not simply its causal relationships, but rather its conceivable effects. James's suggestion is here again rather similar to Grice's account of speaker meaning. For in that account meaning is not determined directly by the actual effects of some utterance but rather by its intended effects. Causality is a factor in both accounts, but it is a factor mediated in both cases by a person's understanding.

But even if that prima facie objection can be so easily rebutted the resulting picture remains hazy. For one thing, if we now explicitly include among the 'objects' whole thoughts or propositions, how are we to understand in that case what is meant by 'conceivable effects'?[37] For another, James's slogan unlike Grice's may seem in direct danger of circularity. In seeking an account of the meaning of some term we have to consider other 'conceptions', that is apparently, other meanings. Such an account might succeed in explaining the meaning of one term by reference to the meaning of others, but it cannot, except circularly, offer a general account of meaning itself. Even Grice's appeal to speakers' intentions has sometimes been criticised in this way, in the belief that intentions can be identified only in some linguistic way. But Grice, at least nominally avoids that circularity by appealing to primitive intentions which are supposed to antedate the conventions of a public natural language. When James appeals instead not to such primitive intentions but only to other 'conceptions' the potential circularity seems more evident.

The first of these apparent difficulties arises in an even more acute form in Ramsey's later version of pragmatism, when he said: 'The essence of pragmatism I take to be this, that the meaning of a sentence is to be defined by reference to . . . its possible causes and effects.'[38] For in that version it remains ambiguous whether it is the sentence or its meaning whose effects are to be considered, and dubious whether it makes sense in either case to speak of such causal relations. James's problem has to do only with the conceivable effects of some object when the object is itself a thought. There is here, however, a clear natural answer, though it is one which demonstrates the principle's indeterminacy. It is natural to say that in the case of thoughts the causal relations involved are those in which the thought functions, for example in drawing inferences, correcting, modifying or adjusting other thoughts, and so on. Such a response plainly requires that we talk psychologically of objects of consciousness rather than linguistically of sentences, at least initially, but this requirement emerges anyway from the passage quoted from the *Principles*. It fits naturally into James's general conception of thoughts as items with a functional role within some system of belief. But although James seems clearly committed to such idioms an account of causal or functional relationships in consciousness plainly stands in need of further explanation. It raises, in particular, the question whether we should understand the mind or consciousness along Cartesian dualist lines or along materialist lines. James inevitably faced such an issue in his account of psychology, but Peirce's principle leaves the issue entirely open.

The further difficulty concerned a potential circularity in James's appeal to other conceptions in elucidating meaning. Here James has available a wide variety of responses, though it remains unclear which he would have been prepared to accept. One possibility would be simply to concede the point, but in a typical pragmatist fashion to insist on the importance of clarifying specific uses of terms within a particular context. An example would be to clarify the use of 'substance' within the framework of the debate between Locke and Berkeley. What is important here is less the general account of meaning than the specific use which philosophers make of some obscure terminology. To take such a view would be, so far, to give up any more theoretical quest for meaning; it would be to follow the strictest Wittgenstein therapy[39] and deal with individual cases without attempting to bring them under any more general account of meaning.

But James might still retain some interest in a more general theory. He might claim, for example, that there is no hope anyway of giving a non-circular account of meaning, perhaps for the reasons that Quine later offered.[40] The idea here would be that there is some insuperable barrier to prevent any attempt to break out of the circle of intentional terms of which 'meaning' is one. James's procedure, in accounting for the meaning of some terms by reference to other 'conceptions' patently does not break out of that intentional circle, but it may be suggested that this is all that can be done. A general account of meaning, then, is nothing more than a complete elucidation of the conceptions which make up some language. Inevitably such an account will contain circularities, but this may motivate a holistic conception of meaning rather than the abandonment of any general account. We saw earlier that, quite independently of these problems about meaning, James was influenced by such holistic considerations.

The third objection, too, seems to attract a natural response. It would be a handicap to any account of meaning if it drew no distinction at all between causal relations and meaning relations. It is therefore a requirement for a theory of meaning that not all causal relations should be included within such a theory. But it seems likely that James's idea was only that conceivable effects form a kind of pool of data from which some sub-set might be selected in recording the meaning of some term. Such references to conceivable effects might be used to differentiate between hypotheses in a pragmatic way, but it would not follow that all such data would have to be included in a record of the meaning of some item. In the earlier case James's claim that pragmatic meaning was all there is was interpreted to mean only that no other reference was necessary rather than that there was simply no difference between pragmatic and conventional meaning. So in this case it is natural to interpret James's appeal to conceivable effects as a reference to such a pool of data rather than as a commitment to a strict identity of causal and meaning relations.

The discussion of these criticisms shows clearly enough the need for further clarification of James's position. James's formula, as the fourth objection correctly claims, is too imprecise as it stands to bear the weight of the required theory. Yet the earlier objections can be given formal answers which point in the direction any such theory would have to take. Of course, it is still an objection that at several points in the discussion there is more than one path for such a theory to take. They show, for example, that the method is primarily concerned with individual cases in which the use of some term is obscure or confused. The appeal to 'conceivable effects', extended to include the inferential or conceptual role of the item within some system of belief, may then serve to clear up the confusion, to differentiate what may have seemed to be identical hypotheses, or to provoke a suspicion that some hypothesis is untestable or even meaningless. What such a method might aspire but patently so far fails to do is to support the pragmatic guidance in Peirce's principle with some more general account of meaning.

Such a more general account would make use of two subsidiary ideas which the prima facie objections have brought to light. The first of these is a link between individual, or pragmatic, meaning and conventional meaning within some language. At this point James's account needs elaboration of the sort provided by Grice's 'communication-intention' theory of conventional meaning. The second is the inclusion within James's account of a causal or functional framework for thoughts which would indicate their conceptual role in inference or deliberation. James's independent account of concepts or hypotheses as functional items within systems of belief naturally encourages the elaboration of meaning in this way, but it raises serious problems which involve James's attitude to the philosophy of mind and psychology. Peirce's principle cannot resolve these issues, but serves only to unearth them. But something may conceivably be learned at this stage from James's treatment of the other pillar of pragmatism, namely his genetic theory of what is meant by truth.

3

The Theory of Truth

James's theory of truth, one of the twin pillars of his pragmatism, itself has two central aspects. First there is the strict account of truth itself, and second the wider links which the strict account has with other notions such as belief, meaning, and behaviour. It is somewhat artificial to draw such a distinction, but under the first heading I shall outline the main features of James's account and his attempts to defend that account against criticism. Under the second heading I shall consider more closely the connections between the account of truth and the notions of belief, behaviour and meaning. Two of these issues remain from the previous chapter. On one side it remains to be seen whether any further light may be thrown on James's view of meaning as a result of the examination of his theory of truth. On the other side it might be asked which of the twin supports for pragmatism has priority. It may be suggested that the two supports, the method and the theory of truth, have parity of status; but if it turned out that the method rested on a theory of meaning and that theory itself rested on the account of truth, then there would be reason to revise such a view.

Even within what I have called the 'strict' account of truth philosophers often draw distinctions between different types of account. It is, for example, common to separate attempts to define truth from attempts to provide a 'criterion' for truth. In another dimension they have sought also to distinguish epistemic from semantic accounts of truth and to divide these from metaphysical or ontological accounts. Though such distinctions should not be merely disregarded, they are not always clearly drawn; and even when they are clearly drawn it may remain questionable whether the separation is not artificial or over-simple.[1] There is some ground for thinking that James himself took such a sceptical view of traditional theories of truth.

Consider, for example, how a 'correspondence' theory of truth might be characterised. It would be natural to represent such a theory as at least offering a definition of the predicate '. . . is true'. But simply to legislate that that predicate may always equivalently be replaced by '. . . corresponds to the facts' is by itself a quite idle manoeuvre. Such a definition will seem entirely uninformative, though it could be supplemented by a further attempt to elucidate such terms as 'fact' and 'correspond'. A theory which explained such a correspondence relation in detail for certain elementary sentences of a language and then explained how such a correspondence relation for other sentences could be derived from that elementary basis might provide such a supplementary theory. Accounts of such a kind have been offered, or sketched, by such philosophers as Tarski and Austin,[2] though Tarski was more interested in formal and Austin more interested in natural languages. Tarski's account of truth in particular has come to be regarded as a valuable model with which to understand the semantics even of natural language. In such a case, though, the value of the enterprise lies less in its potential elucidation of 'fact' and 'correspond' than in the formal apparatus of the derivation.

A purely verbal definition of truth as correspondence might, however, be supplemented in another way. Certainly one motive for adopting some such correspondence theory has always been a faith in the existence and identity of facts. So some correspondence theorists may take their definition of truth as an overt commitment to facts and to some form of realism, though such a commitment is not strictly necessary. Austin, for example, plainly thought that there was merit in the notion of a correspondence to facts, but it is doubtful whether he would have wished to commit himself to any form of metaphysical realism. Equally someone might be prepared to accept the formal apparatus of correspondence theory but still believe that the notion of a fact itself was derived from some other source. To think, for example, that the notion of a fact could be explained only in terms of a coherence among beliefs might be to accept some form of correspondence together with a coherence theory. In the light of all this while it may be important to be sensitive to the different types of truth theory, it is evidently also important not to take the labels of such theories at face value. To do so is rather like prescribing drugs on the basis of their brand names rather than their chemical constitution.

It was suggested earlier that James's apparent disregard of traditional divisions between types of truth theory might be the result of a deliberate dissent from them rather than a merely cavalier carelessness. Two preliminary grounds might be given for such a view. First James's account fits naturally into that earlier description of a theory which accepts the notion of a fact but treats it as derivative from certain coherence relations between beliefs. In this way his account patently straddles the space traditionally left between correspondence and coherence theories of truth. The second point has to do with James's initial characterisation of his theory as a 'genetic' account of what is 'meant by' truth. Since it is common in philosophy to contrast genetic accounts of some phenomenon with accounts of the meaning of some term, James's characterisation plainly stands in need of further explanation. That need is reinforced by considering that James also says that he is giving a definition of truth, though not a criterion, and that his task is logical rather than psychological. These claims may indicate some confusion on James's part, but they may also indicate a conscious wish to deviate radically from philosophical tradition.

1 The strict theory of truth

What struck James's contemporaries and opponents most forcibly in his account of truth was his apparent equation of truth with usefulness or expediency. Many critics, including Moore and Russell,[3] felt unable to overcome the difficulty that we do not normally equate, and indeed normally oppose, these ideas. It is, of course, easy to find cases we would ordinarily describe as inexpedient, or useless, truth as well as of expedient, or useful, falsity. James himself was well aware of this, but treated such initial objections as shallow, and the characterisation of the theory to which they are counter-examples as a slander.[4] He thought the critics had failed to notice that the equation held only for the *generally* expedient or useful, and for that only *in the long run*.

He did not believe, any more than his opponents, that what might be useful or expedient for some individual to believe was consequently true. Nor was his theory intended to be committed to the view that what some community generally believed at some time was therefore simply true. On the contrary James wished to stress the general fallibility and revisability of our beliefs, and the extent to which our beliefs are constrained by other beliefs which may form part of our current stock or may be candidates for acceptance in the future. These caveats may not suffice to disarm all these natural objections. They may lead us to complain at least that James has formulated his theory in regrettable and misleading ways, but they suggest that the initial objections are not yet decisive against the theory. It may also be thought unclear how these provisos remedy the initial defects, but that may encourage us to look more closely at James's elaboration of his theory.

As often in philosophy the theory can be approached by asking what it was intended to deny. Two aspects of such a rival theory can easily be found. First James patently wished to reject the idea of truth as an 'absolute', 'in the singular and with a capital T',[5] as he put it. For him the accessible and important primary use of 'true' was the ordinary way in which we identify truths, in the plural and with a small 't'. Second he wished to reject certain aspects of a correspondence account of truth. James represents philosophers such as Bradley as canvassing the notion of truth as an absolute, that is as something which is attained only when our beliefs are unrevisable, guaranteed, and finally true. For James, such an idea was wholly unrealistic and indeed a standard example of the 'vicious abstractionism' to which he thought philosophy, and especially rationalist philosophy, was liable.

The ideal of an ultimate, complete and unrevisable Truth, as opposed to the partial and temporary truths we ordinarily trade in, was canvassed in Bradley's *Appearance and Reality*. James thought that if such an unattainable ideal were identified with our conventional commerce in truths, or even if the latter were to be measured against that ideal, then we would arrive at a 'preposterous position'.[6] Certainly all our ordinary dealings in truths will then appear to be at best questionable and at worst quite unjustified. As with other manifestations of the 'absolute' James was prepared to grant it some minimal, derivative and residual force, as a regulative reminder of better truths to discover or further revisions to make, but he thought that such an ultimate Truth was unattainable.[7] He took the view that no theory is ever a complete transcript of reality, and that there need be no ultimate or final Truth. Unlike Peirce, who denied the latter view, James expressed serious qualms about that denial. At one point he says: 'The absolutely true, meaning what no further experience will ever alter, is that ideal vanishing point towards which we imagine all our temporary truths will one day converge.'[8] And on another occasion: 'There is nothing improbable in the supposition that an analysis of the world may yield a number of formulae all consistent with the facts.'[9] Like Quine James was not prepared simply to accept the ideal of a final unique truth. As in terrestrial travel the horizon is something we may aim at, but there is no hope of finally arriving without some further horizon presenting itself.[10]

Certain forms of correspondence theory were also part of James's target. He was prepared to concede some trivial truth attaching to correspondence definitions of '. . . is true', and he was at pains to stress that his own account was realist and assumed the existence of facts. But he did not believe that an informative correspondence theory could be wholly correct for two types of reason. First he thought that a correspondence relation could not adequately cover all the cases in which we naturally speak of truth. He thought that few of our beliefs ever are directly confronted with the relevant facts, because, as he says, truth lives on a credit system. It is an essential part of James's epistemic holism that a belief has to co-exist in a system of other beliefs and to work with them. It would be impossible to verify or check all, even a majority of, such beliefs. We accept most of them on trust, on credit, and in terms of a loyalty to testified apparent success in the past.[11]

James held also that many of the terms in our beliefs, which we might call 'theoretical' terms and which he called 'ejects',[12] were simply not susceptible of direct face to face confrontation with the facts. The more complex and theoretical our beliefs the less plausible it is to imagine them corresponding to some discoverable fact. 'The overwhelming majority of our true ideas admit of no face-to-face verification'.[13] To cling to the idea of a correspondence in these cases is simply to distort the procedures by which we verify or falsify, accept or reject, the beliefs in which such terms figure. James's general picture of verification procedures in such cases is very like the holism of what has come to be called the 'Quine-Duhem' thesis.[14]

James adds, under this first head, a crucial long-term claim, namely that what we call verification procedures are not the only kinds of consideration which determine the working of our beliefs. James recognised that such procedures form a vital part of the operation of scientific beliefs, but he wished also to stress the similarities between these scientific and other, non-cognitive, cases. Even in the case of non-cognitive beliefs James thought that we could still usefully consider their working, and he tends to represent these operations as parallel to those available in the scientific case. Typically, though, these non-cognitive operations concern what might be called generally 'satisfaction' rather than verification procedures. It is important to stress that for James these verification procedures are included among the working of our beliefs, especially in the scientific case. 'True ideas', James says, 'are those we can assimilate, validate, corroborate and verify'.[15] But he thought not only that other parallel 'satisfaction' procedures worked equally importantly in the non-cognitive cases, but also that even in science satisfaction had a role to play. He says, for example: 'Truth in science is what gives us the maximum possible set of satisfactions, taste included, but consistency with previous truth and with novel fact is always the most imperious claimant.'[16] Even in the case of science, then, but especially in non-cognitive contexts, the notion of truth involves operations among our beliefs which cannot be associated with the idea of a bare correspondence with fact.

Those lines of argument, which restrict the scope of any correspondence account, still allow for some cases just such a direct correspondence. But James's second, and more positive, objection restricts the value even of that limited appeal to correspondence. For although James wished to preserve a realist appeal to facts, he thought that a positive theory of truth rested that realism on a more profound idea, namely the working of our beliefs. For James that mode of operation, in which beliefs are accepted or rejected, revised or challenged, and in which accepted beliefs lead to action, was the central element in the notion of truth. It was that central element which the pragmatist theory was designed to capture. James puts the point in the following ways:

> Truth for the pragmatist becomes a class name for all sorts of definite working values in experience. For the rationalist it remains a pure abstraction.

> It (the pragmatic theory) converts the absolutely empty notion of a static relation of 'correspondence' between our minds and reality into that of a rich and active commerce between particular thoughts of ours and the great universe of other experiences in which they play their part and have their uses.[17]

It is in this context that James insists on the awkwardly formulated claims that 'truth happens to an idea ... it becomes true, is made true, by events'.[18] It is also this direction of interest which reveals James's application of pragmatic method to the problem of truth. The enquiry is to show what truth is 'known-as', what its 'cash-value' or 'fighting weight' might be, as against the static and abstract accounts of traditional philosophy. It led in particular to the contrast which James took over from Schiller between 'truth as claimed' and 'truth as validated'. That contrast is clearly linked to James's concern with truths in the plural, and with the workings of our ascription of truth in practical contexts. We ascribe and claim truth on a revisable and defeasible basis, which may never be finally validated. James evidently believed that the traditional accounts of truth had concentrated on the abstract concept of a finally validated truth itself, while he was interested in the way it operated in the context of our beliefs.

Traditional philosophers will be inclined to criticise James for aiming at the wrong target. It is easy to draw a distinction between the ways in which we operate with, the practical ways in which we come to ascribe, truth and the predicate which we ascribe in those operations. No doubt our ascription of truth on particular occasions is tentative and provisional, but it may be said that this is irrelevant to what we ascribe. The same tentativeness may attend our ascription of other predicates, such as redness, but this would not entitle us to identify such a predicate with truth. Traditional philosophers were therefore inclined to offer accounts of truth itself and not of the general circumstances in which the predicate is ascribed. James might have been prepared to concede something to such a line of argument. He was, as we saw, prepared to admit some residual value for what he conceived as the 'absolute' conception of truth. He thought, for example, that his own pragmatist account might have such a conception wrapped around it, but he still held that the substance of any theory of truth must be found in its working.

It is in somewhat this way that James might begin to justify his startling equation of truth with usefulness or expediency, but so far nothing has been said explicitly of what, in this context, the useful or expedient are useful or expedient *for*. In the first instance the notion of truth, according to James, is related to what it is useful or expedient to believe; and in the second it is related more widely to the notion of successful action. It is a central part of James's theory that the concept of truth functions in the working and acceptance of beliefs, and that these items are crucial in determining the success or failure of individual or communal courses of action. In so far as our beliefs lead to general success so far we ascribe truth to them and retain them in our credit system. James is sometimes tempted to put these points by reversing what may seem the natural order of such concepts. In this case the claim would then be that our beliefs are not successful because they are true, but that they are described as true because they are successful. James himself actually licenses both such orders when he allows as equally appropriate the claims that some belief is true because useful and that it is useful because true.[19]

It is important to recognise that at least in the context of scientific enquiry James wished to stress the notions of verification or corroboration. For it was another common complaint against James that in talking of usefulness, or still more of 'satisfaction', he had obliterated any reference to evidence, testing, or verification. It should now be plain that James had no such intention, for the notions of usefulness and of satisfaction already include a reference to such standard testing methods at least in the appropriate contexts.[20] As we have seen James thought that an over-emphasis on such considerations was itself misleading, because it encouraged a mistaken view of science, drew too sharp a distinction between cognitive and non-cognitive beliefs, and wrongly fostered approval for a general correspondence theory of truth. Even in the scientific context James wished to include verification as only one consideration operative in the working of such beliefs. For even in that context the idea of verification is not the terminus of the account of truth but only one particular stage in it. James wished to explain verification itself as subordinate to other, more wide-ranging, goals. For him the duty to seek truth was not an end in itself but something enjoined, as he says, 'for excellent practical reasons'.[21] Theory construction and testing, and more generally the operation of beliefs in any context, are means to other vital satisfactions, that is, they have survival value.

It is in this way that James speaks of the harmonising of our beliefs, or of their getting us into a satisfactory relationship with other parts of our experience. He speaks also, of course, of certain ideas or beliefs as 'leading' in fruitful directions and terminating in some testing procedure. These harmonies and satisfactions are not merely what is pleasing or agreeable to the individual or to a community at some time, but rather what foster successful, beneficial, long-term action. It is for this reason that James stresses the otherwise odd claim that truth is a species of the good. The notions of verification, correspondence with fact, realism, all play a part in our systems of belief, but even in the scientific context they are subordinated to more general, biological, evolutionary, goals. James's psychological interests and his Darwinian background are clearly apparent here.

Two general problems clearly arise from James's account. The first is to consider whether that account is satisfactory for the standard case in which we ascribe truth, that is the cognitive case. The second concerns James's evident wish to extend that standard case to cover also non-cognitive beliefs, in morality, for example, or religion. The two issues are plainly linked. For James thought that cognitive and affective considerations were involved in the working of all beliefs. If there was a difference between them it was to do with the mix of such considerations and not simply with their bald presence or absence. Given that even in the non-cognitive cases we identify beliefs, and that for James the problem of truth had to do with the working of beliefs, it was natural that he should envisage the extension of truth from the cognitive to the affective context.

These different issues are not always properly separated. In his *The Origins of Pragmatism*, for example, Ayer says:

> In particular the notion that a belief is to be accounted true if it gives one satisfaction to hold it is applied by James only to beliefs of the third class (those whose function is to satisfy our moral or emotional needs), and to them only with reservations. It has, however, been almost universally assumed by James's critics that he puts this forward unconditionally as a general criterion for truth.[22]

Ayer is importantly right here in his rejection of the naive view that for James beliefs are true, for individuals, in so far as they give those individuals satisfaction in holding them. But his account is misleading in its suggestion that James drew a totally sharp distinction between moral and scientific beliefs. For this overlooks the fact that James regarded emotional satisfaction as important even in the scientific case; and it fails to stress James's conviction that even in the moral case individual satisfaction has to be weighed against other considerations, just as it does in science.

2 James's response to criticism

James was forced to recognise that his account of truth was open to strong criticism, but he persisted in believing that this was due more to misunderstandings of the doctrine than to the doctrine itself.[23] In a number of responses to his critics, mainly collected in *The Meaning of Truth*, he sought to clarify the doctrine further, to answer criticisms, and to take the battle into the enemy camps. Some of his responses might be thought to confuse the issues rather than to clarify them, but others, such as his response to Russell, deserve closer attention. But it should also be noted that he was prepared to make some further provisos or concessions in his view. For one thing he admits that the doctrine needs further work in order to elucidate the factors which determine the acceptance of belief in scientific contexts. He did not think that the logic of science had progressed far enough to be able to offer a detailed account of such verification procedures. But though he was prepared to concede a certain incompleteness in the account at that point he was in no doubt that the account pointed in the right direction for such further work.

James also conceded that 'satisfaction' was not a sufficient condition for truth, though he still believed it to be necessary. This concession indicates, what might in any case be evident, that James's term 'satisfaction' is ambiguous. The term might be used, narrowly, to signify the emotional satisfactions with which such things as testing procedures are *contrasted* in science; but it might be used, in a wider sense, to stand for some *overall* satisfaction, including testing procedures, which accompanies the acceptance of some belief. To say of the first kind of satisfaction that it is necessary but not sufficient for truth may be, then, only to repeat the point already made, that emotional factors are only one among many such factors determining the acceptance of belief. This would not add anything to what has been already said of James's account, but it is perhaps all that James meant by his concession. But he might have intended to say that even overall satisfaction is itself only necessary and not sufficient for truth. Even this might be given some sense within the scope of what has been already said of James's theory. For it might mean no more than that any particular acceptance of belief is in principle always open to later revision. What gives such satisfaction to one man now may not give such satisfaction to others, or even to him at a later time. Such a claim, too, adds nothing to what has been already said.

But James might have wanted to claim that overall satisfaction is not equivalent to truth. This, however, would be a serious concession in danger, indeed, of rendering his own theory inconsistent. For that theory claims in some way to *define* truth, to give the meaning of truth, in terms of such a notion as that of overall satisfaction. But if that latter notion is not sufficient for truth, then it seems incapable of fulfilling James's requirements. Many of James's critics would undoubtedly have said that this was the basic stumbling-block in the way of their acceptance of the pragmatic theory. Even overall satisfaction in general and in the long run fell short of their conception of truth. Such conclusions might be avoided if James's view of meaning or definition were unconventional; and this is suggested by his response to Russell's criticisms.

Russell could not resist the common objections to James's doctrine. Like other critics he objected to the apparent equation of truth and usefulness. He says at one point: 'I have always found that the hypothesis of Santa Claus "works satisfactorily in the widest sense of the word"; therefore "Santa Claus exists" is true although Santa Claus does not exist.'[24] But it is enough to rebut this account of James's theory that Russell seems to regard the question of 'working satisfactorily' as excluding all the normal tests which provide us with evidence on the matter, and on which Russell relies in his own view that Santa Claus does not exist. If these are included, as they should be, in the wider sense of 'working satisfactorily', then it is difficult to believe that even Russell found the hypothesis to work satisfactorily. The worst objection that could then be derived from the exchange is that James does not tell us specifically how the various divergent factors operate in determining the acceptance or rejection of such hypotheses. But this, too, has been already admitted by James.

Russell, however, had other objections to make. In one he claimed that if a true proposition is one the consequences of believing which are good, then to believe a proposition true must be to believe that the consequences of believing it are good. Russell thought it self-evident that the question 'Have Popes always been infallible?' was quite different from the question 'Are the consequences of believing Popes to be infallible good?' One problem here is that the objection is in danger of collapsing into the earlier, inadequate, point. The difference between the two questions will be strongly apparent if we confine good consequences to moral outcomes, or emotional benefits. But if we extend such consequences, as James intended, to cover evidential procedures, action-guidance, and ultimately survival value, then the difference is less easy to make out. Indeed once that point is made then James has available in principle a strong counter-attack. For it is open to him to ask Russell what *other* considerations bear on the first question which do not bear on the second. Russell indicates on occasion that his answer would be that the relevant facts make the difference, but it has been shown already that James did not deny this. Though the notion of a fact may itself be dependent upon the working of our beliefs, James was quite ready to admit such a notion within the extended framework of what he called good consequences. He would, therefore, have taken the view that the only alternative available to Russell was some transcendent appeal to ultimate facts of the kind indicated by a Bradleian absolute.

Though it is not likely that Russell would have construed his appeal to facts in that way, James's position undoubtedly has defensive resources which Russell overlooks. At one point James says 'At each and every concrete moment truth for each man is what that man "troweth" at that moment with the maximum of satisfaction to himself.'[25] This has suggested the following idea, that if one is asked to list on one side of a piece of paper all the things he believes and on the other side all the things that are true, it appears that there could be no discrepancy between the two lists. At least it makes no sense to suppose that a man might really compose distinct lists, in which items appeared in the second which either did not appear in, or contradicted items in, the first. A cautious man might leave the second list blank, or include in it only a sub-class of the items in the first list. But it is clear that no rational person could suppose that some item was true even though he did not believe it. In that case supposing an item to be true just is to believe it. James might have used such an illustration to support his contentions that there is a necessary link between truth and belief, and that the former notion rests in some way upon the latter. Against this Russell's position faces the challenge of locating truths or facts independently of any beliefs, as in the right hand column; and this seems at best very difficult. A modest man might, of course, have the idea that none of his beliefs will turn out to be true ultimately, but James would have regarded such a pessimism as indicating only that heuristic idea of an ultimate truth, which he was prepared to accept.

Russell also drew from that earlier claim the conclusion that James's theory was in danger of an infinite regress. For if to believe p is to believe that the consequences of believing p are good, then that latter belief will also entail the further belief that the belief that p has good consequences itself has good consequences, and so on. Simply to believe p then seems to entail an endless series of ever more complex beliefs and this may seem quite unplausible and unacceptable. One counter that James makes to this objection is quite inadequate. He implies that Russell's point requires that believers must already have established that their beliefs have good consequences before holding their beliefs. It would, certainly, be quite unplausible to make such a requirement for the holding of any belief, but Russell does not need to make any such claim.

A better response would be to query the seriousness of such a regress. It is, after all, well known that the notion of truth itself breeds just such a regress in the form 'If it is true that p, then it is true that it is true that p'. That entailment will also generate an endless series of more complex statements, and yet it can be treated as an inevitable and quite trivial feature of the truth operator. Once that comparison is made the parallel regress of beliefs may seem less worrying. It may be suggested that the anxiety is confusedly produced by the conviction that when we believe that p we are not simultaneously aware of, say, the more complex fifth order belief generated in the regress, let alone the whole infinite series of such beliefs. Such an anxiety is confused, though, since it adds the assumption that whenever we hold a belief we are distinctively aware of holding it and of all its logical consequences. This neither formed part of the original claim, nor has it independent plausibility.

James did not offer these responses, but instead gave some indications of the way in which he conceived his doctrine as an account of the meaning of truth. The point can be introduced by considering a natural response to Russell's point. It is well known that we cannot infer from

(1)   Colin believes that the Archbishop's envoy is in Libya

that

(2)   Colin believes that Terry Waite is in Libya.

For even if Terry Waite *is* the Archbishop's envoy, still Colin may not know or believe this. Now it is natural to offer a similar rebuttal of Russell's argument. For that argument could be put in the form:

(3)   If someone believes that p is true; and for p to be true is for the consequences of believing p to be good; then that person believes that the consequences of believing p are good.

45

The infinite regress will then arise from this inference so long as the inference is valid. But, it may be said, it has been already shown that the inference is not valid, since even though for p to be true *is* for its consequences to be good, still the believer may not himself know or believe this.

This attempted rebuttal does not work, although James does offer a suggestion along these lines. The evident reason for its failure is that Russell attributes to James not merely the identity of a proposition's truth and the good consequences of believing it, but their synonymy.[26] He says:

> According to the Pragmatists to say 'It is true that other people exist' *means* 'It is useful to believe that other people exist'. But if so, then the two phrases are merely different words for the same proposition; therefore when I believe one I believe the other.[27]

Once this condition is satisfied, however, then the inference on which Russell relies to generate the regress is no longer open to the original objection.

The point shows something about the appeal to meaning in James's account of truth. Russell is working, quite correctly, with an account of meaning in which the pragmatists' equations are strict synonyms. If James were to rely on the objection from the opacity of belief, then he would have no defence against Russell's argument. We have seen, indeed, that James *does* speak of offering a definition of truth, and of presenting a logical rather than a psychological account of truth, and of giving a genetic theory of what is *meant* by truth. All these claims suggest that Russell was right to insist on the synonymy within the argument, and further that Russell has a clearer grasp of the central concept of meaning than James. The one point that might seem puzzling is James's suggestion that he wishes to give a 'genetic' account of what 'true' means. For this suggests that James had a different conception of meaning from Russell.

That suggestion is confirmed by the best of James's efforts to refute Russell's argument. At one point he says:

> A horse may be defined as a beast that walks on the nails of his middle digits. Whenever we see a horse we see such a beast, just as whenever we believe a truth we believe something expedient. Russell and Hawtrey, if they followed their anti-pragmatist logic, would have to say here that we see *that* it is such a beast, a fact which notoriously no one sees who is not a comparative anatomist.[28]

The suggestion is that Russell's argument commits a new fallacy, in which from

(4) Colin believes something (p), the consequences of believing which are good

we are to infer

(5)   Colin believes *that* the consequences of believing p are good.

Since James thinks it fallacious to infer from

(6)   Colin sees a horse, that is, an animal that walks on the nails of its middle digits

that

(7)   Colin sees *that* the animal walks on the nails of its middle digits

he also thinks that Russell's inference is fallacious. In these cases there is no doubt that the relevant clause elucidating the nature of truth or equinity is a definition of some sort, but the suggestion is that it is a definition of a special kind.

James is right to represent these inferences as fallacious, but he gives little direct help in trying to understand what kind of definition he has in mind. He speaks of separating a 'sure sign, mark, or criterion', which his account does *not* provide, from a 'lurking motive inside of every truth claim', but it is hard to attach a clear sense to the latter description. Moreover there seems positive danger in following the analogy with comparative anatomy too far, since a theory of truth will undoubtedly be of a different kind from a theory of anatomy. Perhaps the central point is that James wishes his own definition of truth, like the anatomists', not merely or trivially to paraphrase our conventional ascription of truth, but rather to fit it into some appropriate developed theory. Then, just as the ordinary man who recognises horses but knows no comparative anatomy could not define a horse in that technical way, so the ordinary speaker could not be expected to define truth in James's theoretical way. Any such definition is then intended to express a new and theoretical classification which is not simply a dictionary definition or a conventional synonym.

These claims offer James an escape route from Russell's objections, but they do not at all clearly indicate where that escape route leads. It sounds impressive to require such a definition to find its place within some developed theory, but it remains obscure what sort of theory would be appropriate. It was noted earlier that James thought of concepts or hypotheses as functional items in experience, and that an account of their meaning would disclose the functions they fulfil. It would, therefore, be quite natural to take James's developed theory to be one in which the role of the truth predicate was disclosed in this way. It is also clear that for James such a theory would be part of an epistemological enterprise, that is, one in which the function of truth is related to our acquisition of beliefs, to their revision or rejection, and to their inter-connections with other beliefs. James's interest in truth is thus sharply distinguished from such a formal account as that presented by Tarski, and it is this difference, in part, which the term 'genetic' indicates. James envisages a theory in which all the factors concerned in what he calls the 'working' of our beliefs will find a place.

James also took the battle to the enemy camps. Throughout *The Meaning of Truth* he considers the merits of various alternative accounts, and finds them all inadequate. Here is a sample:

(1) Russell: There is no problem – some propositions are true, some false: belief is an attitude to propositions which yields knowledge when the propositions are true, and error when they are false.

(2) Pratt: A thought is true when the object of which one is thinking is *as* one thinks it.

(3) Taylor: Truth belongs to a system of propositions which have an unconditional claim to be recognised as valid.

(4) Rickert: Truth is a name for all those judgments which we find ourselves under obligation to make by a kind of imperative duty.

(5) Bradley: A true thought must correspond to a determinate being which it cannot be said to make.[29]

Given what has already been said of James's interest in truth his response to these accounts is predictable and understandable. He thought Russell's claim trivial and misleading. What it positively says of truth, belief, and knowledge is not informative, and its claim that there is no problem seemed obscurantist. James, surely rightly, believed that he had at least identified a problem. He felt more sympathy for Pratt's view, but thought that it too concealed rather than solved a serious problem. For if we ask, as James did, what it is for an object to be *as* we think it, then we unearth James's problem beneath the surface form of the definition. Such a question might also elicit an answer of a Tarskian form, but there is no reason so far to think that such an answer excludes rather than complements James's projected epistemological enquiry.

Taylor's account gets closest to the 'absolutist' view which James wished principally to reject. It remains unclear why there should be just one system of propositions with an unconditional claim to validity; it remains doubtful if we ever could be faced with an unconditional claim; and the reference to validity provides a serious danger of circularity in the definition. James thought Rickert's account quite unhelpful, and contrasted it with a pragmatic attempt to give a cash-value to the kind of duties involved. James, as we have seen, wished certainly to associate truth with moral values and goodness, but he also wished to understand these in the biological context of goals such as survival. Of Bradley's claim James says that it is easy to understand why he made it. The motive was to express some commitment to an independent reality. James acknowledged the same commitment, but he thought that Bradley's terms 'correspond', 'determinate being', and 'making' remained unclear.

4

Extended Truth

1 Truth, belief, meaning and action

James's projected epistemological account of the working of our beliefs, designed to elucidate the notion of truth, is not totally without further elaboration. Part of the project might be expected to surface in his radical empiricism, and another part concerns that extension to the scope of truth which assimilates the non-cognitive, affective, considerations to the cognitive case. But even within the narrower context of the cognitive ascription of truth James offers some account of the wider system in which truth is to find its pragmatic place. For James wished strongly to emphasise the inter-connection between truth on one side and belief, meaning, and action on the other.

James often indicates his view of the general relationship between truth, belief, and action, even though he does not devote any single passage to the clarification of these connections. He says such things as 'All feeling is for the sake of action',[1] or 'The essence of consciousness is to instigate action',[2] and 'Perception and thinking are only there for behaviour's sake'.[3] In these claims action and behaviour are treated without differentiation, and, unless a specific need arises to distinguish them I shall follow James. Elsewhere he says that 'Truth is only that which inclines belief',[4] and speaks of belief as 'measured by action'.[5] These claims fit quite naturally into the account of truth given so far. The basic phenomenon to which truth is primarily attached is the individual 'trower's' belief. Such an individual accepts, and is often forced to accept, beliefs in order to respond in action to the current circumstances. Truth therefore depends in some way upon that basic phenomenon which James calls the inclination to belief; but belief is itself measured by action and so is in some way subordinate to it.

The resulting picture has been partially drawn before. Human beings are biological organisms living and acting in a specific environment. For such

49

creatures to survive, or flourish, it is essential that they adapt their behaviour successfully to that environment. In so far as behaviour is rational, guided by reasons and choices, it must make some reference to belief, but presumably some methods of accepting or rejecting beliefs will tend to be successful while others will not. The successful strategies will, at some developed stage of consciousness, be marked by consciously formulated beliefs to which we eventually give the title 'true'. Even before that stage is reached, however, such strategies may still exist and still guide action. Action, or behaviour, here seems to be the most basic phenomenon, while belief, truth, and meaning, are in some way dependent upon that basic item.

This emphasis on action is part of the popular conception of pragmatism, and it is, so far, entirely justified. But if that emphasis is expressed in terms of priorities or dependences among such concepts as belief, truth and action, then the popular conception is ill-focussed for several reasons. At least two basic requirements would need to be met if the terminology of priority or dependence is to be accepted. First there would have to be some criterion to determine the order of priority or dependence; second the very terms of the dependence relationship would have to be made clear. Under the first heading, for example, the notion of dependence might be construed in a weak or a strong way. Consider the relationship between words, or what they signify, and sentences. To many traditional philosophers it seemed obvious that the former items were basic and the latter dependent upon them. For without words there would be no possibility of constructing sentences. It was only later that the opposite order of dependence was canvassed in which words, or what they signify, depend upon the places, or roles, they occupy in sentences. The later claim has been associated with Frege, Wittgenstein, and Quine, and might be captured in the slogan that a word has meaning only in the context of a proposition.[6] It would be natural to think that the two claims, the traditional and the modern, are in conflict, but the simplest way to deal with the problem is to treat the two claims as compatible. We may then say that there is a dependence in *both* directions, and allow that this defines a weak claim for such a dependence. A strong claim for the dependence of A upon B would assert that A is impossible without B, although B is quite possible without A. The weak claim would be only that each is impossible without the other. Since James does not express his envisaged priorities or dependences in these forms it remains unclear whether he conceived a strong or weak form for such relationships.

Whichever form of dependence is at issue, however, it is equally important to know the precise terms of the dependence relation. If we talk, for example, of belief and action then the order of their dependence may turn on specific aspects of each. It seems reasonable to say, as James does, that belief is measured by action and so subordinate to it, but such a claim is clearly ambiguous. It might mean that the *success* of belief is measured by the success of action; or it might mean that the *ascription* of belief is determined by action. Either of these claims, moreover, might be accepted while it is also claimed that in some way action depends upon belief; that is, that at least for deliberate action some prior belief is required to produce it. Certainly James would not have wished to deny that belief may be causally prior to action in that way, even though he also plainly thought that action had some priority over belief.

If we turn to the claimed dependences between belief and truth, then it might be argued on James's behalf that it would at least be impossible to ascribe truth where there was no belief. But such a claim faces two related problems. For first it requires the assumption that truth can be ascribed only to belief, and it further raises the question whether such a dependence is weak or strong. It might be that without belief the ascription of truth would be impossible, but also the case that without the ascription of truth belief would be impossible. The two points come together in this way. If we do not accept the assumption that truth can be ascribed only to belief this may be because we envisage the ascription of truth to sentences or propositions, even where these do not happen to be vehicles of belief. But then it may be said that the notion of a sentence or proposition is that of a potential vehicle of belief, so that the reference to belief is reinstated in a weaker form. The further difficulty is then that if this weaker form is compared with the reverse order of priority we seem to end up with only a weak dependence instead of the stronger one-way dependence originally envisaged. We then produce two parallel claims of the form:

(1)   It would be impossible to ascribe truth if there were no possibility of holding beliefs.

and

(2)   It would be impossible to hold beliefs if there were no possibility of ascribing truth.

Such claims seem unacceptably weak, but James might instead turn to another idea, namely that while a creature might have beliefs but not itself have any conception of truth or of belief, it would be impossible for a creature to have a conception of truth without having both a conception of belief and beliefs. Such a claim is intuitively plausible, offers a strong dependence between these items, and is further not open to the earlier objection about truth's being ascribed only to beliefs. For all that would be needed to establish a conception of belief is the idea of a sentence's, or proposition's, being a potential vehicle of belief. It is also proof against one possible immediate objection to the effect that it is possible to have a conception of truth without actual beliefs. For in answer to this it may be said that nobody could have a conception of truth without grasping that truth is a predicate of belief; but in grasping such a claim a belief has been already formulated.

51

Even these claims are threatened by some current lines of argument, in which a more complex, 'hermeneutic', relation is canvassed between such things as belief, desire, and action. Davidson, for example, expresses part of such claims in the following way:

> Both (beliefs and desires) are essential to the explanation of behaviour and neither is more directly open to observation than the other. This creates a problem for it means that behaviour, which is the main evidential basis for the attribution of beliefs and desires, is reckoned the result of two forces less open to public observation. Thus where one constellation of beliefs and desires will rationalise an action it is always possible to find a quite different constellation that will do as well.[7]

In the same paper Davidson argues against the view, here ascribed to James, that it is possible for a creature to have beliefs without having a concept of truth or belief. If Davidson's argument were compelling, then the view ascribed to James could no longer be held.

The argument for Davidson's conclusion is formally very simple. He says:

> Can a creature have a belief if it does not have the concept of belief? It seems to me that it cannot and for this reason. Someone cannot have a belief unless he understands the possibility of being mistaken, and this requires grasping the contrast between truth and error – true belief and false belief. But this contrast, I have argued, can emerge only in the context of interpretation, which alone forces us to the idea of an objective public truth.[8]

The suggestion is that the ascription of belief to some creature carries with it the recognition, on the part of that creature, of the contrast between truth and falsity, which is in turn dependent upon a context of interpretation which locates the creature in a speech community with the public apparatus of language and meaning.

The argument can be represented as a chain of implications of the following kind: For any creature to have a belief it is required
(3)   that it understands the possibility of mistake
(4)   that it therefore understands the contrast between truth and falsity
(5)   that it therefore participates in a context of interpretation
(6)   that it consequently is a member of a speech community
(7)   that it therefore has the concept of belief.
Of these steps (5)–(6) seems unquestionable as reflecting the sense of Davidson's technical term 'context of interpretation'. There might be residual doubt, however, about step (6)-(7), on the ground that being a member of a speech community may not entail recognition of the concept of belief if the language of that community has not made room for it. At least such a point indicates that there may be some variability in concepts of

belief. For perhaps different communities with different levels of development and different interests might have a grasp of a concept of belief somewhat different from, and more rudimentary than, our own. These are interesting speculations, but it is steps (3)–(5) which seem most dubious.

The weakness in these steps lies in their apparent ambiguity. Plainly if the notions of 'mistake', or 'truth' and 'falsity', are to permit the further steps after (5), then they must be understood in a strong sense, in which they form part of a context of interpretation and so of a public communicable language. Yet it is not hard to construe such notions in a far weaker sense which patently does not involve any such complex developed background. James's own position invites us to envisage creatures who have acquired strategies for survival through some process of trial and error, and who might be said to have primitive beliefs which guide their actions. It might consequently be said that they already have some conception of success or failure in action, and so some appreciation of mistakes, and yet that they evidently have no developed concepts of truth or falsity of the kind envisaged in steps (5)–(7).

One difficulty here, which Davidson acknowledges, is the argument's tendency to produce conflicting intuitions to support each side of the dispute. Certainly Davidson could not simply legislate that the notion of belief can be ascribed only if it was of the strong kind required to validate steps (5)–(7). But by the same token he could say that we could not, without begging the question, simply legislate that a primitive belief could be ascribed on the basis of a weaker interpretation of (3) and (4). What can initially be done, however, is to spell out the kind of case that supports the weak interpretation. We have to imagine, then, a creature which has developed a successful strategy for achieving some goal, say quenching its thirst, and then to consider its behaviour if that strategy should turn out on some occasion to be unsuccessful. We have to imagine how it would react if the previously successful strategy of walking to the water hole were obstructed by drought or the presence of a predator. Clearly if the creature has no conception of success or failure at all, if for example its behaviour can be classified simply as a tropism, then we would expect little change in the behavioural repertoire. But we have little difficulty in imagining cases where the response indicates recognition of an obstacle and some awareness of an appropriate modification to the strategy. In the light of such examples Davidson needs some non-question-begging argument to reject them on top of the argument in his paper. There is a suggestion that his account of the complex, 'hermeneutic', relation between belief, desire and action might offer some such support.

It is, however, worth noticing briefly first not only that James would have rejected Davidson's argument but also that he would have regarded it as an example of his 'psychologists' fallacy'. At one point James describes the fallacy as 'the confusion between the constitution of the thing as known by the psychologist and the constitution of that same thing possessed by a mind which the psychologist is examining'.[9] The suggestion is that Davidson's argument so far unwarrantably ascribes to any creature with a belief the complex and sophisticated background in which we talk of error and of truth and falsity of belief. Davidson equates the recognition of a mistake with the recognition of our concept of a mistake.

There is an indication that Davidson takes such a view because he is impressed by the 'hermeneutic' relation between beliefs, desires and action. For the argument may be that since there can be no direct behavioural way of identifying beliefs and desires independently, some additional assumptions are needed which form part of the 'context of interpretation'. It may then be said that the simple counter-example can be constructed only by violating that hermeneutic claim, and that this is not permissible since, as Davidson puts it, 'any other constellation of beliefs and desires will do as well' to rationalise the action. It is as if we have to solve an equation with two unknowns when we have data enough only for one unknown. Davidson does not believe, any more than Quine does in his comparable arguments, that such radical indeterminacy is practically unresolvable, but, like Quine, he is inclined to suppose that such practical resolutions require background assumptions, analytical hypotheses, a priori principles of rationality or charity, or the context of interpretation.

The form of such arguments, common though they are, is obscure. Two points might be made. First, as we shall see later, James in his radical empiricism refuses to accept general arguments of this kind which appeal to a priori principles in order to supplement a supposed set of basic empirical data. Like Austin, James thought that such traditional styles of argument involved a needless appeal to 'trans-empirical' principles, which then rested upon a wholly unrealistic account of the basic data. Second, however, in the specific case of beliefs and desires Davidson evidently challenges his opponents to explain how the primitive case outlined earlier can be supported against this objection. What made it plausible in that case to talk of beliefs on the basis of a behavioural repertoire was the presupposition of an already determined basic desire. The assumption was that the creature had, and was currently influenced by, the basic need for water, and it was in relation to that fixed parameter that the behaviour was interpreted in terms of belief.

So long as it is possible to fix some such basic desires, to identify what psychologists have tended to call 'instincts', then the remaining unknown, belief, can itself be identified. Endorsement of such a strategy has not been confined to psychologists. Hume's conclusions about the role of instincts in the development of our own more sophisticated patterns of behaviour is of the same sort. It is difficult to see why such a procedure should presuppose a priori principles of rationality, or of the context of interpretation. Hume's views, indeed, are specific denials of such claims. It is consequently difficult to see Davidson's argument as compelling.[10]

2   An outline theory

Such an appeal to a basic desire coupled with an ascription of primitive beliefs on the basis of behaviour is the starting point of a programme outlined by Grice, which seems to fit James's ideas remarkably well. In his 1975 paper 'Method in Philosophical Psychology'[11] Grice outlines a programme in which, starting from such a primitive basis, more complex, fine-grained, psychological descriptions can be progressively applied. James does not himself pursue such a programme in this way, but I shall take it as a possible model with which to understand how James's basic ideas might be developed.

Grice begins with the same basic problem as Davidson to do with the complex and interlocking relationship between belief, desire and action. To offer an explicit definition in behavioural terms of

(8)   A believes p

of the form

(9)   Given that A desires X, A is disposed to act in ways (Y) which will realise X if p is true

involves two circularities. First it assumes the identification of specific desires, when the corresponding definition of desire will presumably require the independent identification of specific beliefs. Second (9) is at least not a necessary condition for (8), since, even though A may believe p, he may fail to do Y, or even to be disposed to do Y, if he does not realise that Y is the way to achieve X if p is true. This defect might be remedied if we write in place of (9)

(9a)   Given that A desires X, A is disposed to act in ways (Y) which *he believes* will realise X if p is true.

But (9a) remedies that defect at the expense of producing another, more blatant, circularity.

Unlike Davidson, however, Grice does not conclude that the relation between these psychological states and behaviour is inscrutable. He says, on the contrary,

> The idea suggested to me by this difficulty is that we might be well advised as a first move to abandon the idea of looking for explicit definitions of central psychological concepts and look instead for implicit definitions, to be provided by some form of axiomatic treatment; leaving open the possibility that, as a second move, this kind of treatment might be made the foundation for a different sort of definition. Such a procedure might well preserve an attractive feature of behaviouristic analyses, that of attempting to explain psychological concepts by relating them to appropriate forms of behaviour.[12]

In particular Grice makes two moves to achieve his goal. First he relies, as the counter-example to Davidson relied, on the idea that certain basic instincts or desires might be identified in terms which relate the physical conditions of an organism to its survival. Thus certain obvious consequences of failing to find or absorb food or water serve as the starting-point for the identification of a primitive desire for food or water. Once such a desire is fixed then associated patterns of behaviour related to the search for food or water and their success or failure may be associated with judging, or belief, as well as wanting. Grice notes that complications arising, for example, from the frustration of such standard behavioural repertoires would need to be taken into account, but the earlier discussion suggests that these would reinforce rather than undermine the general programme. For the suggestion there was that certain behaviour may be associated with the recognition of an obstacle or an error, while other behaviour cannot be.

Second Grice offers various procedures through which the basic position might be developed to achieve more complex, sophisticated, psychological descriptions. Central to these procedures is the idea of 'internalisation' in which what may be implicit in a level of development at one stage becomes explicit in a subsequent stage of development. Grice distinguishes carefully between different kinds of internalisation, stressing, for example, the contrast between 'first-order' and 'second-order' internalisation. The former would be exemplified by the transition from an observer's report

(10) A will in the future judge p,

to

(11) A future-judges (p)

or from

(12) A judges either p or q

to

(13) A or-judges (p,q).

The latter would be exemplified by the transitions from (11) or (13) respectively to

(14) A judges (in the future, p)

or

(15) A judges (p or q).

In a similar way Grice also suggests that an explicit notion of belief might be introduced into more developed systems in terms of a higher-order judging. If some creature at one level of development has the capacity to judge p, it does not follow for Grice that that creature has the concept of belief. In this way the developmental programme makes explicit room for the possibility that Davidson wished to exclude, namely the occurrence of belief without the concept of belief. Grice suggests plausibly that a creature which not only judges p, but has also the ability to judge that it judges p would have attained not only beliefs but also the concept of belief.

Grice's programme of development has three features which particularly fit it into the scheme here attributed to James. First it is implicit in the account that successive stages of the development, like the starting-point itself, are governed by a general biological goal of 'survival-utility'. This is initially expressed in the fanciful terms of the 'genitorial programme', in which a genitor or creator sets out to design, and with the help of an 'engineer' produce, successively more complex creatures. But the myth of the genitor is no more, it appears, than a picturesque way of referring to those biological goals. Grice says, for example:

> I think of the genitorial programme . . . as being primarily a heuristic device. I would, however, hope to be able to retain a less vivid reformulation of it, in which references to the genitor's purposes would be replaced by references to final causes, or (more positivistically) to survival-utility.[13]

At each stage in the later developments, consequently, Grice appeals to the supposed advantages to survival which the changes would be expected to bring. James, of course, bases his own account of the priorities among beliefs, truth, and action upon the same basic appeal to biological goals and survival-value.

A second similarity arises within the programme of internalisation in which Grice suggests a higher-order notion of 'acceptance' as related to the basic notions of judging and willing. He sketches such transitions from

(16)   A judges (p): A wills (X)

to

(17)   A judicatively accepts (p): A volitively accepts (X).

He further sketches a transition from

(18)   A judicatively accepts (p)

to

(19)   A accepts (It is the case that, p).

The first of these transitions, in which a generic notion of 'acceptance' is related to the more specific 'judging' and 'willing', has a similarity to James's wish to assimilate what I have called the 'cognitive' and 'affective' cases of belief. To treat judging and willing in this way is to move towards James's idea that the two broad types of belief should be treated in parallel, and further that the parallel should be marked by the common use of the truth predicate. It is to go some way towards James's account of truth in which the notion rests on the working of our beliefs, whether those beliefs are cognitive or not.

The second transition allows for the introduction at some stage of an explicit operator, 'It is the case that . . .', which it is natural to see as the forerunner, or even equivalent, of the predicate '. . . is true'. Just as Grice is prepared to envisage creatures with beliefs but no concept of belief, so he is also prepared to envisage creatures who might have beliefs but no explicit operator of the form 'It is the case that . . .', or 'It is true that . . .'. Though clearly James does not offer a detailed programme of Grice's sort, the priorities which that programme outlines are close to those on which James wanted to insist. Both of these particular points match James's idea that the notion of truth is dependent epistemologically upon more primitive notions such as belief and desire, whose roles in guiding action are dominated by general biological goals such as survival.

A third similarity has to do with Grice's conception of the transitions from lower- to higher-order states. In this, and other, contexts Grice treats such patterns of development in a Kantian style as showing the conditions which make some phenomenon possible. Though there is dispute about the nature of Kant's transcendental arguments, there is no doubt that they have a character which might be called 'genetic'. They map a theoretically possible way in which some complex phenomenon might develop out of simpler phenomena coupled with certain general conditions. They offer an example of 'analysis' in philosophy which, though presentable in a formal way, nevertheless has a developmental character which marks it off from the usual analysis of concepts. James might not have welcomed such an affinity with a Kantian transcendentalism, but this would have been mainly because he, like other nineteenth century theorists, mistook the nature of Kant's arguments. At their best they are essentially ways of marking priorities or dependences among concepts, of just the sort that Grice and James were concerned with. Such a comparison at least begins to explain what James had in mind when he spoke of his theory of truth as a 'genetic' account.

The programmes sketched lightly by James and more fully by Grice point in the same direction, but neither has progressed far. Their features are, I think, sufficiently similar to regard Grice's as an elaboration of James's ideas, or to justify the claim that Grice is a pragmatist in a way that James would understand, but they do not yet establish the theories as true. For one thing the programme remains a sketch, whose details need elaboration. That objection is in principle remediable, but there may be other objections which are not. I shall consider three possible criticisms, the third of which in any case recalls an admitted gap in the account. For James's envisaged theory was to relate belief and action not only to truth, but also to meaning, and nothing has yet been said of that.

The three objections are:

(i)　That the programme's starting-point, namely the identification of certain basic instincts or desires in behavioural terms, fails to take into account the 'intentionality' of desire.

(ii)　That the programme is internally unclear in its appeal to dependence or priority, and that in particular it remains unclear whether it supports a strong or only a weak form of dependence.

(iii)　That the programme's order of priorities must be wrong. Belief, it may be said, cannot be the foundation for the notion of truth, since belief requires a content which already invokes the concept of meaning. Moreover, if the notion of meaning itself rests on that of a truth condition, then the content of belief, and belief itself, will rest on the notion of truth rather than the other way round. On such a view 'belief' is simply a name for that adventitious relation which occurs when some creature captures a content in a certain psychological way.

i *The intentionality of desire*

James knew of Brentano's idea of intentionality and indeed made extensive use of it in his psychology and his radical empiricism. The objection here, however, is not that James was generally ignorant of intentionality, but that it is mistakenly excluded from the programme's initial identification of desires. The most succinct formulation of such a criticism is in Wittgenstein's response to Russell's account of desire in his *Analysis of Mind*, a work in which Russell strongly acknowledges the influence of James. I shall consider the point in the light of comments made on it by Baker and Hacker in their *Scepticism, Rules, and Language*.

Wittgenstein ascribes to Russell the view that a desire is 'a feeling of discomfort which causally generates a behaviour cycle which terminates in a condition of quiescence'.[14] The desire is then said to be *for* the state of affairs which produces that quiescence. Wittgenstein objected in these terms:

> I believe Russell's theory amounts to the following: If I give someone an order and I am happy with what he does, then he has carried out my order. (If I wanted to eat an apple, and someone punched me in the stomach, taking away my appetite, then it was this punch that I originally wanted.)[15]

Baker and Hacker comment on this:

> To know that a state of affairs which is realised is the object of one's desire is to apprehend an internal relation. . . . (But in Russell) recognition of the realised object of desire is conceived as an external relation. This in effect makes it an open question whether what somebody sincerely *avows* to be the object of desire really *is* so . . . But this is absurd . . . What is desired is not ascertained by experiment, but rather it can be read off the expression of desire . . . The relation between a desire and its fulfilment is . . . forged in language.[16]

On the face of it the same objections should apply to James and Grice, in so far as they envisage determining desires by experiment in behavioural terms. Moreover, it may seem as if such an argument could re-activate Davidson's earlier claims. For the objection, so understood, seems to rest on the claim that desires cannot be experimentally ascertained, but require a language, a language-user, and the possibility of sincere avowals of desire. To take such a view is to endorse Davidson's claims about a 'context of interpretation'.

There are, however, decisive reasons not to take the argument in this way. Baker and Hacker plainly restrict their interest to the self-ascription of desires, whereas the pragmatist programme is interested, for reasons already made plain, in the other-ascription of desires. No doubt it is correct to say, of oneself, that generally experiments are not necessary in order to identify one's own desires, but it is no less plausible to envisage the use of experiments in ascribing desires to others, especially where those others are too primitive to have developed a language. In the pragmatist programme it is assumed for these basic desires that the desirer cannot itself identify the desire in that way. A reference to language, to intentionality, is, indeed must be, present in the theorist's ascription of desire, but not necessarily, if the programme is right, in the consciousness of the desirer. The references to language, to intentionality, are necessary in the theorist's account; how else could he ascribe desires? But it does not follow that those references are already present in that form in the desirer itself. To suppose so would be again to commit James's 'psychologists' fallacy'. It is by no means obvious from what Wittgenstein says that he would in any way have disagreed with this.

Davidson's claims cannot be re-activated in that way, but it may still be said that the pragmatist account, like Russell's, is still open to the main objection. If desires are defined in terms of patterns of behaviour which terminate in quiescence, then Wittgenstein's examples present a problem even if they are not interpreted in the way that Baker and Hacker interpret them. For they suggest simply that on such a definition anything which produces quiescence will then count as the object of the desire. Since death will quite generally produce that result we may seem forced to the view that in all our wishes it is really death that we desire; a view which adds a new dimension to the old scholastic ambiguity that the end of life is death.

But the pragmatist programme is not vulnerable to this gross objection, and neither is Russell. The former at least, as we have seen, does not begin by offering explicit definitions of desire in behavioural terms. It could not then accept the definition which is objected to any more than Wittgenstein could. The initial basic desires are identified, too, not only in behavioural terms, but also in terms of biological goals, such as survival, and the organism's physiology. Such additional materials plainly can be used to avoid the conclusions which Wittgenstein draws. Beyond that, as we have seen, Wittgenstein's plea for the inclusion of intentionality is admitted in the programme, though at the initial stage only at the level of the theorist's ascription of desire. Russell, though more vulnerable to such a point than Grice, nevertheless also shares the same theoretical aims as the pragmatist programme and can similarly escape the objection.

ii *Dependence and priority in the theory*

The second objection had to do with internal unclarities in Grice's programme about its notion of dependence and the nature of the theory itself. It remains unclear whether the relation of dependence should be understood in the theory in a strong or weak way, and also what might determine the acceptance or rejection of the theory. As to the first of these it has to be conceded that the relations in the theory are not fully elaborated. In some cases Grice spells out the connections by identifying, as the theory requires, different patterns of behaviour associated with different levels of development. He distinguishes between, for example, the reports 'A judges p or A judges q' and 'A or-judges (p,q)'. To make the former true all that is needed is that A make one judgment, which may be p or may be q; but the latter involves A's considering two judgments and adopting a form of behaviour appropriate to their relation, for example showing hesitancy or indecision while keeping both options open. But such elaboration is not generally available for the transitions in the theory.

It may consequently be unclear whether the theory licences strong or only weak dependences. The theory itself, however, shows, and if confirmed would establish, the possibility of one item (A) without another (B) together with B's emergence on the basis of A, coupled with other assumptions. In that way the theory demonstrates a strong relation of dependence between A and B, but it might be objected that the theory does nothing to establish that this is the *only* way in which A and B might be related. Such an objection is like one frequently raised against Kant's priority arguments, that they may show one possible way of constructing experience, but do not demonstrate uniqueness for the solution. Perhaps another theory could be constructed in which either B is independent of A, or even A itself depends upon B. In the former possibility, if it forces us to accept both A and B as basic, we might still prefer the Gricean theory on the grounds of economy, but that consideration would not help in the latter cases. What would be needed there would be some other ground for preferring one of the theories to the other, where the only grounds available seem to involve empirical evidence.

Clearly there are empirical constraints on the acceptance of specific psychological theories of the sort Grice envisages. There can be no doubt that James would have welcomed, indeed insisted on, just such a claim. For him the philosophical discussion should move towards, and terminate in, the formulation of empirical hypotheses which may then be accepted in the light of empirical evidence. Probably the same would be true of Grice, at least if my classification of him as a pragmatist is just. But in Grice's case we should distinguish between his philosophical ideas about the forms of such psychological theories, and the specific psychological theories which might be constructed under those forms. The former would produce a general template, or blueprint, for theories of the latter type. Both such theories are vulnerable to empirical constraints, but these constraints will apply directly to the specific psychological theories and only indirectly to the philosophical blueprint. The specific psychological theories would, for example, depend upon the identification of basic desires for some species, and these would be determined by those creatures' physiological needs and their environmental situation. The envisaged transitions, too, from one state to another would be vulnerable to the discovery of creatures whose pattern of development followed a different path. In that case the background blueprint would provide nothing more than a theoretical possibility, which might be realised in some other creature but does not hold for this one. Though it is true that Grice, and still more James, do not elaborate these constraints their existence offers a way of establishing the strongest form of dependence.

iii *Belief, content, and meaning*

James also speaks of his account as a genetic theory of 'what is meant by' truth, and we saw earlier how that reference to meaning confused critics such as Russell. That earlier discussion showed that James's conception of meaning-elucidation was not that of providing analytic equivalents, or dictionary synonyms, but rather that of exhibiting the function of such a notion as that of truth within a Gricean-type theory. We should here distinguish, as I earlier did, between a strict theory of truth which would show the working of our beliefs and its outcome in decision and action both in the cognitive and affective cases, and the wider theory in which truth is related to belief and meaning. But there is no reason to doubt that James would have been prepared to accept both as connected branches of one general theory of truth.

Nothing, however, has yet been said of meaning in its relation to belief and this produces two problems. One is simply that of locating the notion of meaning within the order of priorities already sketched. The other, internal, problem is that of ordering the relations between pragmatic method and the theory of truth. The main difficulty in the first problem is that the notion of belief requires a content, and the latter notion requires the idea of a meaning which that content expresses, or is. The difficulty is compounded if it is assumed that the required notion of meaning can be found in a theory of truth conditions such as Tarski's formal truth theory. For such priorities indicate an order at odds with that envisaged by James. James conceives of truth and meaning as dependent upon belief, but the alternative view makes belief depend upon meaning, and meaning in turn depend upon truth through the notion of a truth condition. The difficulty in the second problem has been canvassed before. It is that if pragmatic method rests on a conception of meaning, and meaning itself rests on the notion of truth, then the method will depend upon the theory of truth rather than the other way round.

One way of dealing with these problems would be to invoke another part of Grice's programme, namely his 'communication-intention' account of meaning.[17] The suggestion here is that just as more sophisticated psychological states may develop out of more primitive such states, so an abstract notion like meaning may develop out of primitive intentions. Grice paints a picture of primitive communication in which one creature may, for example, attempt to warn another of impending danger. Such an attempt will be successful provided the second creature correctly recognises the first creature's intention, and Grice's idea is that such a success might provide a foundation for the more stable and public co-operative conventions of a natural language. Grice's idea is not, as some early commentators supposed, to 'analyse' conventions of an existing natural language so that they could be replaced by equivalents mentioning only intentions. If that were Grice's aim, then he would be open to the familiar objection that some intentions can be formulated, and formed, only within the framework of a developed natural language. If that were true then plainly not all such conventions could be analytically reformulated in terms of primitive intentions. Understood, however, in the 'genetic' way outlined earlier Grice's theory is not open to such an objection. He is not, then, offering analytic equivalents for linguistic conventions, but rather showing how they might develop step by step out of some basic intentions and primitive co-operative wishes.

If such a programme is fitted on to the scheme envisaged already, then we obtain a parallel account of meaning and language. That is, just as complex psychological states such as recognition of a concept of belief are to be represented as developing out of basic forms of judging and willing, so the more complex semantic ideas, such as that of a public convention, are to be represented as developing out of primitive intentions. Since such intentions will themselves rest on basic judgings and willings, we can expect that the semantic development will fall within the general psychological scheme. There will be, then, not two distinct, serially ordered, developments so much as one general development in which cognitive and semantic complexities arise in parallel. It is scarcely possible to determine within so general a sketch exactly how these would be related, but what is important to James is preserved in such an extended Gricean programme, namely the priority of belief over both truth and meaning. Belief and the working of beliefs, are to be the basis of both the notions of truth and meaning, and this allows for the possibility of giving a formal account of natural language meaning in terms of truth conditions. That would not be incompatible with James's view so long as the notion of truth itself rested on that of belief, rather than the other way round. James was fond of likening the notion of truth to other abstract ideas such as those of health, or wealth, beauty or goodness. For him these were simply sophisticated ways of referring compendiously to the complex practical phenomena in which they were manifested. 'Beauty,' he says, 'is pleasure objectified.'[18] It seems likely that he would have taken a similar view of truth and of a formal truth theory. Such a theory would then be simply a formal representation of the workings of our beliefs.

In the light of such a view it is not difficult to outline the relations between pragmatic method and the theory of truth. In one way the enquiry into truth must proceed along pragmatic lines, and that may make the method seem prior to the theory. But if the stronger versions of the method themselves rest on a conception of meaning, and the notion of truth is required for the latter, then James's procedure may seem circular. The method is used to enquire into truth, but the notion of truth is itself required in order to establish the notion of meaning on which the method rests. But it is now plain that James would not have wished to make truth basic to the method, even if a theory of meaning could be constructed on the basis of a truth theory. For what is basic to both truth and meaning is the working of belief. The working of belief is the basic datum for notions such as truth and meaning as well as for the clarification of issues in pragmatic method. In this way, and with appropriate provisos, James was right to say that the method provides no substantive claims; it merely points to the data which are to be used to resolve all such issues. The method and the theory of truth reinforce each other, but they are not objectionably circular in the way suggested; both are predicated upon the fundamental importance of beliefs and their working.

It may still be thought that the first problem remains, that the requirement that belief have a semantic content is an insuperable obstacle to James's programme. Two further points might be made to resist such a view. First, though it has been admitted that the ascription of belief requires a content a distinction has been drawn between the way such a content may be realised by, say, a language-less creature and an observer with a language which he uses to ascribe that belief to that creature. The order of priorities canvassed in the pragmatic programme is one in which beliefs are ascribable without the concept of belief being ascribable. By the same token belief contents may be ascribed without the concept of a content being ascribed, or even ascribable. The distinction is that which arose earlier in the discussion of the intentionality of desire, and it is one on which James frequently insists. It may seem more plausible to ascribe desires, or instincts, in some primitive way without worrying about their content, but both beliefs and desires require a content of some sort. If it is possible to overcome this difficulty for desire then it should be possible to do the same for belief.

Such a response will seem less satisfying than a positive demonstration of the way in which such ascriptions might work. Such an account, however, has been offered in Brian Loar's account of Ramsey's theory of belief and truth, and in his extended account of propositional attitude psychology.[19]

In Loar's view what is fundamental is the functional role of beliefs, just as it is in the pragmatist programme. The ascription of content is conceived as similar to the 'indexing' of a temperature by the allocation of a number to measure or scale it. In the case of belief such 'indices' are primarily dependent upon the functional role of the belief which will then determine its content and so the meaning of any sentence which the believer may use to express the belief or which an observer may use to ascribe the belief to the believer. Three features in Loar's theory offer a hope of filling out James's, and Grice's, programme.

The first of these is that Loar is prepared to treat belief as a foundation for theories of meaning and truth. He says, for example,

> The third condition (that a belief ascription does not give the content of a belief by referring to a sentence or utterance of the ascriber's as having a certain meaning) . . . would permit belief to have a foundational status in the theory of meaning.[20]

Second, he insists on the idea that the functional role of a psychological state determines the proposition which captures the content of belief. For a creature with a language such considerations will determine what some sentence of his means to him, or to some wider population of which he is a part. Loar says, for example,

> The causal properties of the mental factors of a belief determine its objective factors – i.e. what proposition captures the content of the belief. It seems fair to say that for Ramsey the theory of *belief* and the theory of *meaning* are one and the same: what makes a sentence of Z's mean p is whatever constitutes a mental relation to that sentence as being the belief that p.[21]

Third, he fits this account of belief onto an account of truth which is in some respects Jamesian, and which allows the development of a formal truth theory as itself dependent upon the fundamental notion of belief.

Loar's and Grice's theories, which complement each other in some ways, make it seem at least plausible that James's sketch of a pragmatist programme could be filled out. It is true that the suggestions are still highly programmatic, though Loar's is by far the most detailed account of such a theory so far.[22] They suggest that James's ideas about a theory of belief, in its strict or wider forms, are not to be put aside simply because he expressed his views in the dubious equation of 'true' and 'useful'.

5

Radical Empiricism

In the preface to *The Meaning of Truth* James outlines the three central tenets of radical empiricism. These are, first, the postulate 'that the only things that shall be debatable among philosophers shall be things definable in terms drawn from experience': second, the statement of fact 'that the relations between things, conjunctive as well as disjunctive, are just as much matters of direct particular experience . . . as . . . the things themselves': third, a generalised conclusion, 'that therefore the parts of experience hold together from next to next by relations that are themselves part of experience'. James adds to this conclusion that 'the directly apprehended universe needs no extraneous, trans-empirical, support'.[1]

It was pointed out in Chapter 2 that some of these tenets are closely linked to James's pragmatic method, even though he was at pains to dissociate the two doctrines. The postulate in particular looks with hindsight very close to part of pragmatic method. It is true that the method could be construed as neutral with respect to experiential ways of settling disputes. Then it would be understood simply to outlaw any issues where there is no possible decision procedure, that is, where we fall into what James called 'interminable metaphysical disputes'. Certainly in such contexts as those of mathematics or logic, which James was prepared to regard as 'a priori' in the *Principles*, he did not require experiential tests, and criticised Mill for so doing.[2] But he also believed, as other empiricists have, that even these special contexts, though not directly related to experience, were nevertheless indirectly related to it. In practice, of course, James was in any case far more interested in philosophical issues where there was some clear link with experience, so that his own use of the method tended to match his acceptance of the postulate.[3]

The second item, the statement of fact, is clearly more complex. It concerns essentially the difference James wished to mark between traditional empiricists, such as Locke, Hume, or Herbart, and his own 'radical' empiricism. James was in general friendlier to empiricism than to what he called 'rationalism', but he also believed that traditional empiricists had made one big mistake. It was not that they dwelt more on the parts of experience than on experience as a whole, for James was inclined to follow them in this.[4] Rather it was that they had too restrictive a conception of what those parts might be. James expressed this point by distinguishing between parts and relations, and between what he called disjunctive and conjunctive relations. He thought that traditional empiricists had separated the parts of experience from the relations between those parts, and had restricted the basic content of experience to exclude most of what James called 'conjunctive' relations. This view is not immediately intelligible or evidently correct.

Traditional empiricism might be represented in terms of three interlocking principles.

(1) A Principle of Economy, which enjoins the acceptance of as few basic resources as possible.

(2) A Principle of Atomism, which identifies the basic *content* of experience solely as discrete sensory particulars.

(3) A Principle of Analysis, which claims that legitimate experience can be derived from the basic content only by the application of logical rules.[5]

Of the three principles the first is a heuristic injunction of the type that Russell frequently invoked under the title 'Ockham's Razor';[6] the second deals with the basic resources of experience as far as the *content* is concerned, while the third deals with the basic resources of the derivation of experience, as far as its *form* is concerned. I shall use the general term 'resources' to cover both kinds of item involved in (2) and (3). Clearly the principles are not formulated with total precision, but this allows for variations within the general frame which nevertheless still deserve the title 'empiricism'.

The first principle effectively draws a distinction between what is basic in experience and what is derived, or dependent, and it simply enjoins the restriction of the former only to what is strictly required. Such a principle may be necessary for empiricism but it plainly is not sufficient. A Kantian might accept the principle but insist that some basic items not recognised by empiricists were also necessary. Traditional empiricism then adds to the first principle a second, in which the basic content of experience is identified in terms of discrete sensory particulars, impressions or ideas. Such a principle is supported less by general argument to the effect that no other items are necessary than by a strong, even ideological, conviction that there could be no such other items. This second principle is what divides empiricism from Kantianism. For Kant wished to question that ideological conviction by showing that certain other items than sensory particulars were required for experience.[7]

These two principles naturally invite a third, which defines the resources used to derive our complex experience from the identified basic content. It would, of course, be possible for someone to accept the first two principles but to reject the third. Such a position would leave us only with the basic, discrete, fragmentary impressions included in the basic content, and so unable to recover the central features of our developed experience. It would leave us with an extreme scepticism, even a solipsism of the present moment.[8] But some form of scepticism notoriously might still arise even if the third principle is accepted. For the extent of the successful recovery of that developed experience will patently depend upon the strength of the particular principle of analysis itself. If that principle should turn out to be unexpectedly weak, then certain portions of our ordinary experience may have to remain unaccounted for. Notoriously this is frequently regarded as the natural outcome of traditional empiricism, and it invites two opposed responses. In the first the empiricist principles are upheld, but at the cost of treating some parts of our ordinary experience as erroneous, illusory, or unjustified. In the second the empiricist principles are questioned or rejected, perhaps even on the ground that they have palpably failed.

In such a characterisation it is easy to see that the first two principles have a reciprocal relationship to the third. The weaker the basic resources of content the stronger will need to be the principle of analysis in order to recover any dependent item of experience. By the same token the weaker the principle of analysis the stronger will have to be the basic content in order to derive some dependent item. Hence for those philosophers who wish to reject a traditional version of empiricism because it fails to recover some item of our ordinary developed experience, two broad strategies are available. One will be to strengthen the resources of derivation, in the principle of analysis, but to accept the restrictive basic content of empiricism; the other will be to leave the resources of analysis untouched but to enrich the basic content. It would, no doubt, be possible to combine both strategies, or even to reject the whole framework within which empiricism operates. But it is reasonable to suggest that Kant chooses the first of these strategies and William James the second.[9]

James complained of traditional empiricism not only that it encouraged scepticism, but also that such a scepticism itself encouraged the rejection of empiricism.[10] Such a rejection, moreover, might result in the denial of the additional conclusion which James added to his three radical empiricist tenets. For dissatisfaction with a sceptical outcome might lead us to adopt the Kantian strategy of appealing to what James calls 'trans-empirical' principles, that is, principles of the sort Kant held to be synthetic a priori in his own epistemology. Actually James here is less than fair to Kant, since the notion of a trans-empirical support is ambiguous. In one, weak, sense it indicates only the rejection of the empiricists' exhaustive distinction between analytic and synthetic truths and the acceptance of synthetic a

priori truths. In another, stronger, sense it allows a reference to inexperiencable items. Kant's synthetic a priori truths were explicitly denied
that stronger reference and allowed only an 'immanent' function in relation
to our experience. But for our purposes it is only the weaker claim that
needs to be considered. James did wish to reject a Kantian synthetic a priori
classification, and so far was prepared to accept the traditional empiricist
principle of analysis. He consequently took the view that it was wrong to
escape from a threatened scepticism by a Kantian route which denied
empiricism, or at least that feature of its analytic apparatus.

The natural, perhaps only serious, recourse left to James was to question
the remaining principle of atomism. The suggestion he wished to make was
that a consistent, and improved, version of empiricism can be obtained by
remedying the factual falsity of that traditional principle. What is given in
basic experience, then, is more than merely the discrete sensory particulars
of the traditional empiricists. What is basically given must also include
relations between these items, and conjunctive as well as disjunctive
relations between them. It was pointed our earlier that there was a danger
in reading James's term 'radical' as 'extreme' in his characterisation of his
own empiricism. Though it still remains unclear how James thought of
disjunctive and conjunctive relations, this account already shows that
'radical' empiricism is a more generous, tolerant, version of the doctrine
rather than a more restrictive or extreme variety.[11]

James cites several examples of the standard empiricism he wished to
reject in this way. In the *Principles*, for example, he quotes from Bain: 'The
stream of thought is not a continuous current, but a series of distinct ideas,
more or less rapid in their succession.'[12] Elsewhere he also cites Hume's
famous appeal to 'distinct existences': 'All our distinct perceptions are
distinct existences, and . . . the mind never perceives any real connection
among distinct existences.'[13] In the same passage in the *Principles* James
makes explicit the point noted earlier, that an unduly narrow conception of
the basic content of experience may so encourage the strengthening of the
principle of analysis as to admit the existence of a priori or trans-empirical
principles. Thus the sensationalists, as James now calls the traditional
empiricists, simply reject the reality of most relations, while the intellec-
tualists admit their reality but say that they can be known only through an
'Actus Purus of Thought, Intellect, or Reason, all written in capitals'.[14]

James accepted that traditional empiricists were committed to a recognition of some relations in experience. Bain's distinct ideas, and Hume's
distinct existences, imply at least that the distinctness of these items is
presented to us. Such relations of distinctness or difference James calls
'disjunctive' relations, but he thought that these did not exhaust the range
of presented relations and that what he called 'conjunctive' relations must
also be added to the basic content of experience. James was also prepared to
accept that traditional empiricists had admitted some small number of such

conjunctive relations, such as similarity, or perhaps simple spatial or temporal relations, among their basic content, but he believed that that small number must be greatly increased.

In many passages James illustrated the sort of relations he would count as conjunctive. Among these, for example, he included what he called the 'great envelopes of experience', that is space, time, and the self. Space is presented to us as a sense of 'voluminousness', time as an 'echo of the objects just past, and in a less degree perhaps, a foretaste of those about to come', and the self as a sensible continuity of thought. The general idea of a continuous transition stands as a mark of such conjunctions as do the ideas of change, activity, similarity, and relations indicated by particles such as 'with, near, next, like, from, toward, against, because, for, through, my'. At one point in his notes he said 'If there were telepathy there would be another conjunction'.[15]

Such lists indicate clearly enough the direction of James's radical empiricist extension of the basic content of experience, but they also raise some serious problems. Most obviously there is the problem of providing support for such an enriched empiricism. In the end, as James's description of the tenet as a statement of fact indicates, the issue is simply an empirical matter, though he does also offer a range of supplementary arguments for his view. Scarcely less problematic is the need for some criterion to indicate which items in our experience are *not* to be counted as basic. Though the empiricist principles outlined earlier do not specifically state that some items in experience must be non-basic, they naturally imply such a conclusion. For to deny such an assumption would make the principle of analysis redundant, and empty the other two principles of substantial sense. There may be a suspicion that James's enriched version of the content of experience is at least in danger of reducing his version of empiricism to that kind of triviality.

There are hints, indeed, that James's ideas were more revolutionary in this way than he sometimes admits. In *Some Problems of Philosophy* he offers as a definition of reality: 'Anything is real of which we find ourselves obliged to take account in any way'.[16] Since empiricists have been inclined to treat as a criterion for reality bare inclusion among the basic contents of experience, such tolerance might, though it need not, be construed as a refusal to exclude anything from the basic class. Later, too, as we shall see, James associates his empiricism with what he calls 'natural realism' which in turn is associated with common sense beliefs. This, too, might, though it need not, be treated as a commitment to a common sense realism which refused to follow that empiricist ontological criterion.

Despite these points there is good reason to deny that James in effect reduced the empiricist principles to emptiness. Two points in particular are decisive. First, even in the *Principles*, James tacitly draws distinctions between what is basic and what is derived from, or developed out of, what

70

is basic. In relation to space, for example, what is given is the original sense of voluminousness, but our subsequent discrimination of different spatial dimensions, our development of complex and subtle metrical systems, and our construction of formal geometries, are not themselves given.[17] They are later developments out of what is basic. Second we have noted previously that James's theory of truth was committed to an account of theoretical terms which do not correspond to any presentable fact. The existence of 'ejects', as James called these terms, was a central reason for his rejection of a correspondence theory of truth. But this implies that such terms cannot themselves be basic, but need to be explained in some way by reference to what is basic.[18]

If these commitments bring James firmly back into the empiricist framework, they nevertheless leave some questions unanswered. James plainly accepts the principle of analysis in some form for those items which he regards as non-basic, but that form itself remains unclear. It is common to distinguish between 'analytic' and 'genetic' relations between concepts, and to suppose that although traditional empiricists were sometimes confused about the contrast the former is the more accurate and less misleading form for empiricism. That distinction might be illustrated by the contrast between providing an analytic equivalent for some claim, or set of claims, and providing an account of the way in which some associated discrimination might be learned. It is, further, a common requirement for the former that the analytic equivalent should provide a 'reductive'[19] analysis, that is, should make reference only to some simpler, or lower-level, set of concepts. A theory such as phenomenalism, for example, often associated with empiricists, is generally taken to provide an analytic, reductive, account of the meaning of statements about physical objects in terms purely of statements about sense-experience, or sense-data. The suggestion is that such an analytic account of meaning should be sharply separated from any account of the way in which the concept of a physical object might be learned.

James's own 'analyses', and the models provided by the Gricean programmes, hardly seem to fit such paradigms. On one side James's psychological interests naturally incline him towards an account of the way in which some discrimination might be learned. In the spatial case, for example, part of such an account would explain how, on the basis of a sense of 'voluminousness', we come to recognise and mark three spatial dimensions. In such a case there is no question of providing an analytic reductive account. Our explicit recognition of spatial dimensions simply marks what is already implicit in the original sense of voluminousness; it is not reducible to it. Similarly in the case of 'ejects' it is not James's intention to reduce or eliminate such terms in favour of others, but rather to give an account of the way in which they function within some theory. Neither of these cases fits neatly into the analytic reductive pattern.

But although such cases incline James towards the 'genetic' accounts, there are other aspects of his treatment which do not fit that case either. For one thing, although James seems not to aim at analytic or reductive accounts of meaning, he is nevertheless interested in elucidating meaning. His account of ejects as fulfilling some role within a theory is precisely designed to elucidate their meaning. That view is further supported by his generally 'functional' treatment of the meaning of terms, and specifically by the functional analysis of the meaning of truth. Russell took James to be providing analytic, and possibly reductive, equivalents for the notion of truth, but it appeared that James's conception of meaning was different from this. The Gricean models further complicate the issue, for they provide a 'genetic', developmental, account of certain notions, and yet provide it in a way which is both open to empirical constraints and able to elucidate meanings. For Grice envisaged both what he called an 'axiomatic' treatment of his views and also the production of formal definitions for contentious concepts on the basis of such a theory. These complications might simply indicate residual confusion on the part of James and Grice, like that which is supposed to have afflicted traditional empiricists. But it is also a possibility that the simple distinction between 'analytic' and 'genetic' accounts is too restricted to cope with these variations. Light may be thrown on this by the later discussions of James's accounts of the self and of the physical world.

The puzzles in James's conception of analysis are also evident in his generalised conclusion of radical empiricism. If we are not permitted to go beyond experience, and if experience consists basically of parts and relations between those parts, both of which are directly presented, then the conclusion may seem to follow almost trivially. But that conclusion might then be construed either as a commitment to a reductive analysis, or as a statement of James's empiricist holism, or as an account of some other form of analysis within that latter framework. It seems likely from the cases cited so far that James did not understand his conclusion in the first way, as a reductive analysis, but rather in the third way, as a functional analysis.

1   James's rejection of atomism

James bases his denial of atomism in the *Principles* less on philosophical arguments than on the needs of, and empirical evidence from, psychology. This is not at all surprising, given that this basic divergence from traditional empiricism is captured by the second tenet of radical empiricism, which James calls a statement of fact. Nevertheless there is a problem here about the relation between James's psychology and his philosophy. It was noted earlier that James drew a sharp distinction between psychological and metaphysical issues. It may be that in the *Principles* he concerns himself with the empirical questions and leaves philosophical argument for another

72

occasion. Moreover, there is a natural location for that postponed consideration, in the *Essays in Radical Empiricism* and those issues will be discussed with James's treatment of the physical world. For the present, therefore, I shall make no distinction between these issues. Even in the *Principles* James does not confine himself to the rehearsal of facts in denying atomism, but produces some arguments for his view as well. It is those arguments that I shall now consider.

At the very start of his discussion of sensation and perception James objects to the empiricist appeal to simple sensations on the ground that sensations never *are* simple. He was prepared to accept some distinction between sensation and perception, and to admit that the latter was more complex than the former. But he claimed that many who had acknowledged these points had done so in a misleading or mistaken way. For they had admitted sensation as a 'fractional *part* of thought in the old-fashioned atomic sense which we have so often criticised'.[20] Sensations are not discriminable parts of perception, and in adults and subjects beyond the new-born stage a 'pure' sensation is scarcely a possibility. In other passages James makes clear his view that Locke's programme of constructing complex intellectual items out of simple sensations was impossible.[21]

James attempts to support his hostility to atomism in several ways. In one he argues that our sensations over periods of time are never the same, or at least 'that there is no proof that the same bodily sensation is ever got by us twice'.[22] The reason for our natural belief that we can sometimes experience exactly the same sensation again is, according to James, that we naturally identify the sensation in terms of its *object* and then suppose that the identity of the object guarantees that of the sensation. We may hear the same note repeated on a piano and identify the two sensations in terms of that same note, but it does not follow from this that the two sensations were even qualitatively the same. James adds two 'presumptions' in favour of his view. First he cites the familiar case where repetition becomes tedious, so that our sensations change without our noticing while the same note is repeated. It is in this way that phenomena such as successive colour contrast sometimes come as a surprise to subjects who have nevertheless been experiencing them all their lives. Second he says that 'every sensation corresponds to some cerebral action' so that 'for an identical sensation to recur, it would have to occur in an unmodified brain'. But for James this is an impossibility, since 'to every brain-modification, however small, must correspond a change of equal amount in the feeling which the brain subserves'.[23]

These arguments are open to serious objection. There are, first of all, some unclarities in James's thesis, which can be summarily resolved. Is he talking of numerical identity or only of qualitative identity? Here the answer must be that he is talking of the latter and not the former.[24] Even atomist empiricists would not have claimed that two temporally separated sensations were numerically identical, but they presumably were committed to the claim that the same type sensation, qualitatively identical, might be experienced on distinct occasions. Further is James arguing that, because individual sensations can never be wholly separated from their neighbours and felt associations at any particular time, two temporally separated sensations will always have different surroundings, and so be qualitatively distinct? Such a view is objectionable in the context because we may not accept that a difference in surroundings establishes a difference in the quality of the sensation itself; but much more because the claim *assumes* what James is trying to prove, namely the continuity in experience which the premiss expresses. The argument is circular, though James's view could still be supported by empirical evidence.

Other ambiguities in his position are less easy to resolve. James hesitates in his text between claiming that he can prove that no identical sensation ever recurs, and that at least the opposite atomistic view could never itself be established. Again he appeals to features of the brain and to relations between the brain and sensations in ways which seem questionable. For one thing James strongly rejects, in other parts of the *Principles*, the idea of a simple one to one correspondence between brain states and psychical states. He is scornful of what he calls 'psychic chemistry' in which complex sensations result from a supposed fusion of simpler sensations. He describes this as the mistake of 'fusing without a medium', and he took the view that the fusing could be accounted for in terms of brain changes which then finally resulted in some sensation. It might be said that the charge of assuming the processes of 'psychic chemistry' can be levelled against traditional empiricist psychology,[25] but the target is not the same as the present one. Nor is it easy to see how such an attack can be reconciled with the view he now takes. For if every brain modification must correspond to a change of feeling, then it seems that the physical fusion must be paralleled by a corresponding psychic fusion.

It might also be doubted whether the brain *is* a permanent record of all its previous transactions. To take such a view is to regard the brain as a sort of indestructible, cumulative, bank statement, in which every transaction is permanently recorded and can be traced back to its origins. For this reason a repeated transaction will be different from the original operation. But the picture is not obligatory. Why should the brain not sometimes act like a magnetic tape in which, in order to record one transaction an earlier one is erased? In such a case the brain would be more like a position on a chess board. The board and pieces have exactly the same configuration when a position is repeated, for the causal history of the moves is not recorded on the board itself. There can be no doubt that the brain does record past history, but why should it always function in that way? Even if it does always so function, why should we not determine the identity of sensations independently of that causal history?

James's arguments here plainly raise more questions than they answer, but perhaps they distract attention from the main point. Perhaps he should have avoided the claim that he could prove the atomist assumption wrong and content himself with showing the weaknesses in that assumption. There are indications that James also pursued that tack. He is prepared, for example, to concede some merit of a theoretical kind in the atomist claim. He speaks of it as a 'convenience' with, however, only a 'symbolic value' to which nothing in nature corresponds. He says 'A permanently existing idea . . . which makes its appearance before the footlights of consciousness at periodic intervals is as mythological an entity as the Jack of Spades',[26] and he likens the atomist theory to the idea that electricity is a fluid. According to James the atomist view that our sensations come in neat discrete packages, separately and distinctively identified, has a convenient simplicity but distorts the phenomena. He would not have wanted to deny value to such a heuristic simplification, for he believed that theory worked precisely through such simplifications, but he wanted to insist that they may mislead us into mistakes.

One difficulty which James points to in the atomist view is plainly correct. Our conventional means of identifying sensations through descriptions of their objects is demonstrably not sufficient to establish the qualitative identity of the sensation itself. Whether or not the brain is a permanent record of all past experience, and however it is related to our sensations, still we recognise that two discrete sensations may be qualitatively different even though we describe them in the same terms. We may describe two auditory sensations as of the same piano note, and yet accept that the sensations were qualitatively different despite this described identity. Since atomists wished to identify the simple basic sensations such circumstances show that we have not yet identified them if we use such descriptive resources. Requirements implicit in such a view are that the basic sensations should be simple and determinate; our identification of such sensations must allow no more determinacy than, and must capture no more than, the simple character of the basic sensation itself. These requirements have been expressed by atomists in the claims that the basic sensations must be no further analysable, and that they must not 'go beyond' the particular sensations themselves.

At one point, in *A Pluralistic Universe*, James gets close to a statement of such requirements. He says of T.H. Green

> Green more than anyone realised that knowledge *about* things was knowledge of their relations; but nothing could persuade him that our sensational life could contain any relational element. He followed the strict intellectualist method with sensations. What they were not expressly defined as including they must exclude.[27]

For what James here calls the 'intellectualist' method states the requirement that at least the basic sensations have one simple, determinate character which therefore exactly captures their nature. It is this highly abstract picture of simple sensations, driven by the requirements already noted, which James wanted to reject. Though the aim among empiricists was to identify the humblest, most basic, particular elements of the content of our experience they were driven in this way to deploy resources which were of a highly abstract, theoretical kind. It is presumably in this way that James conceived of their procedure as both theoretical and intellectualist.

An atomist theory characterised in this way is known to be open to serious objections and dangers. It has encouraged all the complaints against empiricists that they never succeed in making clear what the simple basic contents of experience are. It led Russell and Wittgenstein in their logical atomist period to require of the basic atoms that each reference to them should be logically independent of the others, so that they then had great problems in identifying those atoms. It might lead even to the absurdity of trying to characterise what is essentially particular in terms which are both intelligible and yet do not go beyond what is immediately presented.[28] For it is difficult to see how we could capture such a particular intelligibly except by describing it, when any such description seems to go beyond it. Perhaps such evident problems can be overcome. We have seen that James would be prepared to accept some such purified atomist view, so long as it is recognised as a theoretical or symbolic simplification. But then the test for such a theory would be its success in accounting for our experience, and James believed that such a test revealed only failure. For it produced as a necessary consequence the idea that 'our thought is composed of separate independent parts and is not a sensibly continuous stream', a view which, he claims, 'entirely misrepresents the natural appearances'.[29] Ultimately it is this factual distortion which sinks the atomist view.

James goes on in the *Principles* to appeal to an introspectively obtained better description of the 'stream of consciousness', to which he adds some explanation for the empiricists' error. In the descriptions the sensible continuity relates a present sensation or thought to what has preceded it and what currently surrounds it. Even where we admit a discontinuity in our experience, for example in sleep, James points to the continuity of memory which normally connects the waking experiences with what was felt before going to sleep. James offers many graphic accounts of this continuity, talking, for example, of different phases of our experience as 'transitive' or 'substantive', and likening these respectively to the flights and perchings of a bird. Throughout these phases consciousness is, for James, literally continuous, so that one phase or element shades or dissolves imperceptibly into another with no sharp breaks. Such distinct phases are said to be like the joints in a bamboo cane; they represent different types of experience, but they belong to the same continuous phenomenon.

James diagnosed the atomists' failure as a result of over-attention to our language. Because we are simply more interested in the substantive than the transitive phases of our experience it is the former which get marked most obviously as names in that language. There is, then, a strong temptation to use these terms alone to stand for the basic content of our experience, and if the temptation is too powerful we become committed to an atomist picture. In that picture what stand out are the discrete, substantive, elements of experience together with the relations of distinctness which separate them. Such a view then has the task of constituting a continuous, conjunctive, experience on the basis of such punctiform data, and James thought such a task impossible.

James wished to admit as equally basic items in our experience those transitive or relational features which we mark with other verbal forms, such as the prepositions listed earlier. At one point he is even tempted to redress the atomist balance by claiming that these are names, too, and associated with particular feelings within the stream of consciousness. On such a view the atomist failure is a failure to notice that there are other, less conspicuous, names in our language, which also stand for particular aspects of our experience. Later, however, he adopted the more plausible view that we should not treat these particles as names at all. In *Some Problems of Philosophy* he provides a reductio argument against the view that to have meaning a word must name some discriminable item where he says: 'By this rule every conjunction and preposition in human speech is meaningless. The truth is that neither elements of fact nor meanings of words are separable as our words are.'[30] On such a view the atomist fault is in part a failure to notice the function of non-naming words in the language, in part also a failure to recognise that the naming view of meaning is itself wrong.

2 The account of the self

James's account of the self is the most obvious illustration of a conjunctive relation, and so of the traditional empiricist failure to admit such relations among the basic contents of experience. It is in his treatment of the self that James provides the most striking descriptions of continuity, in talking of the contrast between the flights and perchings of a bird or the joints and canes of bamboo.[31] The empiricist difficulty in this case of reconstituting a continuity out of the punctiform data seems particularly serious, for it threatens the legitimacy of our notion of the self. James believed that the admission of conjunctive relations would eliminate that danger.

James recognised clearly, however, that his own account of the self owed much to those empiricist predecessors. He says:

This description of personal identity will be recognised by the instructed reader as the ordinary description professed by the empirical school . . . and it is to the imperishable glory of Hume, and Herbart, and their successors to have taken so much of the meaning of personal identity out of the clouds and made of the Self an empirical and verifiable thing . . . But in leaving the matter here and saying that this sum of passing things is all, these writers have neglected certain more subtle aspects of the Unity of Consciousness . . .[32]

James thought that these failings in the empiricist theory encouraged the appeal to a transcendent 'arch-ego', which he associated with Kant's 'transcendental unity of apperception', and described as a 'windy and ineffectual abortion'.[33] He regarded the oscillation between the two theories as a typical example of the way in which one philosophical view feeds off the defects of its rivals. James held that *both* theories are wrong but that what *motivated* each was entirely right. He aimed to satisfy these motivations by amending the empiricist theory without falling into arch-egoism.

James also contrasts these two rival theories with what he calls 'spiritualism', a doctrine he associates in the *Principles* with a mind-body dualism. He believed that a cash-value for spiritualism could be found in a role for consciousness as a selecting agent, but after his discussion of the self he seems to regard such metaphysical issues as either resolved or side-stepped. For the account of the stream of consciousness offered an adequate empiricist psychological account of what he called the 'central fact of consciousness'. These wider issues of the mind-body problem indicate a division which James drew between psychology and metaphysics. He tends to reserve the latter term for those issues which, though arising out of psychology, cannot be resolved by psychology itself. As a naturalistic science psychology, he says, must rest content with noting the 'functional' relationship between mind and brain.[34] It is interesting that in this context James talks of mathematical rather than causal functions, but these background issues must be considered later in the section on psychology.[35] What is important and distinctive in James's account of the self is the empirical nature of the stream of consciousness and the lessons to be learned from it about the traditional philosophical problem of the self.

For although James places his discussion within psychology in this way he also implicitly draws a further distinction between a purely empirical enquiry into persons and the traditional philosophical problems of the self. He distinguishes what he oddly calls 'constituents of the self' among which are on one side the 'material, social, and spiritual selves', and on the other the 'pure ego'.[36] In so doing he separates a purely empirical enquiry into, for example, the way in which a man's behaviour may change according to the different roles he occupies, from the traditional Humean problem about the nature of the self. We might say in the former case, if the behavioural differences were sufficiently striking, that the man was a 'different person' in the two contexts, but what we would normally mean by this is merely that he adopts different attitudes. Normally we are in no doubt that such differences of attitude are combined with sameness of person. It is this wider notion of 'same person' which is Hume's and James's quarry.

The specific problem James saw can be derived from Hume's discussion. For Hume the idea of the self must be either simple or complex. If simple it must be related directly to some perceptible impression; if complex it must be analysable into a series of such impressions. The initial difficulty arises from the recognition that no simple impression of the kind required by the first option can be located. Hume argues for this partly on empirical and partly on conceptual grounds. Whenever I try to catch an impression of my self I succeed in locating only some specific impression with its own content. Nor perhaps *could* I expect to succeed in such an enterprise. For any specific impression must be owned by some person and so apparently presupposes the very idea of the self which is at issue. Beyond that the idea of the self is presumably the idea of a persistent identity over time. Even if there were some elusive but persistent impression which always accompanied my experiences, its career throughout the time of my existence must be something complex rather than simple. Hume consequently fails to find any simple thread of identical material along which the beads of our distinct impressions might be strung.[37]

It has, therefore, to be supposed that the self is a complex idea to be analysed into simpler components. True to his standard practice Hume indeed offers such an analysis in terms of the series of our experiences and relations of resemblance between them. But he contrives also to suggest that the resulting account is unsatisfactory. For it seems to fail to support our intuitive beliefs about the identity of the self, by apparently replacing them with the inferior notion of a qualitative similarity over time. Such an account of identities, whether of objects or of the self, is, according to Hume, 'attended with a fiction'. He says

> For when we attribute identity, in an improper sense, to variable or interrupted objects, our mistake is not confined to the expression but is commonly attended with a fiction either of something invariable and uninterrupted or of something mysterious and inexplicable, or at least with a propensity to such fictions.[38]

The suggestion is that we have no justification for our belief in an invariable and uninterrupted, or mysterious and inexplicable, self, though we are inevitably led to such a belief. Hume himself acknowledged the strength of such fictional beliefs, and so the apparent weakness of his own analysis. It was that apparent weakness which indicates the natural motive towards postulating some rival a priori or transcendent 'arch-ego'. James agreed that there were weaknesses in Hume's account, but he did not believe that that rival view was the correct way to deal with them.

James's requirements for a solution to the problem are clearly outlined in conformity to his pragmatic principles. He says:

> All the experiential facts find their place in the description unencumbered with any hypothesis save that of the existence of passing thoughts or states of mind.[39]

> It is impossible to discover any *verifiable* features in personal identity which this sketch does not contain – impossible to imagine how any transcendent, non-phenomenal, sort of arch-ego . . . could shape matters to any other result . . . than just this production of the stream of consciousness, each section of which should know, and knowing hug to itself and adopt all those that went before, thus standing as the representative of the entire past stream.[40]

The informal terms 'hugging' and 'adopting' here are versions of the technical term 'appropriation' which James uses to mark the central continuity of experience on which consciousness of personal identity rests.

The hypothesis that James canvasses is that because consciousness is a continuous stream each phase in it can never be wholly divorced from its predecessors and successors. Each such phase is linked to earlier, and will for a time be linked to later, phases in the stream. In his treatment of time James uses the metaphor of the saddleback to indicate the same kind of continuity. Our present experience, or that substantive part of it in which we are interested, may be represented as a point, but if so then it is a point, like a link in a chain, with direct attachments to what has immediately gone before and what will immediately come afterwards. Moreover, those immediately preceding links in the chain will be similarly linked to still earlier phases in a way which may enable us to recall events in our quite remote past. A Proustian sensitivity may succeed in linking a present taste to a large range of inter-connected prior experiences which it appropriates thus to itself. These relations of direct and indirect appropriation are what James relies upon to resolve the Humean puzzles about the self.

James concedes at the end of his account that the act of appropriation still remains obscure, though he tries to remedy this by adding three further points about it.

(1) A thing cannot appropriate itself, but can only appropriate other items to itself.

(2) Its appropriations are less to itself than to the most intimately felt part of its present object, the body, and the central adjustments, which accompany the act of thinking, in the head.

(3) These 'warm' parts of such an object in the act of thinking provide a firm basis on which to rest the consciousness of personal identity, even if thought were unconscious of itself.[41]

These points, especially (2) and (3), indicate the central role James envisages for the body and bodily feelings, in this as in other contexts. James characteristically contrasts the 'warm' and 'intimate' feelings accompanying an appropriation with the 'cold' knowledge we may acquire secondhand of our own earlier life. James here indicates that all mental states are associated with bodily feelings, such as the sense of our body as a 'cubic mass' or of those central adjustments in the head. These provide the immediate locus for the required warmth and intimacy of our appropriations. At one point he expresses such claims by urging, in a Watsonian fashion, that the Cartesian or Kantian 'I think' might be better replaced by 'I breathe'.[42]

The great merit of economy which James sees in his hypothesis is that it relies upon nothing but actual phenomenological occurrences in consciousness, their felt features and conjunctive relations. Of his view he says: 'The passing thought is the thinker',[43] and his most arresting metaphor is that of a herd of cattle in which ownership may be invested in two different ways. In one, the usual, way the owner is not himself a member of the herd and can be identified independently of it. In the other ownership is passed round the members of the herd in turn, so that the owner has no existence independent of the herd itself. Hume's solution is partly like the latter view, and the transcendent account like the former. Any weaknesses in the latter account may encourage us to look outside the herd for an independent arch-ego, but James believed that there was no need for, or profit in, any such search.

James thought that common sense was inclined to embark on such a search, and was encouraged to do so by the apparent weakness in Hume's account.

> Common sense insists that the unity of all the selves is not a mere
> appearance of similarity or continuity, ascertained after the fact. She is
> sure that it involves a real belonging to a real owner, to a pure spiritual
> entity of some kind.[44]

He thought that his own account provided the right answer to such common sense yearnings, or their philosophical counterparts, but it was an answer which showed those yearnings to be both unsatisfiable and needless. James puts this by charging the empiricist account with the errors, noted earlier, of 'psychic chemistry' and 'fusing without a medium', but he believed that his own account was free of these mistakes and should satisfy the demands of common sense. He says

> But in our account the medium is fully assigned, the herdsman is there,
> in the shape of something not among the things collected, but superior
> to them all, namely, the real, present onlooking, remembering, 'judging
> thought', or identifying 'section' of the stream. This is what collects –
> 'owns' some of the past facts it surveys, and disowns the rest – and so
> makes a unity that is actualised and anchored . . .[45]

For James the only legitimate ownership in this context was the way in which the 'title' of a collective self may be passed, or inherited, from one passing thought to another. He says of this: 'It is a patent fact of consciousness that a transmission like this actually occurs. Each pulse of consciousness, each thought, dies away and is replaced by another.'[46] Each successive thought or feeling has the associated feelings of warmth and intimacy which link it with a central body and with its immediate neighbours in the stream. In appropriating these latter directly it also indirectly appropriates other items which they directly appropriated. At any stage in our lives the sense of personal identity is no more than this, actual or potential, link between current and more remote members of the stream. James sums this up by saying 'Who owns the last self owns the self before last',[47] and so opens up the possibility of a link with a whole series of past experiences. Though no specific passing thought could capture the whole series of a person's experience, the suggestion is that consciousness of one's identity can be adequately captured at any time by appeal to some such appropriative thought. At least there are no *other* items to which appeal can be made. Such particular appropriative thoughts stand as 'representatives' of the entire past stream. They provide the cash-value for the complex notion of self consciousness.

James's account seems to deviate very little in substance from a standard empiricist view. But in that case it may seem as though he must be open to the standard objections raised against the empiricist view. At this stage it may seem that James differs from Hume not in any substantive way but only in his attitude to that substantive account. Where Hume shows anxiety at the likelihood of omitting some vital factor in the analysis, James offers reassurance that nothing has been omitted.[48] The standard objections to such a view, however, purport to show that the analysis cannot be adequate, so that something must have been left out. The question remains, then, whether James can answer these objections and so provide a reasoned basis for his reassurance.

Two types of objection concern first the problem of circularity and second the adequacy of the appeal to memory. Although James's 'appropriation' covers more than merely memory it must employ memory to establish more distant links with past experience. Any objections to the appeal to memory will be objections to the account as a whole. In the first of these problems it is objected that the appeal to specific experiences, passing thoughts, and their appropriative powers will be circular if it already invokes the idea of a person who remembers or appropriates. If James's account is to be satisfactory then it must avoid such a circularity. The second is a more complex objection which relies on the facts that memory is both unreliable and incomplete. A man may seem to remember some past experience which he did not genuinely have, and then the appeal to appropriative passing thoughts will not be sufficient to identify those experiences in the stream which constitute a person. Equally he may forget substantial tracts of his past experience, and then memory cannot be necessary for membership in that stream. A variant on such themes concerns the transitivity of memory. A man may at time T_3 have an experience E_3 which appropriates an earlier experience E_2, which at T_2 itself appropriated a still earlier experience E_1, and yet at T_3 fail to remember E_1. E_3 then may fail to appropriate E_1, even though the person at T_3 is undeniably the same person as at T_1. This situation may arise even if we require of appropriation only that it should be a disposition or power to remember past events.

James offers a clear answer to the first objection. He would agree that to invoke the self as the appropriator of earlier experiences would be circular, but his account is specifically designed to exclude this. What performs the appropriation is not for him any mysterious 'arch-ego', but only the passing thought. He has no need to appeal to anything other than accepted items, such as thoughts or experiences within the stream of consciousness, in order to activate the appropriation relation. James thus firmly denied any need to appeal to an independent self, and criticised, quite correctly, a philosophical claim, which he wrongly ascribes to Kant, that at every moment in consciousness we are aware of such a self.

To the second objection James responds in so matter of fact a way as to suggest that he did not see it as an objection at all. He allows that our memories are fallible and far from complete. He notes other vagaries of memory, such as that older people may remember vividly earlier periods of their lives and yet forget what has just happened in their current experience. His response to these facts is to claim that in such cases a person has changed, and he speaks of the 'me' shrinking with memory deterioration and loss.[49] It is also quite natural to take appropriation as a non-transitive relation, simply on the factual grounds adduced earlier.

But both of these points leave problems. The former points about memory raise the question whether appropriation should be taken as a transitive or a non-transitive relation. The latter point might be concisely expressed by saying that if appropriation is a non-transitive relation it cannot account for identity which is transitive. These are serious difficulties for any account which purports to give objective, third-person, criteria to determine whether some described person is identical with the one who did such and such, or had such and such experiences. But it remains doubtful whether James had any such intention.

The issue comes out clearly in Ayer's complex and subtle discussion of James's theory. Ayer defines a notion of 'confamiliarity' in the following way:

Two experiences belong to the same self, and are confamiliar, if either they are sensibly compresent or continuous with one another, or there is a relation of indirect sensible continuity between them, or one of them directly or indirectly appropriates the other.[50]

This captures nicely James's formal requirements. Ayer further recognises that the notion of confamiliarity, and its constituents in the definition, must not invoke a notion of the self on pain of circularity, but he believes that James can avoid this. Still the definition is open to counter-examples, in which, for example, sets of experiences are confamiliar while belonging to different persons, or belong to the same person without being confamiliar.

The latter cases are best illustrated in terms of gaps in the continuity of experience. Such gaps would have to be drastic, for James allows for standard periods of unconsciousness such as sleep. He points out that in these normal cases the gap *is* bridged by memory, so that the discontinuity does not seriously affect the appropriation relation. But Ayer imagines a person who suffers total amnesia with respect to his past experiences after a period of sleep or unconsciousness. In such a case we have, apparently, two sets of experiences, one before and one after the onset of amnesia, but no warm and intimate relations between them. We may stipulate that after the disability there is not even a possibility of the person's recovering a memory of his earlier life. However, despite the separateness of the two sets of experiences we may still intuitively regard the person as the same. If so, then apparently James's account does not match that intuition.

Ayer has an ingenious device to resolve this problem. He invokes the notion of bodily continuity, to bridge the gap between the two phases of the person's life, but he defines the body as the locus of a set of confamiliar experiences. He is aware that an appeal to bodily continuity alone might render James's appropriation relation redundant, but in defining the body in terms of sets of confamiliar experiences Ayer hopes to retain James's stress on appropriation. In the envisaged case we can note that the body identified through the pre-amnesia experiences is continuous with that identified in the post-amnesia experiences. The amnesiac himself, ex hypothesi, can never have more than that 'cold', second-hand, knowledge of his pre-amnesia existence which James distinguishes from the 'animal warmth' of genuine appropriation. But the rest of us may support our intuition that there is only one person and not two persons in the case by an appeal to Ayer's device. This alone makes it clear that Ayer is seeking, on James's behalf, a third-person criterion for identity.

One difficulty in Ayer's account arises from his treatment of the similar case of multiple personality. For in such cases we also have, we may suppose, sets of experiences which are associated with a single body but are not confamiliar. There may be two sets of experiences, within which the confamiliarity relation holds although that relation does not hold between them. In such a case, too, we could employ Ayer's device and use the factor of bodily continuity to determine that there is only one personality and not two. Ayer, however, takes the view in this case that we might allow there to be two people inhabiting the same body, though it is difficult to know why this case should be treated differently from that of the amnesiac.[51] But this difficulty is less important here than the question whether Ayer's device adequately conforms to James's account.

The other counter cases concern confamiliar experiences which, however, belong to different persons. Ayer notes that these arise in a striking way out of independent aspects of James's notion of 'pure experience'. In that doctrine James takes the view that two people may share exactly the same experience, and that this possibility is the basis for our beliefs in a public world of objects and in the existence of other people. The difficulty Ayer points out is that if we concede this intersection of two such experiences, then we seem committed to the claim that there are not really two people involved. For any subsequent experience which appropriates the intersecting experience will then appropriate indirectly all the experiences which that experience appropriates. But those indirectly appropriated experiences will cover what we normally think of as two distinct persons' experience before the point of intersection. It is as if sharing any experience with another person literally unifies you with that person; a disorder we might call the contagion of identity.

It is easy to see that this latter problem will arise for James only if he is seeking what I called earlier an objective, third-person, criterion for personal identity. It is a mark of such a criterion that the appropriation relation should be transitive, just as identity itself is; and further that its application should be available to test a person's identity independently of his own claims about it. Indeed if James is faced with a choice between treating appropriation as transitive or non-transitive he faces what looks like an awkward dilemma. If it is regarded as transitive, then we have the problems of amnesia, and the difficult intrusion of considerations about bodily identity, as well as what I have called identity contagion. If it is regarded as non-transitive, then it seems unable to match the transitiveness of identity.

If we choose the latter alternative, however, at least the two earlier problems do not arise. The man who suffers amnesia after a period of unconsciousness cannot now appropriate any of his earlier experiences. We may feel inclined to appropriate them to him, as it were on his behalf, because we intuitively wish to treat the two sets as belonging to the same person. He himself may come to learn of his past experience, second-hand, in the cold way in which a historian might learn facts about the past experiences of his subject. But if appropriation is associated with the non-transitive relation of a 'warm' memory of those past experiences, then he cannot appropriate any in the previous set. We may say that after his amnesia the man may still have, or acquire, a sense of his identity on the basis of such non-transitive appropriation, but that sense will not extend to any of the pre-amnesia experiences. For him such experiences will be simply nothing. On such an account James's conception of appropriation is as a first-person determinant of one's sense of identity.

The same solution is available to the problem of identity contagion. Even if it is true that people may share the same experience there generally is a separation in the routes back from those experiences which are associated with the two different people. For P_1 the experience E_5, which was shared with P_2, will appropriate experiences E_2 and E_1 which he had but were not shared with P_2, while for P_2 it will appropriate experiences E_3 and E_4, which she had but were not shared with P_1. On the non-transitive, first person, account of appropriation two such streams of consciousness may intersect without becoming identical. Moreover, although I have implied that the earlier appropriated experiences were genuine, it is clear that on the first-person account it is not necessary to make such an assumption. Whether the 'memories' are genuine or not they may still contribute, perhaps importantly, to a person's sense of identity. On the non-transitive, first-person, interpretation it is understandable that James should treat the cases of memory failure or error in so casual a way.

That latter point suggests already that James was interested, contrary to Ayer's assumptions, in non-transitive appropriation rather than transitive. James would not then be offering a third-person criterion for personal identity so much as an account of a first-person *sense* of our own identity. Two objections may be raised to this. It may be said first that James's discussion is based on the third-person problem; and it may be argued in any case that the price for abandoning the latter problem is too high. If we weaken James's account of personal identity in this way, then he simply fails to solve, even address, the real problem of third-person identity.

It is true that James's discussion is not totally clear on the distinction. He does, for example, separate what he calls a 'subjective' from an 'objective' psychologist's treatment of the problem, and he opts for the latter rather than the former.[52] This may have encouraged readers to regard him as standardly tackling the third-person issue. But this distinction is not quite what it seems. Throughout the passage James stresses the dangers of the 'psychologists' fallacy', that is the error of reading into the subject's experience items from the investigator's experience. James makes it clear, as his own emphasis on the stream of consciousness does, that he is concerned to give an adequate account of that personal consciousness. His appeal to an objective, psychological, enquiry then seems to indicate no more than a desire to give an accurate account of that consciousness, rather than to raise all the complex third-person issues about personal identity.

That suggestion is confirmed by the form in which James presents his views. He speaks almost always of the 'consciousness of identity', of the self as 'felt', and of the 'sense' of our own identity. Indeed the major section in which he presents his considered view is entitled 'The Sense of our Personal Identity'.[53] In an earlier quotation he speaks of the required 'warmth' as 'providing a firm basis on which to rest the consciousness of personal identity'.[54] At one crucial point he summarises his view by saying 'Resemblance among the parts of a continuum of feeling constitutes the real and verifiable personal identity which we feel.'[55] It seems undeniable that James's primary concern was with this first-person sense of identity, and that appropriation was intended as a non-transitive relation on which that sense rested.

Still it may be objected that such a view drains James's account of any serious interest. It may be claimed that after all the weakness in Hume's account was that it seemed to omit reference to a substantial self which might resolve the problems about third-person identity. If James evades that issue, then he cannot remedy that weakness as he patently aimed to do. It may further be said that James's account, construed in a first-person way, cannot explain what 'constitutes' personal identity, or what it 'consists in', and that it is these issues about the nature of persons which present the important and genuine problems.

I offer one short and a second longer, but inconclusive, response to such queries. The former characterises James's account not as an attempt to resolve *all* questions about personal identity, but rather as an attempt to provide a basis for that notion. On such a view the basis for the full notion of personal identity lies in the *sense* of our identity, and that is to be found in the relation of appropriation within consciousness. Such an account plainly could not answer every question about personal identity, and could not be expected to answer specific questions of identity of the form 'Did P_1 commit the crime on January 30 1985?'. James's basic considerations might find some place even here, for P_1 might be the sort of person who, having read of the crime, now believes that he remembers committing it and 'confesses' to the police. But the police will then presumably wish to employ further criteria to reject the confession and the claimed identity.

It might be objected even to such a modest claim that a sense of personal identity either could not be located adequately within private consciousness, or could not serve adequately as a basis for personal identity. Sociologists might claim that personal identity has a social dimension which cannot be omitted; and philosophers may invoke Wittgenstein's private language argument to dismiss any appeal to a private consciousness. James could answer both objections. To the sociologists he could point out that he has already made provision for a social dimension within what he called the 'constituents of the self'.[56] For one of these is identified in just such social terms. To the philosophers he could reply that his account of our sense of identity occurs in a context where the existence of both physical objects, such as bodies, and persons is assumed. James's account is not an attempt to locate a private experience divorced from an outer world;

his own reference to bodily sensations makes that plain. I take it that Wittgenstein's argument is an attack not on such ordinary ascriptions of private, mental, features but on a certain erroneous philosophical view of such privacy. There is no reason to think that James has fallen into that view.

Second, it may be said that to treat James's account as incomplete is not yet an adequate defence. For no philosophical account of personal identity would expect to answer specific identity questions about the person who committed a particular crime. These are empirical questions, while a philosophical account is designed to answer the background conceptual questions about identity. Judged by such a standard, it will be said, James's account is incomplete not only in the inevitable way of failing to answer empirical questions, but also in its failure to answer the conceptual questions it is supposed to answer. For it is conceded that James's account does not say what personal identity, in a full third-person sense, 'consists in'.

To this objection, which assumes a clear and readily understandable distinction between empirical and conceptual issues, I offer the second, inconclusive, response. If the objection were to be accepted then we should be prepared to accept that distinction, but I shall argue that we should not be so prepared. Since, however, it is not feasible to consider all the variant accounts of such a distinction that might be given I restrict myself to one suggested by Parfit's account of personal identity.[57] The argument is inconclusive in two ways. First because it considers only one such account, and second because even that one account is too complex to be fully dealt with here. Because I am concerned with only one specific part of Parfit's views I may distort his overall position. I shall therefore ascribe the views to another philosopher, similar to, and even in these respects indistinguishable from, Parfit to whom I give the name 'Perfect'.

Perfect aims to give an account of the nature of personal identity over time, to indicate what that identity 'consists in' and what features it necessarily has. Initially his account seems quite like James's. For it rests on a psychological relation of 'connectedness' which is close to, if not identical with, James's relation of 'appropriation'. Like James's relation Perfect's has a central reference to memory, and like James Perfect is even prepared to include within connectedness a reference to false memories, or what he calls 'quasi-memories'. But since Perfect, unlike James, wishes to give an account of full identity and not just of a sense of identity, he cannot rely solely upon connectedness. As we have seen, and as Perfect stresses, connectedness, like appropriation, is a non-transitive relation while identity is transitive. Consequently Perfect appeals instead to a related notion of 'psychological continuity', which is explained as 'the holding of overlapping chains of *strong* connectedness'.[58] Since it is claimed that such continuity is transitive it may serve in an account of what identity consists in.

Clearly at this point Perfect goes explicitly beyond the account so far ascribed to James, and in such a way as to indicate a potential defect, an omission, in James's account. For the appeal to psychological continuity offers, in a way appropriation does not, a third-person, conceptual, *reduction* of full personal identity to that relation. Perfect, indeed, regards his account as 'reductionist'[59] and contrasts it with other accounts which treat personal identity as involving some 'further fact'. In this respect, too, Perfect's account is in part like James's. For among the further fact theories will be those which appeal to what James calls a transcendental 'arch-ego', and James, like Perfect, rejects these. But it is also true that Perfect's further fact theories range more widely than this, and there is a suggestion in Perfect's 'revisionist' tendencies[60] that he would include quite ordinary conceptions of the self among them. James would not have followed him there.

It may not be obvious how Perfect's 'psychological continuity' can be transitive while connectedness, on which continuity is based, is non-transitive. If we express strong connectedness in terms of memory then the continuity relation may be introduced as a valid inference from

(1) X_1 does, or can, at T_1 remember enough of X_2

and

(2) X_2 did, or could, at T_2 remember enough of X_3.

The conjunction of (1) and (2) will then entail

(3) X_1 is psychologically continuous with X_3

but is compatible with

(4) X_1 does not, and cannot, at T_1 remember enough of X_3.

In these formulae the subscripts indicate dates and the X variables range over persons identified at those dates. Perfect's formulae differ from James's account of appropriation for the latter expresses a relation between feelings, or passing thoughts, rather than temporally dated persons.

The question arises, for the cases where (3) and (4) both hold, how (3), or (2) on which (3) is based, could be established. One way of establishing (2) would be for X_1 now to remember, or be able to remember, enough of X_3 in remembering X_2. But that possibility is excluded by the truth of (4), so that the only way of establishing (2), when (3) and (4) both hold, would be to do so in the cold, third-person, way. That way would be open to X himself and also to anyone else who had the relevant information. Since it is these cases which distinguish non-transitive connectedness from transitive continuity it seems fair to conclude that the latter is a third-person relation which could in principle be established as well by others as by the person himself. Construed in that way Perfect's continuity relation diverges radically from James's appropriation, as I have explained it.

Such a continuity relation faces some serious difficulties if it is claimed that full personal identity over time just consists in such a relation. For it may be said that the characteristic ways in which we ordinarily ascribe identity to persons conflict with the third-person ways in which we might try to establish (2). We are very rarely in a position to check claims such as (2) in cases where (4) is true and yet we do ascribe identity extensively in such cases. Typically what we do is to uncover facts bearing on such things as bodily continuity or character resemblance, and then infer psychological continuity if the facts cohere sufficiently well. Obviously large gaps in the record of bodily continuity, which may arise if the period over which identity is considered is large, will cast doubt on the identity. But if we ascribe identity on such a basis we then may simply infer that psychological continuity must have held. We might elaborate that latter belief by supposing that if we could draw the time scale sufficiently finely it would have been possible to demonstrate chains of overlapping connectedness, even though there is now no direct way in which such a claim could be established. Viewed from this angle psychological continuity may seem dependent upon other ways of determining personal identity.

One way to answer such an objection would be to insist on a distinction between what identity *consists in* and our ways of determining such identity. Parfit thus says

'Criterion of identity over time' may mean 'our way of telling whether some present object is identical with some past object'. But I shall mean 'what this identity necessarily involves, or consists in'.[61]

I shall ascribe to Perfect the view that issues about what identity consists in are conceptual while those about determining identity are empirical. Such an ascription may seem unfair, but at least it would not do to object merely that these new terms are unclear.[62] For they are intended to mark exactly the unclarities of the earlier terms. What the new terms additionally suggest is that the conceptual issues can be settled by some rational methods for determining the meaning of identity without empirical references, while the empirical issues cannot be settled in that way. Among the former methods will be tests to determine whether it is logically possible to have psychological continuity without identity of person, or identity without psychological continuity.

Perfect carries out numerous tests of these kinds. It is neither feasible nor necessary here to consider them all, for what is at issue is not so much the answers we give to these tests as the considerations, empirical or conceptual, which are to determine those answers. In general pragmatists would be unenthusiastic about the attempt to determine the meaning of identity claims independently of their role in experience. They might not reject Perfect's distinction between empirical and conceptual issues out of hand, but they would require further elucidation of it. James, in particular, might be expected to follow that general line in virtue of his belief that the meaning of expressions is determined by the function which those express-ions fulfil, but there is also a more specific divergence here between James and Perfect. Since appropriation is not a transitive third-person relation it will not settle all issues that might be raised about personal identity. It leaves room for cases where appropriation holds but identity does not. The objection to James's account is that he erroneously omits to resolve even the conceptual issues about what personal identity consists in, and so gives only an incomplete philosophical account. A philosophical account may omit consideration of particular empirical cases, but cannot, without serious inadequacy, fail to resolve the conceptual issues. How far James might be able to defend his view by querying the distinction between empirical and conceptual issues can be examined in the Teletransportation case.

In the Teletransportation case a man on Earth is scanned by a machine which records every detail of his body so that it, with all its associated mental states, may be re-created out of different material on Mars.[63] The scanning process destroys the original body, but the person re-created on Mars will be indistinguishable physically and mentally from the original Earthman. We might say, if it did not beg the question, that Marsman will behave exactly as Earthman would have behaved if he had been simply transported to Mars. Certainly from a third-person point of view Marsman's associates, however close, will not detect any difference between him and the Earthman they knew before. The story builds strong connectedness between Marsman and Earthman into the former's consciousness, or at least just as much as existed in the latter's consciousness. On certain assumptions, then, psychological continuity will exist between Marsman and Earthman. Consequently if we take the view that these are two different people, then we deny that continuity is sufficient for identity.

James could take the view that Marsman's ability to appropriate all or most of Earthman's experiences does not suffice to make him identical to Earthman. He could take the view that Marsman, miraculously, has the same sense of identity but is not the same person; just as he could take the view that a madman who managed to achieve the same 'warm' memories as Napoleon might nevertheless not be Napoleon. But the difficulty which James's, and any similar common sense, view faces is to explain why there are two people in the Teletransportation case, and not just one. That difficulty is underlined by the subsequent indistinguishability between the two. Less immediately, but more importantly here, James faces the challenge of saying what the two identities 'consist in', and this may seem very serious if we have to appeal only to conceptual and not to empirical considerations. The suggestion is, again, that James has simply failed to answer the conceptual questions about what personal identity consists in.

But that suggestion, and the challenge on which it rests, are over-simple. It seems quite impossible to disregard empirical considerations in assessing the case, and this can be seen in the story itself. For the scanner is said to 'destroy' the original body, and this may well be why we incline to reject the identity. We have no experience of survival after bodily destruction, so that there is already a natural presumption that Marsman is not Earthman. Perhaps the story could be amended so that the body is not destroyed, but simply disappears from view, so that we have no idea what has happened to it. If we further suppose that the body on Mars was not re-created out of new materials, we may be still less inclined to reject the identity. But we may equally be disinclined to admit the identity until other issues have been settled. We will still ask: What has happened to the original body? How is the Mars body reconstructed? What sort of a machine do we have here anyway? How does it really work? These questions must involve empirical considerations.[64]

It would, no doubt, be possible to legislate about such matters and so to over-ride all these empirical issues. Perhaps, indeed, there is a natural temptation to do this once we accept the strict distinction between empirical and conceptual issues, but I take it that such a move would be of no value in this context. It would be to replace what seemed to be arguable issues by arbitrary stipulation. If that is so, then we are left with enough doubt about the objection to James to regard his position as at least defensible. Parfit, in embarking on his Teletransportation story, notes that other philosophers, such as Quine and Wittgenstein, have expressed reservations about appeals to such fantasies. He quotes Quine's view that

> The method of science fiction has its uses in philosophy . . . but I
> wonder whether the limits of the method are properly heeded. To seek
> what is 'logically required' for sameness of person under
> unprecedented circumstances is to suggest that words have some logical
> force beyond what our past has invested them with.[65]

Though Quine does not express his view in exactly the standard pragmatist form it is plain that his sentiments here are thoroughly Jamesian.

6

Pure Experience

The three tenets of James's radical empiricism outline a framework for a more extended epistemology. They indicate the corrections he wished to make to traditional empiricism's atomism and its consequent failure to appreciate conjunctive relations, and they prepare the way for the major illustrations of those conjunctive relations. The most obvious of these is provided by James's account of the self and its transitive stream of consciousness. But in the *Essays in Radical Empiricism* and *The Meaning of Truth* James offers other illustrations in his treatment of the central problems of knowledge. That treatment conforms very plainly to his three tenets of empiricism and to his pragmatism. It stresses the holistic way in which each part of experience rests on other parts and insists that relations between the parts of our experience may themselves also be parts of that experience. It emphasises too the function which ideas have in our experience. As in his account of truth that function is described mainly in terms of those ideas 'leading' our beliefs or enquiries in certain directions via 'intervening' experiences towards a 'terminus', which may verify them or fail to do so.[1]

In this extended epistemology James outlines four related problems. These have to do with an individual's knowledge of an external physical world, the public shared character of that knowledge, his access to other minds, and the relation between percepts and concepts in knowledge. James has a pervasive image in which these problems are stated, namely that of the possibility of intersection between different lines. One person's mental states may be portrayed as a continuing stream of consciousness with the characteristics and the sense of identity which James described. Similarly we may conceive of a physical object as a continuing item following a linear path through space and time. When some person experiences such an object the two lines intersect, usually to diverge again soon afterwards. The most obvious exception to that natural divergence arises, of course, from the case of one's own body. James sees his general problem as that of explaining the intersections arising from the four cases already cited.[2] Put in these terms his specific problems are:

(1) How can a mind and a physical object intersect?
(2) How can two minds intersect with the same physical object?
(3) How can two minds intersect with each other?
(4) How can percepts and concepts intersect?

Though there are patent differences between the four cases James does not always treat them quite separately. His discussion of one such case tends to involve consideration of others as well. Though there are dangers in this James nevertheless has some justification for it. For first he is concerned mainly with the notion of 'intersection' itself and with the attempt to give cash-value to the general metaphor. Second it is in any case clear that the four cases overlap. It is easy, for example, to outline our ordinary conception of an intersection which involves all four possibilities. Such an example would be that of two people simultaneously perceiving one and the same object, characterising it in the same way, and at the same time recognising the other's experience. Shaking hands with another person might be offered as one paradigm of such a complex intersection.

In each case James tries to show positively how such intersections are possible, and to refute philosophers who have supposed them to be in some way impossible or dubious. As in his treatment of the self James believes that the arguments against, and puzzlement about, the possibility of intersection derive from philosophical error. The characteristic mistakes already ascribed to traditional empiricists, such as their neglect of conjunctive relations, play some part in this, but James now notes other faults in Cartesian dualism, idealism, and what he calls Bradley's rationalism. If there is one central mistake in this context it is for James simply that of 'double-counting'. He says:

> what I maintain is that any single non-perceptual experience tends to get counted twice over . . . figuring in one context as an object or field of objects, in another as a state of mind; and all this without the least actual self-diremption on its own part into consciousness and content. It is all consciousness in one taking and all content in another.[3]

James's problems here are clearly about cognition and within a general framework of epistemology, but it has sometimes been thought that his doctrine was primarily ontological. In this way that I have called his extended epistemology has come to be associated with the ontology of 'neutral monism', though James himself does not use that term. In that doctrine the central idea is that the typical division of reality into two exclusive and exhaustive ontological categories, the mental and the physical, is not basic. Instead each of these two categories is taken to be derived from some other ontological ancestor. The stuff of which that ancestor is composed is the basic monistic material of which reality is composed, and, since the physical and the mental are to be derived from it, it cannot be itself either mental or physical. It was this picture which Russell publicised and associated with James in *The Analysis of Mind*. Russell puts the doctrine in this way:

> The stuff of which the world of our pure experience is composed is, in my belief, neither mind nor matter, but something more primitive than either. Both mind and matter seem to be composite, and the stuff of which they are compounded lies in a sense between the two, and in a sense above them both like a common ancestor.[4]

Russell is quite right to ascribe to James an appeal to 'pure experience', but there is some doubt about the extent to which James would have simply accepted Russell's ontological account of it. For one thing, and superficially, James was typically critical of the 'through and through' monism of Bradley or Royce, and by contrast generally links his own pragmatism with pluralism rather than monism. The point, however, is not decisive since James believed the debate between monists and pluralists to be confused and ambiguous. He is prepared to admit that there may be some ways in which monism is true,[5] and his own account of 'pure experience' might be one of those ways. More seriously Russell's ontological doctrine faces in any case severe difficulties. Russell may have been tempted to speak of a common ancestor of the mental and physical by analogy with his use of that notion in the philosophy of mathematics. But in that context the idea of a root or source from which other ideas may be derived has a specific cash-value. In the new context the metaphor is more difficult to cash.

No doubt the philosophical tradition which divides reality exclusively and exhaustively into the mental and the physical is over-simple. Even so it rests in part on the difficulty of identifying items which make no reference to either category. The supposed neutral category, more basic than either the mental or the physical, has no obvious or natural description and this presents a problem for James in his attempt to characterise 'pure experience'. On one side he tends to describe it as 'experience', or even 'feeling' and 'sensation',[6] which incline it towards the mental; on the other he describes it as 'stuff' or 'material',[7] which incline it towards the physical. James's descriptions might be regarded as commendably even-handed in their refusal to show favouritism to either derived category, but the aim was not to employ both categories so much as to employ neither. As a solution to the ontological problem James's policy succeeds only in casting doubt on the whole idea.

Both Russell and James make use of an argument which further shows the weakness of this ontological account. The argument rests on the identification of what might be called 'hybrid' cases,[8] where we find both mental and physical aspects perhaps inseparably related in some particular item. James uses such a case to argue that the *purely* mental or the *purely* physical are rarely, if ever, presented to us. He draws attention to a particular class of experiences, which he calls 'appreciations', where such hybridisation has special importance. Such hybrid cases might certainly be used to discredit a naive dualism, in which it was supposed that the mental and the physical are generally given to us in a neat and pure form, but their value for the ontological conclusion is quite unclear. James himself puts his point in these ways:

> If 'physical' and 'mental' meant two different kinds of intrinsic nature, immediately, intuitively, and infallibly discernible, and each fixed forever in whatever bit of experience it qualified, one does not see how there could ever have arisen any room for doubt or ambiguity.

> This proves how hard it is to decide by bare introspection what it is in experiences that shall make them either spiritual or material. It surely can be nothing intrinsic in the individual experience.[9]

Those points are clearly relevant to James's positive view that we divide items into physical or mental categories in terms of their relations and functions. They form part of his claim that traditional dualism draws too sharp a division between the categories and so distorts their heterogeneity, and this will be examined later. For the present I point out only the weakness of such an appeal to hybrid cases in drawing the ontological conclusion. For first from the existence of hybrids we cannot directly infer that the forms mixed in the hybrid are not basic. Even if some hybrid chemical, metal alloy, or mixed set of genes linked forms which were not separately found in nature we might still suppose that the hybrid itself depended upon those forms. Indeed, since the notion of a hybrid is that of some compound item in which more basic forms are mixed, it seems almost perverse to argue from hybrids to the denial that those unmixed forms are basic. One way of putting the problem would be to represent the argument as having the form:

(5) Hybrids are composed of *both* mental *and* physical items,

So (6)   the forms basic to hybrids can be *neither* mental *nor* physical.

In such an argument the conclusion might be independently motivated, but the premiss by itself seems to have no plausible role in establishing it.

There is a final fallacy which such an ontological doctrine is in danger of committing. It was noted earlier that James contrived to be even-handed between the mental and the physical in his description of the neutral category. The point might be put by saying that for him neither the mental nor the physical could be prior to, or more basic than, the other. Such a doctrine is 'neutral' between the mental and physical in that no preference or priority is accorded to either. It anticipates Ryle's later rejection of what he called 'the hallowed absorptions of Mind by Matter, or of Matter by

Mind'. It seems likely that this was also part of James's view, and again the argument from hybrids may have some part to play in supporting his view. But such a weak thesis is different from the strong ontological thesis so far considered, and it indicates both an ambiguity and a potential fallacy in inferring the strong thesis from the weaker. For it would be hopeless to infer from

(7)   Neither the mental nor the physical are basic to the other

to

(8)   There is some neutral, non-mental non-physical, category which is
       more basic than either.

(8) is certainly compatible with (7), but equally certainly does not follow from it. Yet it is (8) which expresses what I have called the strong ontological thesis. It may be that James would have been, and would have had to be, content with the weaker thesis (7).

These initial problems might encourage the ascription to James of an epistemological rather than an ontological thesis, but even the former is not free from ambiguities. Part of this may be due to the fact that James deals with a complex set of questions, (1)–(4), which are not always clearly separated, but there are other difficulties arising from James's formulation of his own conclusions. I list some of his key comments to give an idea of these complexities.

In some passages, for example, James clearly distances himself from ontological views. He says, for example:

> There is, I mean, no aboriginal stuff or quality of being contrasted with that of which material objects are made, out of which our thoughts are made; but there is a function in experience which thoughts perform and for the performance of which this quality of being is invoked.[10]

A similar message, more succinctly expressed, is given when he says:

> Les attributions sujet et objet, représenté et représentatif, chose et pensée, signifient donc une distinction pratique qui est de la dernière importance, mais qui est d'ordre FONCTIONNEL seulement, et nullement ontologique, comme le dualisme classique se la représente.[11]

> (The terms 'subject' and 'object', 'representation' and 'represented', 'thing' and 'thought', signify a practical distinction of the last importance; but it is a distinction only of a FUNCTIONAL order and in no way ontological, as classical dualism represents it.)

These claims, however, might not strictly deny the strong ontological thesis. They reject the strong ontological divisions of 'classical dualism', and replace them with a functional distinction between the mental and the physical. In other passages James seems to make a clear commitment to the strong ontological claim.

En fin de compte, les choses et les pensées ne sont point foncièrement hétérogènes, mais elles sont fait d'une même étoffe qu'on ne peut définir comme telle, mais seulement éprouver, et que l'on peut nommer, si on veut, l'étoffe de l'expérience en général.

(In the end of the day things and thoughts are not basically heterogeneous, but are made of the same stuff – a stuff which cannot be defined as such but only experienced, and which one may call, if one wishes, the stuff of experience in general.)

My thesis is that if we start with the supposition that there is only one primal stuff or material in the world, a stuff of which everything is composed, and if we call that stuff 'pure experience', then knowing can easily be explained as a particular sort of relation towards one another into which portions of pure experience may enter.[12]

It was that last passage which led Russell to his own 'neutral monism'. James evidently thinks of the strong ontological thesis as a hypothesis related to his general account of cognition. The hypothesis may be justified if that latter account is itself successful. But the hypothesis claims the existence of a basic 'stuff' which cannot be defined, and this, like the difficulty over the neutral terminology, presents a problem for the onto-logical thesis.

In another passage James indicates an awareness of this problem and seeks to resolve it:

Although for fluency's sake I myself spoke earlier in this article of a stuff of pure experience, I have now to say that there is no *general* stuff of which experience at large is made, there are as many stuffs as there are 'natures' in the things experienced. If you ask what any one bit of pure experience is made of the answer is always the same: 'It is made of *that*, of just what appears, of space, of intensity, of flatness, brownness, heaviness or what not . . .? Experience is only a collective name for all those sensible natures, and save for time and space (and if you like for 'being') there appears no universal element of which all things are made.[13]

James here admits the peculiar nature of the strong ontological thesis, and his own qualified assent to it. No adequate general description can be given of the supposed basic stuff because it is understood to be only particular and sensible and not yet characterised in any general way. Once it is so characterised, it will have as many forms as there are 'natures in the things experienced'. The only way of identifying a bit of pure experience is to describe it within the framework of our own language. That language inevitably already contains a strong commitment to a division between the mental and the physical which has, however, strictly to be excluded when neutral pure experience is at issue.

The particularity, and the consequent general indeterminacy, of pure experience are made plain in several passages:

> [It is] . . . a bald *that*, a datum, fact, phenomenon, content, or whatever other neutral or ambiguous term you prefer to apply.

> 'Pure experience' is the name I gave to the immediate flux of life which furnishes the material to our later reflexion with its conceptual categories. Only new-born babes, or men in semi-coma from drugs, sleep, illnesses, or blows may be assumed to have an experience pure in the literal sense of a *that* which is not yet any definite *what*, though ready to be all sorts of whats.

> It is only virtually or potentially either object or subject as yet. For the time being it is plain unqualified actuality or existence, a simple *that*.[14]

Such views echo James's earlier claims in the *Principles* about the rarity of an atomist sensation, and he makes similar provisos in the later works: 'Its purity is only a relative term, meaning the proportional amount of unverbalised sensation it embodies.' Nevertheless James still wants to insist on the link between pure experience and sensation when he says: 'Pure experience in this state is but another name for feeling or sensation.'[15]

Clearly a part of these claims is a denial of certain traditional philosophical doctrines such as dualism and idealism. James associates these doctrines with a strict heterogeneity between the mental and the physical of such a kind as to make knowledge incomprehensible. He believes that traditional 'representative' theories of perception make an unbridgeable gap between our experiences and the objects they represent. He says, for example:

> and the whole philosophy of perception from Democritus's time downwards has been just one long wrangle over the paradox that what is evidently one reality should be in two places at once, both in outer space and in a person's mind. 'Representative' theories of perception avoid the logical paradox, but on the other hand they violate the reader's sense of life, which knows no intervening mental image but seems to see the room and the book immediately just as they physically exist.[16]

It is for this reason that James rejects what he calls the idealism of the English school.

> With transition and prospect thus enthroned in pure experience it is impossible to subscribe to the idealism of the English school. Radical

empiricism has in fact more affinity with natural realism than with the view of Berkeley or Mill.[17]

James is aware that such philosophers claim to be able to reconstruct our knowledge on the basis of their 'representations', but as in the case of the self he does not believe that such a reconstruction from punctiform atomist data can succeed. He consequently speaks of the 'incredibility' of such a philosophy, and describes it as 'cold, strained, and unnatural'.[18] What, it seems, is needed to remedy these defects is a common sense recognition of conjunctive relations within experience, and in particular an admission of an identity between perceptions and physical objects at the point of contact between them.

Two motives are present in such ideas. First James wishes to ally himself with a certain common sense or natural realism, which is strongly opposed to traditional representative theories. Second he believes that such dualist theories make so sharp a distinction between representation and represented as to commit the error of double-counting. Strong heterogeneity between the mental and the physical in this way allows for no possible re-unification between them. James's view by contrast is that there are not two discriminable items in the case but only one, which, however, can be taken in two different ways. In one way, as he says, it is all consciousness, and in another all content.

The image of divergent lines at a point of intersection matches these views exactly. At the intersection there are not two points but only one. Strictly speaking such a point should be identified, in the theory, in some neutral terminology, non-committal with respect to its mental or physical aspects. James, however, has no wish to reject a common sense distinction between such aspects but only to understand it adequately without the distortions of the traditional theories. The neutral point of contact is indeterminate rather than indeterminable, but whatever determinations we make will depend not only on the 'intrinsic' character of the point itself but also on the relations with which we connect it to other points on some line. Whichever line we are interested in, with its unique direction, will determine the further features we ascribe to the point. If we are interested in the associated experiences relating it by appropriation to one consciousness, then we will describe it in mental terms; if we associate it with a subsequent career independent of any specific consciousness, then we will describe it in non-mental terms.

It is in this way that James insists, in his 'paint' metaphors that these subsequent discriminations come by way of addition and not subtraction. In characterising a pure experience as physical, for example, we are not subtracting a physical entity from a mental reality, as perhaps Berkeley or Mill had hoped to do. Rather we are adding to the character of the experience a relation to other such experiences which determine the path of one of the lines diverging from the point of intersection.

> Paint has a dual constitution involving as it does a menstruum and a mass of content in the form of the pigment suspended therein. We can get the pure menstruum by letting the pigment settle, and the pure pigment by pouring off the size or oil. We operate here by physical subtraction; and the usual view is that by mental subtraction we can separate the two factors of experience in an analogous way. . . .
> Now my contention is exactly the reverse of this. Experience, I believe, has no such inner duplicity; and the separation of it into consciousness and content comes, not by way of subtraction, but by way of addition, – the addition to a given concrete piece of it, of other sets of experiences, in connection with which severally its use or function may be of two different kinds.[19]

1 Intersection

The first intersection, between a mind and an external object, is treated by James very much in the manner of his earlier discussion of truth. An idea which a mind possesses, whether percept or concept, may guide the possessor to other experiences which will support or verify the original idea, or fail to do so. James speaks characteristically of such 'leading' ideas and of the 'intervening' 'transitional' experiences which move us towards some 'terminus'. Though he distinguishes between a common sense and other 'more profound' views of such termini, still they *are* the ultimate reality.

> so long as we remain at the common sense stage of thought, object and subject *fuse* in the fact of presentation or sense-perception – the pen and the hand which I now *see* writing, for example, *are* the physical realities which those words designate.

> To call my present idea of my dog, for example, cognitive of the real dog, means that as the actual tissue of experience is constituted, the idea is capable of leading into a chain of other experiences on my part that go from next to next and terminate at last in vivid sense-perceptions of a jumping, barking, hairy body. Those *are* the real dog, the dog's full presence, for my common sense.[20]

James's proviso about the 'more profound' views is not an attempt to cast doubt on the common sense beliefs. The more profound views are those typically supplied by empirical science, in which the more theoretical ideas need to be judged by different perceptual termini. Although some of these theoretical developments may conflict with common sense there is no sign that James wished to use this to canvass any general scepticism. Indeed, though he plainly wished to be guided in his beliefs by the best available explanations in science, his whole discussion is fundamentally opposed to traditional scepticism. In the present context he is concerned only with the structure common to science and ordinary belief, namely that they both seek relevant termini, though the termini in each case may be radically distinct.

What is of immediate importance in James's positive account is the claimed identity between the mental and the physical at the intersecting point of contact between a mind and a physical object. James clearly wishes to insist that at the point of intersection both mental and physical aspects are inevitably present and that the point itself somehow 'fuses' and 'identifies' these apparently heterogeneous aspects. He elaborates his account of such fusions in other such contexts:

> Just as the seen room is *also* a field of consciousness, so the conceived or recollected room is *also* a state of mind.

> As subjective we say that the experience represents; as objective it is represented. What represents and is represented is here numerically the same; but we must remember that no dualism of representing and being represented resides in the experience per se . . . Its subjectivity and objectivity are functional attributes solely.[21]

In order to support his view of such identities James has to explain his opposition to the view that the two aspects are strictly heterogeneous. He does this at one point by questioning a traditional view which holds that the mental and the physical have no attributes in common. James lists large numbers of attributes which he thinks are held both by mental and physical phenomena, and he criticises Spencer in particular for following blindly a dualism which overlooks them. Even extension, an attribute which for Descartes marked an essential separation of the physical from the mental, belongs to both categories according to James. For our thought of a spatial relation, for example, has to be 'adequate' to the spatial relation itself. The suggestion is that this adequacy is required by our identification of the thought as the thought that 'This is spatially related to that'. James is not here denying that the spatiality of such a thought is of a quite different order from the spatial relation itself. But such a difference is accounted for, he believes, not by denying the spatial aspect of the thought, but by noting its different relational, and especially causal, connections in the two contexts. 'The two worlds differ not by the presence or absence of extension, but by the relations of the extensions which in both worlds exist.' It is at this point that James makes his famous remark: 'Mental fire is what won't burn real sticks; mental water is what won't necessarily (though it may) put out even a mental fire. Mental knives may be sharp but they won't cut wood.'[22]

Two problems stand out obviously from this account. The first has to do with the claimed fusion or identity between the mental and the physical at the point of intersection. James's language here, and its colourful imagery, might amount to no more than a metaphorical device to express a certain philosophical standpoint opposed to traditional dualism and idealism. If it is to be more than a mere rhetorical device, then some specific argument is needed to establish the claims. James provides two such specific arguments, but the central one, concerned with our minds' intersection with a common world of objects, has been severely criticised by Ayer. If that criticism were upheld then James's imagery would have no substantial support.

The second problem has to do with James's belief that the mental and the physical, consciousness and content, have attributes in common and so are homogeneous rather than heterogeneous. For James's explanation of the homogeneity may look like a trick. Clearly thoughts about spatial relations are *not* themselves spatial in any ordinary way. James, as we saw, would not have denied this, but his denial may seem unconvincing. It may be said that he simply fails to give due weight to the difference of type between the mental and the physical, or between our representations and what they represent. To take such a view may be to begin to reinstate the classical dualism which it is an essential part of James's doctrine to reject. That rejection rests, however, not only on the points made so far, but also on a radical revision which James proposed to the whole terminology of 'representation'. For James wished to replace that traditional terminology with a notion of 'intentionality' and with other subsidiary notions within an intentional framework. Plainly that proposal also needs to be examined.

(a) *Two arguments for identity*

James offers two central arguments for the identity between intersecting lines at the point of contact. The first of these has to do with the common intersection between different minds and some physical object, and the second with the intersection between two different minds. James runs these together in the first discussion by stressing the importance of our bodies. 'In that perceptual part of *my* universe which I call your body your mind and my mind meet and may be called co-terminous.'[23] But this is not the central example he has in mind, for our experiences may also be co-terminous with respect to some physical object distinct from either of our bodies, such as the Harvard Memorial Hall or a candle. In such cases James emphasises the co-incidences, or confluence, of our experiences. 'If you put out a candle, for example, when I am present, *my* candle ipso facto goes out.' He goes on to say:

> It is only as altering my objects that I guess you to exist. If your objects do not coalesce with my objects, if they be not identically where mine

are, they must be proved positively to be somewhere else. But no other location can be assigned to them, so their place must be what it seems to be, the same.[24]

He therefore concludes at this stage:

The common sense notion of minds sharing the same object offers no special logical or epistemological difficulties of its own: It stands or falls with the general possibility of things being in conjunctive relation with other things at all . . . In principle, then, let natural realism pass for possible.[25]

Although James believes that such a common sense realism is possible, and proof against the philosophical arguments he considers, he also thinks that there is a residual empirical problem. Two people may experience the same physical object at the same time, but they tend to do so in different ways, even within some specific sense. However close one may get to another the two perspectives and the two sets of sense organs may be somewhat different. James therefore finally raises the question whether on these empirical grounds the intersection never takes place. In answering this objection James takes his own view to be finally established.

On pragmatic principles we are obliged to predicate sameness wherever we can predicate no assignable point of difference. If two named things have every quality and function indiscernible, and are at the same time in the same place, they must be written down as numerically one thing under two different names. But there is no test discoverable, so far as I know, by which it can be shown that the place occupied by your percept of the Memorial Hall differs from the place occupied by mine. All the relations, whether geometrical or causal, of the Hall originate and terminate in that spot wherein our hands meet, and where each of us begins to work if he wishes to make the Hall change before our eyes.[26]

He concludes therefore:

In general terms, then, whatever differing contents our minds may eventually fill a place with, the place itself is a numerically identical content of the two minds, a piece of common property in which, through which, and over which they join.[27]

James sees no more difficulty in this shared experience than in its being the same dollar with which I repay you and which you accept in payment; or, in another image, in the same undivided estate being owned by several heirs.

This argument has been criticised by Ayer[28] in the following terms. When we consider whether *objects* named or described in different ways occupy the same space we have at our disposal a series of empirical tests which may or may not confirm such a claim. But when James speaks of *percepts* occupying the same, or a different, place the argument functions in a new and unsatisfactory way. For we do not normally think of percepts as occupying space at all. We may naturally construe percepts as private, sensory, mental items which are distinguished from physical objects precisely by lacking spatial location. If we take such a view, there seems to be no scope for a discussion of the spatial location of percepts, and so no possibility of establishing that two named percepts occupy different locations. In that case, however, the admitted absence of any test to locate percepts in *different* spaces is not a confirmation that they occupy the *same* space. It reflects only our inability to apply any tests for spatial location to what is essentially non-spatial.

If James's argument is understood in that way, then it is indeed demonstrably faulty. Another way of revealing its hopelessness is to notice that on these grounds *any* two percepts could be said to occupy the same place. For on these assumptions we can never have any ground for differentiating their spatial locations, and so are invited to infer that they are in the same place. These are conclusions that James could not have welcomed. They run quite counter to the common sense natural realism he takes himself to be supporting. But it seems also clear that he did not understand his argument in that absurd and fallacious way.

For one thing it is evident that at some stages in the argument it is the objects, such as the Memorial Hall, whose spatial location is at issue. Moreover, when James elaborates the tests to determine such a location these turn out to be primitive versions of the standard empirical procedures which Ayer is prepared to endorse. James speaks of the geometrical and causal relations which terminate at the place in question as if these were quite ordinary empirical features of our experience. Nor is that surprising given that James, at this point in his argument, is considering an empirical objection to this position. James could not have wished to say that these primitive co-incidences, or confluences, were all that determined the identity or location of your and my objects; he notes, for example, the requirements of identity of quality and function as well as that of time. But the suggestion seems to be that these primitive confluences are, as in his account of space in the *Principles*, the basic experienced phenomena on which our complex discriminations of physical objects depend. They are the basic felt conjunctive relations without which our spatial and physical understanding would be different.

It is true that James's text has an ambiguity which encourages Ayer's interpretation. James speaks in this passage of 'percepts' of the Memorial Hall, where earlier he had spoken of the Memorial Hall itself and later talks of the neutral 'content' of two minds. But there are decisive reasons not to ascribe to James the dualist distinction between mental percepts and physical objects on which the objection rests. For it is clear that James's intention is to query and reject any such dualism,[29] and that his accounts of intersection are designed to remove it. Strictly speaking the point of intersection should be described in some way that is neutral between the mental and the physical categorisation, but we have seen the practical difficulties in meeting that requirement. Perhaps the closest James gets to meeting it is in his choice of the term 'content', though even that requires explanation. What is certain, however, is that James's references to objects and percepts are inevitably unhappy ways of achieving strict neutrality. But whatever the difficulties it can be only to beg the question against him merely to *assume* a dualist distinction within his argument and then to object to it in just those terms.

Such a defence of James's argument is implicit in his own discussion but it does not establish the argument's success. That success could be achieved only if the problems over the neutral terminology were satisfactorily resolved. But there is an indication that the term 'content' and James's appeal to intentionality might help here. Even so it may still be said that the defence leaves only a stale-mate. For the argument seems then only to appeal to quite ordinary empirical considerations about the location of objects when it seemed that these very considerations needed justification. If Ayer's assumption of a dualist vocabulary begs the question against James it may equally be said that James's apparent assumption of a common spatial world begs the question against his opponents.

One way in which such a view might be elaborated would be to note that James appeared to canvass a quite general argument about the location of items in a common space. The suggestion is that James relies on the premiss that there is no possible way of showing that two percepts occupy different spaces, simply because percepts are non-spatial. But such an objection can be answered by recalling that James is forestalling a possible objection to his own common sense position. He requires of his opponents that they provide some general argument against the standard empirical procedure which we use to determine the same or different spatial location. James's suggestion is that when we reach the bedrock of the basic felt confluences, the touching of two hands for example, the empirical differences of perspective and sense no longer provide any reason for doubt. Perhaps an idealist might then revive the old, traditional, arguments based on the strict category differences of the mental and the physical, in order to canvass a doubt. But James, in the current argument, is considering an 'empirical' objection, and not such a full-scale idealist scepticism. It remains true, of course, that his own position, and in particular his own terminological proposal of neutrality between the two categories, are intended as an alternative to that idealist view.

It may still be said that he is not here justifying our common sense beliefs so much as merely relying on them, and there is some truth in this. At various stages in James's discussion of these issues he freely admits that he accepts certain common sense assumptions. In the *Principles* these assumptions, for example about the undeniable existence of both minds and physical objects, are listed as part of the framework in which psychology has to operate. In *The Meaning of Truth* James describes his own enquiry into cognition as 'descriptive psychology, hardly anything more',[30] and sets aside the issues of justification which philosophers have traditionally raised. This attitude should be linked to the many passages in which James adopts, as he says, the standpoint of common sense or naif realism. The present argument should also be understood within such a context. It does not so much justify common sense as rebut certain objections raised against it. The characteristic form of such a rebuttal for James consists in a demonstration of the way in which some concept works or functions in our experience. What James attempts in the argument is to make clear how the basic confluences or conjunctions in our experience operate to determine such things as 'same spatial location'.[31]

The second argument in favour of identity at the point of intersection has to do with a problem about the numerically same experience belonging to two different people. It has the same general form as the earlier argument, that is, it consists of a defence against a possible counter-argument, though in this case the counter-argument might be thought on the side of common sense. For the difficulty James envisages is simply that our usual criteria of identity for experiences make two experiences different if they belong to different people. James admits the strength of the belief that for states of consciousness their 'esse' is 'sentiri', that a 'feeling' '*is*' only in so far as it is felt'. For the suggestion is that any feeling must be felt differently by different people, and that this would rule out the numerical identity of any pure experience possessed in common by two different people.

The defence against this argument consists in distinguishing the feeling itself from the awareness of it as belonging to this or that person.

> To be conscious means not simply to be but to be reported, known, to
> have awareness of one's being added to that being . . . The pen
> experience in its original immediacy is not aware of itself, it simply *is*,
> and the second experience is required for what we call awareness of it
> to occur.[32]

James had earlier extensively criticised philosophers who supposed that with every experience there was coupled a recognition of awareness of the self whose experience it was.[33] Once that distinction is granted James believes that the objection disappears.

> even although 'a feeling only is as it is felt' there is still nothing absurd
> in the notion of its being felt in two different ways at once, as yours
> namely and mine. It is, indeed, 'mine' only as it is felt as mine, and

'yours' only as it is felt as yours. But it is felt as neither *by itself*, but only when 'owned' by our two several remembering experiences.[34]

These claims echo other similar points that James makes elsewhere about the bare nature of pure experience as a 'that' not yet distinguished as having this or that character.

As in the previous argument James's position here seems less than decisive. Someone might object that if a feeling is only as it is felt, and this is felt as mine while that is felt as yours, then these must be two distinguishable feelings and so not numerically identical. James's defence requires that we identify a feeling in both cases without that conscious addition, but queries can still be raised. Even if that addition is not present it still remains true that the feeling is mine, in one context, and yours, in another. The feeling must be owned by someone, so that this addition is necessarily connected to the feeling. In another context James considers this question of the necessary ownership of experiences and there takes the strange view that it is simply an empirical matter that we 'have no experience of such things'[35] as unowned experiences. This does not seem a good response to the difficulties in his present argument.

These problems show a need for further explanation of James's position, and the same is generally true of other more familiar difficulties in it. James could, of course, simply stipulate that when we are talking of *pure* experience the question of ownership does not arise. Such a position would not be entirely arbitrary, since James takes the view in this as in other contexts that the further characterisations of the experience depend upon its allocation to different functional lines. This is as true of the divergent lines of personal consciousness as it is of those in which a consciousness is contrasted with a physical object. But it would be circular on James's part to appeal to such claims here, since the imagery itself depends on the establishment of the numerical identity of the intersecting points on such divergent lines.

We are left, as in the other cases, with a puzzle about the role or sense of 'pure experience'. It is evidently of great importance in James's account, and yet also totally inarticulate. It looks like a paradigm of what Wittgenstein referred to when he said that 'a nothing would do as well as a something about which nothing can be said'.[36] For James's pure experience has to be such that nothing whatever can be said about it, if it is to fulfil the very role for which it is cast. Elsewhere James refers to the 'speechlessness' of sensations and criticises Green for not simply accepting this.[37] James believed that such an attitude was part of a disreputable intellectualist wish to degrade the importance of sheer sensory experience. It was an attitude which he associated with the failings of empiricist atomism, for he thought that empiricists were naturally driven to such inarticulate atoms and so encouraged either scepticism or transcendentalism. It now appears that

James's own view is liable to the same fate. Without some ability to characterise the experiences we have no means of determining their identity, and even have no clear means of assessing James's central claim that we are presented with conjunctive relations in experience as well as atomic sensations. Despite these problems James does, as we have seen, offer characterisations of such conjunctive relations and of the pure experience which involves them. But in order to characterise them in ordinary terms James plainly needs some device like the 'bracketing' of phenomenology, or a non-committal set of phenomenological descriptions, which could give a sense to the idea of a neutral terminology.

(b) *Intentionality*

Part of James's negative thesis involves the rejection of traditional 'representative' theories of perception. James characterises these as invoking an intermediary, a representation, between observer and independent reality in order to explain, perhaps justify, our perceptual knowledge. For James such theories make the mistake of assuming a strict heterogeneity between the mental and the physical, creating a 'chasm' between them which cannot be bridged.[38] He believed that such a failure then led philosophers towards a priori principles or the absolute whose role was to remedy that failure. He did not believe, however, that a reference to such 'solving names' achieved any more than to mark the problem, while the problem itself was simply insoluble within that dualist framework. What was needed was to return to a common sense conception in which the 'chasm' presented no real obstacle, since at the point of contact between observers and physical objects there was no dualism of representation and represented but only an identity of pure experience. The difference between the mental and the physical in this context was one of context and function, and not one between existents belonging to heterogeneous categories. To take the latter dualist view was to commit the error of double-counting.

We have seen, however, that James's claims for the identity at the point of contact are ambiguous and open to criticism. His arguments are proof against some of the most powerful objections but they remain in need of further clarification. James's rejection of classical dualism shows, however, the extent to which he wished to revolutionise our terminology for perception and knowledge. It is clear that he intends to deal with the traditional problems not by accepting their assumptions but by re-writing the vocabulary in which they are couched. He does this by offering to replace the terminology of 'representation' with that of 'substitution', 'operation', and 'resemblance'. A central concern in his attempt to construct a new vocabulary was the problem of what he called 'objective reference', that is, what it is for someone to 'mean' or 'point to' some independent item which 'goes beyond' the present experience. It is in this context that James gives an account of what we should call 'intentionality'. James knew of, and appeals to, Brentano's account of intentional inexistence, but he offers his own version of it.[39]

The best examples of what James calls 'substitution' come from our theoretical thinking.[40] James thinks of any theoretical treatment of some phenomenon as providing a clearer, simpler, substitute for the chaos, the 'blooming, buzzing confusion' which our senses present. When a theory has developed sufficiently he recognises that we may no longer be so concerned with the sensory material and operate instead with the conceptual substitutes for it. Abstract mathematical thinking or the refinements of some complex computer program might present examples where the interest is lodged exclusively in the conceptual construction. James accepts both the benefits and the attractions of such substitute thinking, but he believed that it also contained dangers. Though such substitutes enable us to think more quickly and efficiently, they also to some extent distort and falsify the original data. For James no theory is ever a complete transcript of reality, and every abstract or theoretical idea, however useful, needs to 'dip back' into sense experience if it is to function properly.

There are consequently dangers in failing to admit the limitations of substitute theorising. The empiricists' atomism was for James a good example of such a theoretical distortion. Even more seriously we may come to think of our substitutes as superior to the experience on which they rest and so disregard or devalue the senses. For James such attitudes bred the metaphysical excesses of crude Platonism or rationalism, in which reality is identified quite independently of the senses and exclusively in terms of our conceptual systems.[41] It is not too difficult to see the connection between such metaphysical positions and the strict heterogeneity of classical dualism as James conceived it. James thought that much metaphysical and religious theorising committed these faults; it was a central part of his pragmatism to remind conceptual theorists of their humbler sensory origins.

The replacement of 'representation' by 'substitute' might have a value in reducing these distortions. In a negative way it might avoid the natural inclination to fall into a two-world dualism; more positively it might point the way towards a better grasp of the relevant relationships between observer and the physical world. James says at one point:

> The towering importance for human life of this kind of knowing lies in the fact that an experience that knows another can figure as its *representative*, not in any quasi-miraculous 'epistemological' sense, but in the definite practical sense of being its *substitute* in various operations, sometimes physical and sometimes mental, which lead us to its associates and results.[42]

In traditional philosophy the idea of a representation has been confusedly associated with that of a copy, a mental image, which mirrors and so exactly resembles some independent reflected item. The notion of a substitute might begin to change that traditional temptation.[43] It may also suggest that the original for which it substitutes is both accessible, though less easy to handle, and also more basic than the substitute itself.

James pursues this idea in his accounts of 'objective reference', and of the way in which experiences may 'go beyond' themselves to 'point to' or 'mean' some other item. In the *Essays in Radical Empiricism* he argues that we might give two versions of such relations. In one, the 'transcendentalist' account, we think of them as relations across that epistemological chasm between representations and some purported reality totally independent of them. In the other such relations occur simply between different parts of our experience. James, of course, adopts the latter view and links it with his idea of a conjunctive relation. 'A positively conjunctive experience involves neither chasm nor leap. Being the very original of what we mean by continuity, it makes a continuum wherever it appears.'[44] Our experiences, then, have a certain character of 'self-transcendence' but this is not to make a reference to some inexperiencable, independent reality but only to other accessible parts of experience itself. That strict heterogeneity between the mental and the physical implicit in the transcendentalist account is thus to be set aside.

In other contexts, particularly in *The Meaning of Truth* and *Some Problems of Philosophy*, James says more of pointing to or meaning some external reality. His central idea is to explain them in terms of such notions as 'operation' and 'resemblance'. Of percepts, for example, he says that they are cognitive if and only if they both resemble and directly or indirectly operate on some reality. He sums up his account in a similar definition covering both percepts and concepts:

> A percept knows whatever reality it directly or indirectly operates on and resembles: a conceptual feeling or thought knows a reality whenever it actually or potentially terminates in a percept which operates on or resembles that reality, or is otherwise connected with it or its context.[45]

James explicitly attaches little significance to the details of such a definition, and it clearly suffers from some defects. It seems to assume the existence of some reality, though we have seen elsewhere that James does make such assumptions. It does not make clear what it is for a percept to 'operate on' a reality. The concluding catch-all phrase 'otherwise connected with' seems objectionably vague, and the definition seems at least in danger of confusing testability and truth. For to know that some claim is testable requires perhaps only a potential terminus, while to know that it is true might be thought to require some actual terminus. With one exception such problems seem less important than the invocation of James's familiar view of thoughts or percepts leading us in certain directions towards some terminus which may or may not confirm or verify the original idea.

The one surprising exception is that in the definition James still attaches so much weight to the idea of resemblance. It might be thought that this concedes too much to a traditional representative account. Later, however, James makes it plain that of the two notions it is 'operation' that has primacy. He says:

> As a matter of fact whenever we constitute ourselves into psychological critics it is not by dint of discovering which reality a feeling resembles that we find out which reality it means. We become first aware of which it means and then we suppose that to be the one it resembles.[46]

In a note later attached to the same paper James notes as a first defect in it the 'undue prominence' which it attaches to the resemblance relation.[47] These provisos indicate that resemblance is almost dispensed with so that 'operation' is left to give a cash-value to 'meaning', 'pointing', and 'self-transcendence'.

That rejection of resemblance is important in James's attempt to forge a new vocabulary for perception and knowledge. A straightforward resemblance relation requires that the two relata can be simply compared, and this in turn implies that they can be independently identified. But it had always been a difficulty in traditional epistemology that any such independent identification seemed impossible. An identification which involved the subject in some way was not strictly independent; while anything that was strictly independent seemed quite inaccessible, even undiscussable. James responded to this problem by rejecting the dualists' strict heterogeneity between experience and reality or between consciousness and content. But if the two items are not strictly independent then there seems little room for the traditional idea of a straightforward resemblance between them. James notices, however, a more intimate dependence between such items. He points out that we may be torn between treating such relations, between content and consciousness, as contingent or non-contingent. On one side the relation seems contingent, since no empirical thought guarantees its own truth; yet on the other side we identify the thought as the thought that such and such is the case. The thought and its content are thus strictly inseparable, and this may encourage us to treat the relation as non-contingent.

James's initial attempt to capture these special features is typically metaphorical. He says 'A feeling feels as a gun shoots'[48] to indicate the way in which thoughts and their contents are made for each other. But it seems that the point can be made in less metaphorical ways. If we consider thoughts about matters of fact then the thought is simply incomplete without some content, and so necessarily points to some reality beyond itself. That necessary internal relation is, of course, compatible with the thought's falsity, so that thought and reality are also independent of each other. There is, in such cases, both some independence, of an epistemic kind, and also a strong dependence of a semantic kind between the thought and the content which specifies what it is about. Traditional dualism, as James conceives it, stressed the former independence but failed to appreciate the latter dependence.

James associates his own account with Grote's distinction between knowledge by acquaintance and knowledge *about* something.[49] The contrast might be used to separate non-propositional cognitive states, such as seeing some object, from propositional states, such as believing that p is the case, but James is more interested in stressing the epistemic priority of the former over the latter. He believes that the former provides a paradigm for those basic dumb or speechless sensory experiences which form the basis for our more intellectual states. But he notes at one point that there may be some ambiguity in the description of any content.

> If A enters and B exclaims, 'Didn't you see my brother on the stairs?'
> we all hold that A may answer, 'I saw him, but didn't know that he was
> your brother', ignorance of brotherhood not abolishing the power to
> see.[50]

James uses this as a ground for dismissing intellectualist arguments to the effect that if we do not know *everything* about an object, then we do not know the object at all.[51] But it is also an informal recognition of what has come to be called an 'opaque context' in the reporting of cognitive attitudes. We may correctly identify an object of knowledge or perception in reporting another person's state without supposing that the person either does or could identify it under that description.

James does not pursue these points in the way that later philosophers have, but they suggest some sense for his notions of the neutrality and identity of 'pure' experiences. If cognitive attitudes generally require completion by some content which points beyond itself, then that content must be able to identify both the cognitive state and the reality it is about. There must then be a way of expressing such contents which makes them common both to the cognitive state and to the relevant state of affairs. This will be true, for example, of all the four contrasts earlier noted in James's extended epistemology. This can be simply illustrated from the earlier case, involving all the contrasts (1)–(4), of two people shaking hands. Each may have the thought or perception 'We are shaking hands', so that the content is common both to each person's consciousness whether that is perceptual or conceptual. The same content identifies also the corresponding state of affairs, though that does not guarantee its truth. It was this identity relation which James relied on in the earlier argument about the 'adequacy' of our thoughts to the corresponding reality.

That point about the content's identity entails its neutrality, as James conceives this. For if the same content is common to such diverse contexts, then the content cannot by itself differentiate between them. Moreover there must be a way of expressing such distinctions which set a common content into distinguishable contexts. It is, for example, natural to do this by using different operators to mark those contexts. When we talk of a perceptual context we might prefix the content by 'X sees that . . .' and contrast this with a conceptual operator such as 'X consciously thinks that . . .'. To differentiate between two people sharing the same content we need only substitute different names or descriptions for the variable X. To contrast a direct reference to reality with some person's cognitive attitude to it we might use such prefixes as 'It is the case that . . .' as opposed to 'X believes that . . .'.

Some sense can be given in this way to James's claims for the identity and neutrality of pure experiences. The common contents could not be simply treated as ordinary experiences, though they can be easily fitted into contexts where they report such experiences. For the content itself is neutral with respect to such experiences and any reality beyond them which they point to. 'Pure experience' turns out to mean nothing more than 'content', conceived in this way. Earlier we had noted that James favoured this term to mark the neutral aspect of pure experience, and in one passage at least James explicitly makes the connection.

> Admettons que la conscience, la Bewusstheit, conçue comme essence, entité, activité, moitié irréductible de chaque expérience soit supprimée, que le dualisme fondamental et pour ainsi dire ontologique soit aboli, et que ce que nous supposions exister soit seulement ce qu'on a appelé jusqu'ici le contenu, le Inhalt, de la conscience.[52]

> (Let us accept that consciousness, 'Bewusstheit', conceived as an essence, an entity, an activity, or as an irreducible half of each experience, can be set aside; that that basic, ontological, dualism is abolished, and that what we suppose to exist is no more than what we have so far called the content, the 'Inhalt', of consciousness.)

In the same passage James admits that he has given only a sketch for such an account to solve his four epistemological problems, and it is true that a number of provisos should be added to this view.

James does not dwell, for example, on the distinction that might be drawn between propositional and non-propositional cognitive attitudes. Nor does he explicitly mention the distinction between what might be called non-representative states, such as that of being in pain, and representative states, such as perceiving that something is the case. In both cases there is some implicit recognition of such contrasts, for example in his appeal to Grote's distinction and in his second argument for the identity of contents belonging to two different people. But the first point does not affect the claims about the identity or neutrality of cognitive contents; and the second does not affect his central position, for that is concerned precisely with the case of representative cognitive states, that is, with cases where the experience points to something beyond itself.

More serious problems might be thought to arise from James's implicit recognition of opaque contexts in the reporting of cognitive states, and from his failure to offer any systematic account of the identity of contents. The former point creates a potential difficulty because it allows two different ways of identifying contents, associated sometimes with a distinction between 'de dicto' and 'de re' reporting. The latter might be regarded simply as a remediable omission, but might be more serious if there were grounds for thinking that no such systematic account could be given.

It was suggested earlier that James recognised a distinction between two ways of reporting cognitive states. In one what is reported matches what the person himself understands, and in the other references are correctly made to the items of the person's understanding but not in terms which he would recognise. James shows an awareness of this in a much wider context, whenever he considers a psychologist's account of some person's mental state, and it is the basis for his recognition of what he calls the 'psychologists' fallacy'. The distinction, though important, does not seem to present a decisive obstacle to James's central thesis. It might be said that difficulties may arise if we identify contents on no consistent basis, but that so long as consistency is maintained the identity and neutrality of contents can remain as James sees them. Moreover, whether we identify such contents de re or de dicto James's central thesis remains undisturbed. For whichever mode is employed it remains true that a content so identified can characterise both cognitive states and their associated realities. It might still be argued that James is committed to a de dicto mode of identifying contents in terms of his wish to characterise exactly the feeling as felt by the subject. But one difficulty here is that in principle, though patently not in practice, there is no way of exactly capturing that felt experience.

Similar concessions might be made with regard to the lack of a systematic account of content identity. Probably the most natural anxiety here is the feeling that such identity cannot hold between experiences, however similar, which belong to different persons. James, as we saw, argues explicitly against this and shows certainly that there is no reason why we could not identify contents in this way across different consciousnesses. Two such contents would be said to be identical if, for example, they ascribe the same property to the same thing at the same time. That such a numerically identical content can be attributed to two different people is allowed by that criterion. It is no objection that such a criterion deviates from our ordinary convictions about the numerical identity of experiences, for James is consciously innovating in devising criteria of identity for 'pure experiences'. It can still be objected that such an example makes no allowance for more complex contents, expressible in other linguistic forms. The account offered above gave only a sufficient and not a necessary condition for content identity. To satisfy such a demand for a comprehensive scheme of content identity would require some recursive procedure which might build on that example but could not rest with it. There is no doubt that this would be a complex task, but there is no general reason to think that it could not be carried out.

We are left with the idea that James's proposals are feasible in principle and might give sense to his ideas about pure experiences, their identity and neutrality. But in a review of the upshot of such a proposal there is still a major objection. For even if James has described a feasible proposal it can still be asked why we should accept it, and how far it really refutes the traditional account. The characteristic style of James's arguments is one in which he presents a case which the traditional view regards as quite impossible. In several extended passages, which I have not commented on, he considers the opposing arguments on which that traditional view rests and locates the fallacies in the 'intellectualist logic' of its arguments.[53] He takes the view, then, that if there is no positive ground for the traditional view, with its dualist assumptions, we are entitled to change those assumptions and construct a view more in line with our common sense convictions. This is the strategy which leads him to change the traditional dualism, with its unbridgeable chasm, into his own account of content identity. In that account there are positive grounds to support the new assumptions, for example, in his discussion of intentionality, but it would be wrong to think that he had offered a once for all refutation of scepticism about the external world. James does not deal with all the myriad ways in which such scepticism might be supported, though he does consider the examples most familiar to him. In the end of the day James invites us to consider which of the alternative views has more plausibility.

2 Ontology and epistemology

Some residual issues need finally to be mentioned. There is the question whether James is canvassing an ontological or an epistemological thesis; and whether any ontological view is of the strong kind presented earlier. There is the question whether his view is, as Ayer believed, simply a version of phenomenalism, and there is one extended argument, the argument from hybrids, whose role has not yet been clarified.

James's position in what I have called his extended epistemology has both a negative and a positive aspect. Clearly a large part of the former has to do with his rejection of certain traditional epistemological doctrines which he variously describes as dualism, idealism, transcendentalism, and so on. It should not be forgotten, too, that though an empiricist himself he has also a quarrel with the traditional empiricists on these matters.

116

Although he wishes to reject the classical dualist ontology, he also makes it quite clear that common sense is on the side of dualism. In this respect his plausible position seems to be that classical dualists had misconceived the nature of our dualist beliefs, and so had become entangled with the puzzles and incoherences of traditional epistemology. What is further required, beyond these negative points, is some better account of that common sense distinction which we make between the mental and the physical. In the positive part of James's doctrine he attempts to give such a better account.

We have seen, however, that he sometimes seems to replace the dualist ontology with a strong ontological commitment of his own. The suggestion here is that once we reject classical dualism, with its strict and unbridgeable heterogeneity between the mental and the physical, then we may accept a monism in which the basic stuff of existence is something called 'pure experience'. Such a view might be expressed in the strong ontological thesis (8) above. James sometimes himself expresses a rather cavalier attitude towards this thesis, when he says of pure experience that we may call it a basic stuff, *if we like*. We have seen also that he modifies the claim in a number of ways. Elsewhere, too, he shows a similarly uncommitted view of ontological questions generally, when he speaks of anything's existing which we are obliged to take into account in any way.

There must, then, be some doubt as to whether he wished to hold a strict ontological view of this kind at all, but whether he did or not the question arises whether such a thesis is justified in terms of what has so far been said. The answer must surely be negative. If we ask more particularly *what* exists in this basic way James still has no clear answer. Contents do not look like any sort of 'stuff' at all, and they are not supposed to be understood in terms of ordinary subjective experience. They range over what we ordinarily call things, or events, as well as over what we call states of affairs. This is one way in which James's lack of a clear contrast between propositional and non-propositional cognitive states saddles him with an evident disadvantage. But he accepts an even more severe handicap in his view that strictly pure experiences are quite uncharacterisable. For this means that there simply could be no answer to the original question about the nature of the basic monistic stuff. All that we can say is that our knowledge rests ultimately on particular dumb or speechless sense experiences. Such a view is understandable as an empiricist device, but it stands awkwardly as a strong ontology. There is no doubt that James wished to deny the strong ontological thesis of classical dualism, but that denial does not commit him to a strong ontological thesis of his own.

It was suggested earlier that the argument from hybrids might play a role in the strong ontological thesis, though it seemed disqualified from doing so. James clearly intends to use the reference to hybrids as a further argument against a crude dualism and he does so in two related ways. First he appeals to hybrid cases as a way of showing how rare, even impossible, it is to locate pure mental or pure physical items in our experience. Even the body is described by him as the 'palmary instance of the ambiguity' between the mental and the physical. Second he suggests that we have the power of 'projecting' our own responses onto an independent reality, and that this is so even for our basic characterisation of that independent reality itself. If we accept that latter somewhat obscure claim then James can conclude that no items in our experience are purely mental or purely physical, because our own responses make a contribution to everything that we identify. Such a view may dent the belief in a crude dualism, which implies that there have to be examples of the purely mental or the purely physical in experience; but a more sophisticated dualism might avoid this. Such an argument still seems quite unable to sustain a positive conclusion of the strong ontological kind. It suggests the weaker commitment of (7) above, in which neither the mental nor the physical have priority over the other, rather than the stronger claim (8).

James also uses the reference to hybrids to argue that our distinction between the mental and the physical is not ontological at all but only semantic. The two categories, on this view, are simply ways of classifying or sorting the basic contents of pure experience. They reflect simply the basis for our contrast between a subjective, mental, prefix and an objective, physical content to which the former is attached. This weaker claim is quite different from the strong ontological thesis, and even seems to encourage us at this stage not to draw firm ontological conclusions at all. Rather it invites us to clarify further the criteria in terms of which we sort experienced items into one or other category. The general answer James offers here is simply that familiar story about the divergent lines of development, in which one such line with its intermediate and terminal points has one set of physical characteristics which the other notably lacks. In this positive part of his view the suggestion is that we can clarify the division by teasing out and listing the features which typically guide our classification of things as mental or physical. The workings of our beliefs in the two contexts determine the characteristic directions of such divergent lines. Such an account seems epistemological rather than ontological.

James plainly has two related theses even in the positive part of his doctrine. In the first he attempts to establish the feasibility of the identities in his four tasks (1)–(4). Generally, as we have seen, he tries to show how such intersecting identities are possible against the traditional philosophical arguments which claim that they are impossible. In the second, as the argument from hybrids suggests, James envisages a more detailed investigation into the basis for our classification of items into the mental and the physical. It is this second line of enquiry which has been regarded as a phenomenalist programme, and was extensively discussed by Ayer.[54] It is clear from what has been said already that this second positive part of James's view has obvious similarities to such a phenomenalist account, and yet some provisos need to be made. For one thing to concentrate on this part of James's positive view is to neglect its other aspect. For him the claims about the intersecting identities were at least as important as, and perhaps even more important than, the remaining story. Certainly James does little in detail to fill out the remaining story, but he surely also held the view that that story should be understood only within the framework of the claims about identity.

There are, however, additional grounds for not ascribing phenomenalism to James, and I note these summarily. The standard phenomenalist programme is reductive, and aims to show how complex statements about physical objects may be translated into sets of statements about sense experiences. It is naturally associated with the empiricist principles listed earlier, in which atomist sensory data provide the only material content for the construction and formal logic provides the only generative analytic principle for the construction. Even within that framework there are varieties of phenomenalist view. Goodman, for example, required only extensional isomorphism for the two sets of statements, while Ayer required an intensional connection. At one time Ayer required that the intensional connections should be two-way, so that the statements about sense-data were synonymous with those about physical objects, but later, in his discussion of James, he took the view that the former were necessary but not sufficient for the latter. He nevertheless ascribed the stronger view to James, despite the fact that, as he admitted, James showed no interest in discussing the detail of such a programme.

Even within that characterisation of phenomenalism it is clear that the programme is at odds with James's own views. For one thing Ayer ascribes an extreme form of empiricism to James, whereas, as we have seen, *radical* empiricism was intended to be an improved but not an *extreme* form of the doctrine. In particular the atomist assumptions of standard phenomenalism are seriously in conflict with James's views about conjunctive relations. At the least this raises questions about what James's basic material content for the construction would be, but it also raises doubts about whether the construction could be phenomenalist. For James clearly takes the view that conjunctive relations are presented to us and do not need any construction. If we couple that claim with his persistent commitment to what he calls 'naive realism', 'natural realism', or 'common sense realism', then it seems more plausible to take him to be starting with beliefs, or contents, about physical objects, rather than attempting to construct or justify them. When he speaks of the dog's 'full presence', or of the identity of the intersecting points, then he points in a direction away from phenomenalism.

There is a further set of problems in the attribution. When Ayer considers the basic material content for his phenomenalist construction he requires that the basic sense-data should be neutral, that is should not be committed to the existence or non-existence of physical items. He believed that this followed James's own requirements for the neutrality of 'pure experience'. But we have seen that strictly James's neutrality is wider than this. Pure experiences are supposed to be neutral not merely with respect to physical items but to the whole division between the mental and the physical. They are to be non-committal with respect to that dual classification, and so cannot strictly be identified with ordinary, subjective, mental experiences any more than with physical items. Earlier it was noted how Ayer's assumption here led him to characterise and criticise James's first argument for the identity of contents. There, however, it was shown how that assumption distorted the role of James's argument. Put more generally Ayer's conception of neutrality assumes the basic dualist division which it was a part of James's account to reject. One way in which this appears is in James's quite unmistakable rejection of the programme of Mill and Berkeley, both of which are naturally characterisable as phenomenalist. On Ayer's account that rejection is incomprehensible.

One final point might be made against Ayer's view. Phenomenalism, as I have characterised it, is reductive in a traditional empiricist way. James expresses a clear rejection of such empiricist reduction, not only in his rejection of atomism but also in his stress on 'functions'. His positive account of the division between the mental and physical is designed not to reduce the latter to the former, but to give parity to both. What we call ordinary mental experiences and physical items are distinguished, according to James, by the functional and contextual relations among pure experiences. His aim seems to be to sketch that functional relationship rather than to reduce one element to the other. Such an aim conforms well both with his own claims about the 'descriptive' goals of his discussion and with his holistic view of experience and meaning. It was noted earlier that James rejected 'foundationalist' epistemologies, just as he also rejected 'foundationalist' theories of morality. His holism is a partial expression of that rejection. It remains unclearly defined, but its general attitude is out of line with the phenomenalist programme.

On balance, then, I do not think James was canvassing a phenomenalist construction, but Ayer's convictions are understandable. If we ask whether James thought that our beliefs about physical objects were determined, verified or falsified, by the intervening and terminal experiences which he describes, then the answer is not in doubt. James was an empiricist, though not an extreme empiricist, and certainly held that our beliefs about physical objects required no reference to a priori principles or trans-empirical items. Our beliefs about physical objects must be related in some way to our sense experiences, and to the course of that experience. Sometimes 'phenomenalism' is so loosely defined that this would be enough to make him a phenomenalist, but so loose a definition should not be accepted.[55] Ayer has a much tighter conception of the programme, but precisely for that reason his conception conflicts with much of what James says.

7

Philosophical
Psychology

There is inevitably some artificiality in separating James's epistemology from his philosophical psychology. The inclusion of conjunctive relations among the items given in experience is an integral part of both aspects of his philosophy. The part such a notion plays in James's account of the self in the *Principles* alone shows this, but it is also evident in his discussion of particular topics, such as Berkeley's theory of vision.[1] Many of the distinctions James thought vitally important, such as that between knowledge by acquaintance and knowledge about, have prominence in both accounts. Yet the distinctive features of radical empiricism, and in particular the appeal to 'pure experience', are temporally later than, and go beyond, the doctrines of the *Principles*. James, too, draws a sharp distinction in the latter work between psychological and metaphysical issues.

His view of the relationship between the two disciplines is well stated in the preface.

> I have kept close to the point of view of natural science throughout the book. Every natural science assumes certain data uncritically, and declines to challenge the elements between which its own 'laws' obtain . . . Psychology, the science of finite individual minds, assumes as its data (1) *thoughts* and *feelings*, and (2) *a physical world* in time and space with which they co-exist and which (3) they *know*. Of course these data themselves are discussable; but the discussion of them is called metaphysics and falls outside the province of this book.[2]

Elsewhere James notes variants of these assumptions, whose acceptance divides a natural science like psychology from metaphysics. He lists at one point as further assumptions (1) the psychologist, (2) the thought studied, (3) the thought's object, and (4) the psychologist's reality.[3] More generally he characterises the psychologist's attitude as a thoroughgoing dualism. He says of the discipline 'It supposes two elements, mind knowing and thing known, and treats them as irreducible'.[4] It is a measure of the connection between James's science and his philosophy that these last assumptions are sometimes made even in his account of radical empiricism.

Usually once James has identified a problem as 'metaphysical' in the *Principles*, as in the case of free-will, he evades a resolution of the issue in the psychological context. Of a belief in introspection and its salient features he says

> I regard this belief as the most fundamental of all the postulates in psychology, and shall discard all curious enquiries about its certainty as too metaphysical for the scope of this book.[5]

This does not, however, prevent James from discussing at length some relevant metaphysical issues, such as the traditional mind-body problem. One reason for this is its importance for the operation of psychology itself, and another is its close connection with the account of the self which James offers in the *Principles*. A third reason is simply that it is not easy to disentangle the metaphysical from the psychological issues. James's discussion of that traditional problem in the chapters on 'The Automaton Theory' and 'The Mind-Dust Theory' is designed in part to draw these divisions more clearly. Towards the end of that discussion James writes:

> We are back at Leibnizian monadism, and therewith leave psychology behind us and dive into regions inaccessible to experience and verification; and our doctrine, though not self-contradictory, becomes so remote and unreal as to be almost as bad as if it were. Speculative minds alone will take an interest in it; and metaphysics, not psychology, will be responsible for its career.[6]

James's attitude to problems so characterised as metaphysical is not that of the logical positivists. Though he allied his own pragmatism to the positivism he knew, and describes his psychology as naturalistic and positivistic, he did not simply conclude that metaphysical issues were meaningless or empty merely because they were unscientific. The free-will issue was, for James, metaphysical rather than scientific, because it demonstrated a conflict between science and morality. It could not be settled by science, but was not for that reason spurious or nonsensical. James defends metaphysical questioning more generally in *Some Problems of Philosophy*,[7] where he takes a Russellian view of the relations between philosophy and science. More specifically he defends it also in the *Principles* when he says:

> the data assumed by psychology, just like those assumed by physics and the other natural sciences, must some time be overhauled. The effort to overhaul them thoroughly and completely is metaphysics; but metaphysics can only perform her task well when distinctly conscious of its great extent. Metaphysics, fragmentary, irresponsible and half-

awake, and unconscious that she is metaphysical, spoils two good things when she injects herself into natural science.[8]

In the final chapter of his *Briefer Course* James explicitly distances himself from the disparaging use of the term 'metaphysics', and is especially modest about the achievements of psychology itself. He talks of its supplying a 'string of raw facts . . . and not a single law',[9] and describes it as 'only the hope of a science'. He sums up this view in saying:

> When we talk of psychology as a natural science we must not assume that that means a sort of psychology that stands at last on solid ground. It means just the reverse; it means a psychology particularly fragile, and into which the waters of metaphysics leak at every joint.[10]

Clearly one of the metaphysical leaks of which James was most conscious was the traditional mind-body problem. In its more particular form, about the relationship between mind and brain, James was prepared to bypass it for scientific purposes, but at the same time acknowledged the mystery it involved.

> The fact that the brain is the one immediate condition of the mental operations is indeed so universally admitted nowadays that . . . I simply postulate it . . . The whole remainder of the book will be more or less a proof that the postulate was correct.[11]

While he therefore offered physiological explanations for various mental phenomena he was also prepared to concede that 'the relations of a mind to its own brain are of an unique and utterly mysterious sort'.[12]

James's philosophy in general, and his psychology in particular, are probably best known for the notion of a 'stream of consciousness', or for his description of psychology as the 'science of mental life'.[13] It is less remarked that he nevertheless places so much emphasis on physiological explanations that he is, as he admits, strongly tempted by materialism.[14] Further indications of the complexity of his own attitude to psychology can be seen both in his suggested resolutions of the mind-body problem and in his catalogue of the methods appropriate for psychological investigation. With respect to the former it has been said that in the *Principles* there are few traditional solutions to the problem that he does not at some time or other seem to accept. There is in particular serious doubt whether he was prepared to accept some form of inter-actionist dualism, or preferred a weaker parallelism between mind and brain. Though he officially rejects the 'automaton', materialist, theory he is nevertheless tempted by materialism; though he officially rejects any reference to a spiritualist 'soul' in his final account of the self, he nevertheless at one stage allows a free choice between such a spiritualism and a more positivistically austere solution. With respect to the methods of psychological enquiry

James identifies three, namely introspection, and what he calls 'experimental' and 'comparative' methods. Of these it is clearly the first that he thinks most important, though this hardly squares either with his stress on physiological explanations or his inclination towards materialism.

It may be that a clearer way to James's view of psychology is less through his own accounts of its metaphysics and its methods than through his discussion of specific psychological topics. I finally consider what is probably the best known of these in philosophy, namely James's account of the emotions.

1 The mind-body problem

James considers a number of purported solutions to the mind-body problem in the *Principles*. He separates primarily a materialist 'automaton' theory from what he calls 'mind-stuff' theories, but within these broad divisions he also considers epiphenomenalist, parallel, and inter-actionist variants. He quotes from Huxley and Clifford, for example, to indicate an epiphenomenalist automaton theory in which conscious feelings have no more effect on our lives than the colours of a mosaic have in holding the fragments in place.[15] He considers, and temporarily endorses, a version of dualism in which mental and physical events run parallel courses without influencing each other. And over all these variants he is guided by three crucial considerations. First is the need to appeal to a common sense conception of the mind, which would nowadays be described as 'folk psychology'; second is the need to identify clearly insoluble metaphysical issues when they appear; and third is the need to separate those problems from the practical methods to be employed in psychology. James is in no doubt that brain physiology is an indispensable part of psychology, but he sees also that such a commitment does not settle the issue between, for example, materialism and spiritualism.

James considers two arguments against materialist epiphenomenalism and two arguments for it. He is inclined to accept the arguments against the theory and to reject those in favour of it. One of the former, the appeal to consciousness as a 'selecting agency', he regards as offering some empirical support against epiphenomenalism. This leads him to conclude that automaton theory of an a priori or quasi-metaphysical sort is to be rejected as an 'unwarrantable impertinence'. This makes it look as though James is merely expressing an emotional preference, but his arguments have considerable force.

Generally he treats the arguments for automatism as inconclusive. The theory may, for example, point to physiological factors determining behavioural responses even when the cortex is not itself involved. James himself refers to such examples in the opening chapters of the *Principles*. Responses to stimuli may appear on the basis of the neural organisation of the spinal cord, even when that is severed from the brain. Automatists may argue in accordance with a principle of continuity that if such purely physiological explanation suffices for this behaviour, then it suffices for all behaviour.

Such evidence was of the type which led Russell in *The Analysis of Mind* to say that it was humiliating to find how adequate such mechanistic explanations were.[16] But, however striking such evidence may be, James is correct in rejecting the argument. He points out that a principle of continuity works in *both* directions. We might infer that consciousness plays no substantive role in influencing behaviour because we accept the continuity principle and the physiological explanations at the lower end of the scale. Equally we may invoke the principle of continuity to claim that the conscious aspects of the higher levels of behaviour must also be present, in a reduced state, in the lower. James might also have claimed that the principle of continuity itself is in need of clarification and support. Without it both of these opposed arguments commit the fallacy of inferring from what is true of some cases to what is true of all. Later it turns out that James accepts neither of these arguments from continuity. This is important to him because it encourages him to infer that mental phenomena are really novel phenomena, even though they undoubtedly emerge from physiological and material conditions.[17]

The second and third arguments are rather formal exchanges. Part of the materialist armoury consists in a rejection of Cartesian dualism, on the ground that the envisaged inter-action between two heterogeneous substances is quite unintelligible. In one quotation the suggestion is that such inter-action is as absurd as to suppose that the coaches of a train might be held together by the feelings of amity subsisting between the driver and the guard. Such a claim is justified, and James would not have wanted to resist it, but he thought that there was no inference from this rejection of Cartesianism to the truth of materialism. The inference would be valid only if there were no other theories available, but James makes it clear that there are many others.

In this and other passages he appeals instead to a 'common sense' dualism which is right to speak freely of causal links between minds and bodies; but the suggestion is that common sense dualism is not Cartesian dualism and is not committed to the existence of two heterogeneous substances. James does not indicate clearly what form such a common sense dualism would take, and he later suggests that it is safer to accept only a parallelism between mental and physical events. The suggestion is that common sense talk still stands in need of elucidation, but that Cartesianism had not given an adequate account of it.[18] In other ways, too, James gives some priority to folk psychology. He points out that we often need to interpret the detailed accounts of physiological phenomena in terms of such common sense descriptions in order to give some sense to them. And he finally argues that the epiphenomenalist theory is incoherent in its acceptance of a causal link between body and mind in one direction, while it thinks the causal connection in the other is unintelligible.

James offers a final argument in support of the anti-materialist theory, which rests on the idea that consciousness might have some evolutionary or adaptive value. He argues that a brain with so complex an organisation as ours is ill-adapted to function unless it can select from the wealth of information supplied to it. Elsewhere in his discussion of the will James also stresses the importance of selection.

> This is the point where an anti-mechanist psychology must make a stand in dealing with association. Everything else is pretty certainly due to cerebral laws, but spontaneity can't summon items up ex abrupto, only select from those that appear.[19]

This is the sort of case which leads James to speak of 'novelty' in our thinking, when we find that words, or solutions, 'occur' to us and where our only conscious task is to select from them. James believes that this selective attention can be justified on evolutionary grounds, and offers a positive case against materialism.

James's strong emphasis on attention and selection has been followed by later psychologists, and the argument undeniably has some heuristic force. It is presented, in this context, not as a decisive rebuttal of the materialist but only to indicate that materialism is over-simple. James is surely right to regard the argument as less than conclusive. For even if we concede all the claims for an adaptive ability to attend and select, the question still arises of the mechanism in which such features are realised. Merely referring to consciousness and its selective function does not eliminate the possibility of such neural mechanisms any more than a reference to thinking or perceiving does. The materialist will naturally look in the brain for some such controlling function and then the whole issue of the relation of that physical item to the mental phenomenon will re-appear.

The upshot in this first exchange is, then, quite inconclusive on *both* sides. The automaton theorist rests his case on a fallacious argument, unless the continuity principle can be given a clearer and more favourable sense. But James's own preferred alternative is not established either.

The main alternative to the automaton theory is the theory of 'mind-dust'. In this theory the same continuity principle is upheld but works in the opposite direction. Where the automatists regard higher levels of consciousness as no more than very complex material organisation, the mind-dust theorist takes the view that every such material phenomenon must be endowed with a minimal consciousness. James takes the theory to be committed in this way to two highly contentious claims. First is the idea that the mental experiences we normally have are compounds of simpler experiences. Second is the idea that some of these simpler mental features must be unconscious. The first of these commitments is to what James calls 'mental chemistry', and in the *Principles* he unequivocally rejects any such appeal. Later, however, in *A Pluralistic Universe*, and in an article in the *Psychological Review* James modified his rejection.[20] James's attitude to the second commitment, too, seems to undergo a change during his career. In the *Principles* he generally rejects appeals to 'unconscious' mental states, though he acknowledges the existence of hysterical phenomena, automatisms, and what he calls the 'fringe' of consciousness. Later, however, in *The Varieties of Religious Experience* and *A Pluralistic Universe* the ideas of a subliminal, or trans-marginal, experience come to play a more positive role.[21]

James's discussion of the mind-dust theory is again directed towards the continuity principle. He takes the view that some such continuity should be accepted if possible, and should be rejected only after every effort has been made to sustain it. His earlier discussion of the automaton theory rejects the continuity principle as that materialist view conceives it, and in his account of the alternative he makes it clear that the principle cannot be accepted in that form either. He is inclined, therefore, to canvass a certain 'disjointedness' or discontinuity[22] between the physical and the mental, which represents the latter as a genuine emerging novelty.

His case against mind-dust rests on his objections to the two commitments of that theory. Against the idea of psychic chemistry James raises two objections, first that it is an unnecessary and not adequately supported hypothesis, second that it is unintelligible. In *A Pluralistic Universe* when he recalls his earlier discussion he sums it up by saying that the theory of 'combination' was 'logically nonsensical and practically unnecessary'.[23] It is unnecessary because we have more economical ways of explaining the phenomena. The hypothesis supposes that to every specific brain modification there is some corresponding feeling, and that just as the brain states may in some way combine to produce an overall physiological effect, so the mental states also combine to produce a cumulative mental experience. The alternative would be to regard the mental states as arising only when the brain states have already combined to produce their large-scale cumulative effect. On that simpler hypothesis there would be no need to suppose a corresponding mental experience for every brain modification.

James also believes that the former hypothesis has no empirical evidence to support it, and that some empirical evidence from the physical realm counts against it. He points out that in physiology there are cases where an effect can be produced only when a certain level of energy triggers the mechanism.[24] In order for a signal to pass through some part of an electrical circuit it may have to be boosted to reach an appropriate level. The mind-dust theorist might argue formally that since things are different in the mental realm we cannot draw any conclusions from such physical phenomena. But James points out that the theory actually rests on analogies with such physical phenomena, which do not always support it. Repeated pushes on a pendulum will not deflect its swing by greater amounts, but prevent it from swinging at all. Increased breathing into a wind instrument will not always produce a louder sound, but may produce no tone at all. If the case rests on physical analogies, then it limps badly.

These objections put the psychic chemistry hypothesis under some strain, but they are less damaging than the second objection. For James makes the logical point that any such cumulative phenomenon requires a medium in which the combination or synthesis can be manifested, and he argues that this requirement is not met in the mind-dust case. In that case we have what James calls 'fusing without a medium', which he takes to be unintelligible.

> All the combinations which we actually know are effects wrought by the units said to be 'combined' upon some entity other than themselves . . . Just so in the parallelogram of forces the 'forces' do not themselves combine into the diagonal resultant; a *body* is needed on which they may impinge to exhibit their resultant effect.[25]

In the case of the mind-dust theory the only medium that is available is that of the brain itself, but the hypothesis of mental chemistry specifically excludes this. James here hints at the idea that mental terms may be similar to theoretical terms, such as that of 'force', whose primary realisation is in the physical phenomena of the brain. He does indeed class mental terms, like 'anger', as 'ejects', but he does not pursue the idea.[26]

Some more informal points are added to illustrate the unintelligibility of the hypothesis. James contrasts the mixing of green and red pigments to produce a yellow pigment with the absurd idea that we might mix a feeling of green with a feeling of red to produce a feeling of yellow. He also asks how we could understand the fusing of several distinct consciousnesses of separate words to make up a consciousness of the corresponding sentence.[27] The suggestion is that understanding a sentence is not a compound out of those separate understandings of the individual words, but something new and additional to the former.

These arguments offer powerful objections to the *assumption* of mental chemistry. Our common sense dualism tempts us to carry over certain physical analogies to the sphere of mental phenomena which on reflection may seem not just unsupported but even senseless. Although James does not deploy the later vocabulary of Ryle in identifying these mistaken temptations it is clear that he is attempting to sharpen what Ryle called our 'category discipline' in relation to minds and bodies.[28]

The second commitment of the mind-dust theory, to the existence of unconscious mental states, fares no better than the first. James very clearly outlines the case against traditional conceptions of such unconscious states. Perhaps the clearest example comes from his discussion of perception. We naturally draw a distinction between what we literally perceive and what we infer on the basis of such perception. Since we nevertheless characteristically describe what we perceive in the latter terms it has sometimes been suggested that underlying all perception are such processes of inference. Since we may not admit that we have consciously carried out such an inferential process it may seem natural to think that the inference was unconscious. In other cases we may behave as if we had perceived some object while sincerely denying that we were aware of any such perception. Intent on some interesting object at a short distance from us we fail to notice some obstacle in our path and yet take the appropriate evasive action. It is tempting in these and other cases to use the language of unconscious perception or unconscious inference, and to appeal to such unconscious phenomena in explanation of our behaviour.

James's objections vary according to the case in question. Generally he takes the view that such explanatory forms are unnecessary in the light of physiological, or automatic, mechanisms which explain the phenomena better without any dubious commitment to unconscious experiences. One way of coming to believe in such unconscious experiences would be by simply *confusing* brain processes, which are generally unconscious, with mental processes, which are not. Where such physiological explanations are available James says that it is quite unnecessary to postulate this 'additional wheelwork in the mind'; and that to invoke unconscious mental phenomena is either a 'useless metaphor' or a 'positively misleading confusion between' physiology and psychology.[29] In other cases James appeals to rapid loss of memory as a simpler explanation of the subjects' lack of awareness. In still others he continues the task of category discipline by noting the fallacy of inferring from our dispositions to perform in certain ways that we must have performed corresponding occurrent acts in order to carry out those performances.

Once James has rejected the two commitments of the mind-dust theory in this way he raises the question of the relation between the mind and the brain. His initial reaction, as we saw earlier, is to stress the mystery of such a relation, and this is a view he often expresses. However, at various places in the *Principles* he does offer some further clarification of this mystery. On one side he insists that 'no mental modification ever occurs which is not accompanied or followed by a bodily change', a view which he sometimes puts in his own terms as 'no psychosis without neurosis'.[30] It was noted earlier, however, that James seems also to commit himself to the idea that every brain event corresponds to some mental event. He says, for example,

> For an identical sensation to recur it would have to occur the second time in an unmodified brain. But this strictly speaking is a physiological impossibility; so is an unmodified feeling an impossibility, for to every brain modification, however small, must

correspond a change of equal amount in the feeling which the brain subserves.[31]

James seems to commit himself here to a correspondence in *both* directions, and so to the acceptance of

(1)   No mental state can change without some change in the brain

and

(2)   No brain state can change without a corresponding mental change.

(2), however, looks uncomfortably close to the mind-dust hypothesis which James wishes to reject.

It is possible that James did not mean to commit himself to (2), and perhaps confused it with (1). But it may be that he believed he had avoided a commitment to the mind-dust hypothesis by making it clear that (2) refers to a *total* brain state. For this is the view which he offers in his own response to the mind-dust theory. He says,

> The consciousness which is itself an integral thing not made of parts 'corresponds' to the entire activity of the brain, whatever that may be, at the moment. This is a way of expressing the relation of mind and brain from which I shall not depart during the remainder of the book, because it expresses the bare phenomenal fact with no hypothesis, and is exposed to no such logical objections as we have found to cling to the theory of ideas in combination.[32]

James recognises that there are objections even to this hypothesis. He points out that it gives up any attempt to correlate specific features of thought with limited parts of the brain. It achieves a safe minimal relationship at the expense of producing what is almost a truism, namely that our mental states depend in some way upon features of the brain as a whole. Clearly in his own detailed enquiries James did not confine himself to such a truism, but attempted to make more specific correlations between parts of the brain and types of experience. He raised another objection to his minimal view, namely that the entire activity of the brain is not a 'physical fact' at all but only 'the appearance to an onlooker of a multitude of such facts'.[33] James takes this to be a separate objection but it seems to do no more than to repeat the danger of uninformativeness. But the most serious problem is one he does not mention, namely whether such a minimal view avoids an unwelcome commitment to (2). As it stands the commitment is not avoided. So long as it is possible for the brain to change only in some minute way which is insufficient to change our experience, then (2) will be false. But it is the possibility of such changes which do not correspond to mental states which James uses to reject the mind-dust theory. It seems that he would do better to keep (1), but abandon (2).

James has one final possibility to explore before he offers his own view. It is the idea that the required 'combining' of mental features might be carried out in some master brain cell, a 'material monad' as James calls it. The earlier difficulties in combining separate consciousness of distinct words in order to make up a consciousness of the whole sentence might here be answered by supposing a central processing unit in the brain which should carry out the synthesis. It might seem, too, as though such an appeal could avoid the dangers of fusing without a medium, for it would provide just such a medium. James objects to this idea both on the, rather weak, empirical ground that no such master cell has been discovered, and also that there is no reason why we should consider only cells instead of considering even smaller physical units of which cells are composed. The crucial objection, though, must be the one noted earlier, that even if we identified a cell, or region of the brain, in which such central processing was carried out, we would still not have resolved the problem. We might take the materialist view that there is nothing else involved in understanding a sentence; but we might equally take the view that the physical event is only a correlate of the mental experience of understanding. The physical discovery, interesting as it is, has no more power to settle the issue than the discovery of any mechanism in the brain associated with mental states. The issue is about what 'association' means here.

James's immediate conclusions from this extended discussion are quite inconclusive. He says, for example,

> The separateness is in the brain-world, in this theory, and the unity in the soul-world: and the only trouble that remains to haunt us is the metaphysical one of understanding how one sort of world or existent thing can affect or influence another at all. This trouble, however, since it also exists inside of both worlds, and involves neither physical improbability nor logical contradiction is relatively small.[34]

It is hard to attach much weight to that final point. The acknowledged difficulty of understanding causal relations between brains and minds is not lessened by the admission that there are also problems about the causal relations between physical objects. He goes on:

> I confess, therefore, that to posit a soul influenced in some mysterious way by the brain-states and responding to them by conscious affections of its own seems to me the line of least logical resistance.[35]

In the end, however, James appears to take a different view, influenced partly by the weaknesses of positing the soul.

> [The view] does not strictly *explain* anything, but is less positively objectionable than either mind-stuff or material monad creed. The bare phenomenon, the immediately known, which is in opposition with the entire brain-process, is the state of consciousness, not the soul. In Chapter X we shall ask whether the ascertainment of a blank

unmediated correspondence, term for term, of the succession of states of consciousness with the succession of total brain-states be not the simplest psycho-physical formula, and the last word of a psychology which contents itself with verifiable laws, and seeks only to be clear and avoid unsafe hypotheses. Such a mere admission of the empirical parallelism will there appear the wisest course. By keeping to it our psychology will remain positivistic and non-metaphysical; and although this is certainly only a provisional halting-place, and things must some day be more thoroughly thought out, we shall abide there in this book.[36]

Acceptance of a parallelism between brain-states and mind-states, at least of type (1), makes it understandable that James should have spoken of the relation between these as 'functional in the mathematical sense'.[37] For such a relation could be formulated without commitment to a *causally* functional relation.

There is consequently doubt about which view James finally holds, though this is less the result of mere indecision on his part, than a recognition that the issue is presently insoluble. In other cases where James thinks that a metaphysical decision is called for on insufficient evidence, for example in the free-will debate, he is inclined to treat the conclusion as an option. In his final remarks where he offers the positivistic option or a belief in a soul he seems to indicate a similar attitude. The main provisos that need to be made here are first that not every option remains open, and second that the options should not be confused with the practical methods which psychology employs, even though they are bound to be linked to those methods. Beyond that all that can be done is to assess the various considerations inclining us towards one theory or another, and to indicate their importance for the practice of psychology.

It might be thought, however, that such a conclusion could be strengthened by showing that the metaphysical issue is somehow nonsensical. Although James clearly thinks that the issue is presently insoluble he does not take this stronger view. He does not, however, offer any clear indication of the way in which it might be solved. At various stages in the debate it appears that no amount of additional evidence could settle the issue, and this may encourage the view that there really is no genuine problem. A materialist and a spiritualist may both accept the value of physiological explanations of mental phenomena, and yet disagree about the relation of mind to brain. No appeal to such explanations, however striking or extensive, will then decide the issue between them. One residual question here is then about the nature of explanation and the logical relations between explanans and explanandum. Such a question goes far beyond the limits of the mind-body problem, but if it could be clarified that latter problem might be clearer too.

When James indicates that in using physiological explanations we may *need* to interpret the physical phenomena in terms of folk psychology he hints at an order of priority which does not put the physiological material unequivocally in first place. The suggestion is that in order to be of interest as a *psychological* explanation the physiological account has to be interpreted in psychological terms. In recent times the computer model, with its different levels of language, has sometimes been offered as a clarification for this relation. Computer operations are explicable in purely physical terms, but the interest of such models for psychology is at a higher level of interpretation in which we describe its activities in terms of strategies and functions which mimic those of humans. Even if we accept, however, that the physical events need to be interpreted in a psychological way, we might still hold that ontologically the physical basis is prior to the higher level psychological phenomena. This is a picture which James also hints at in his account of the mental features as a novelty which nevertheless emerges from a physical organisation.

Another way of putting a residual problem would be to stress not the explanatory or ontological relations between the mental and the physical, but the semantic relations which hold between them. James's account makes reference to all the various considerations which naturally bear on the ascription of mental terms, that is, the physiological, behavioural, phenomenological factors. The question arises of the connection between such considerations in the meaning of any specific mental term. Such a question cannot be divorced from the issue of explanation, for if we define mental item X in terms of consideration Y, then it would be only a spurious explanation to attempt to account for X in terms of Y. The interplay between, and confusion arising from, such factors has led to difficulty in the conceptual framework of psychological investigation. Such unclarity can be clearly illustrated in James's own account of the emotions, and will be considered with that account. Ideally we should have a clear picture of the semantics of mental terms, and in its absence it is not surprising that the general mind-body problem should be so intractable.

2 Psychological methods

James's hesitancy over the mind-body problem, understandable as it is, is matched by some indecisiveness over psychological methods.[38] Three such methods are identified, namely introspection, and what he calls the 'experimental' and 'comparative' methods. He is critical of all three, but clearly places most reliance on introspection. This priority reinforces the view that James's psychology dealt primarily with 'conscious mental life', and makes use of behavioural or physiological evidence only in a secondary role. James's references to experimental method are the closest he gets to any version of behaviourism, but he is highly critical both of its achievements and its style. He says, for example, that such a method 'taxes patience to the utmost' and that 'the results have as yet borne little theoretic fruit commensurate with the great labour expended in their acquisition'. He is prepared, however, to concede that 'facts are facts', and that the method has 'quite changed the face of the science so far as the latter is a record of mere work done'. If we associate the method with behavioural tests, these disparaging remarks would not have met with the approval of Watson, and no doubt partly account for Watson's own critical comments on James's influence. Watson would have been still more irritated by James's conviction that such experiments are in general secondary to introspective data and have the main function of checking the latter by statistical techniques.

If behaviourists would find James's appeal to introspection hard to swallow, materialists will be no more impressed by James's failure even to mention the use of physiology among psychological methods of investigation. James's view seems to have been that while physiology is indispensable as a means of explaining the mechanism of psychological operations it could not be identified with those operations themselves. Such a view is supported by his common sense dualism, and by his rejection of the continuity principle. For James mental phenomena had their own distinctive existence, access to which was principally through introspection, and presented a genuine novelty with regard to the material organisation out of which they indubitably emerged. The idea, canvassed in recent times by some materialists, that such supervenience might be compatible with an identity between mental and physical events, is not considered by James.

Although, therefore, James did not include physiology among the methods of psychological investigation his own practice gave it great importance. The opening chapters of the *Principles* are concerned with the physiology of the brain and the nervous system, in order to stress their importance in explaining mental phenomena. The feature which he there picks out as distinctively marking mentality within physical organisation is the pursuit and recognition of goals. The account of the self, and indeed almost all of James's detailed accounts of psychological topics, stress the intimate links between our mental life and our body. In his discussion of the mind-body problem, and elsewhere, he takes the view that physiological explanations are to be preferred wherever possible to psychological explanations.

While for James introspection is the primary method of investigation in psychology, he admits its deficiencies and dangers. He dismisses any consideration of its authenticity as 'too metaphysical' but he takes seriously the question of its reliability. For he is not prepared to accept the view of Cartesian dualism that introspection is infallible or incorrigible. Its defects, he says, are the defects of any observational technique, in which mistakes may be made.

He takes more seriously the objection that introspection is bound to be inadequate simply because we cannot both have an experience and simultaneously attend to it, without potentially altering the experience itself. James is content here to rely on an argument he canvasses elsewhere about the impossibility of subtracting a pure awareness from some specific mental experience, as though the latter necessarily was composed of a specific content plus a self-awareness. But he appeals also to Mill's defence which claimed that even if it were impossible to have and attend to the same experience simultaneously, still we may immediately remember the initial experience and attend to and comment on its features retrospectively. Such a view fits in with James's account of conjunctive experiences. For he did not believe that the stream of our consciousness was a discrete string of items either blankly present to, or absent from, our attention. At any particular point in the stream we are aware of the present fading experience and of premonitions of its impending successor.

James stresses not only the weaknesses of introspective observation, which might be checked by experimental methods, but also certain dangers to which it is prone. What is of importance to psychologists is not only the ability to introspect but the reports of such supposed observation.[39] Such reports inevitably involve the use of language, which James believed to be a serious source of error. It was an error due to language which James holds responsible for the faulty atomism of traditional empiricists. There is a natural tendency to cut our stream of consciousness into discrete fragments corresponding to the substantive parts of the stream which we attend to and name. He thinks that such features of language mislead us quite generally, in encouraging us to believe that some thing corresponds to every name and that the absence of a name entails the absence of any discriminable feature. In this general way he echoes Wittgenstein's therapeutic claim that we ascribe to the object what belongs to our method of projection in the language.[40]

Such general errors and distortions are clearly linked with James's account of pragmatic method. They justify the claim made earlier that such a method was evident in the *Principles* even before James formulated it explicitly in the lectures on pragmatism. In the more specific context of psychology, however, James highlights one form of such a danger which he calls the 'psychologists' fallacy'. This is typically expressed in terms of a psychologist's relation to the experience of others, but it could equally apply to a person's comments on his own experience. The fallacy is formulated in several ways. In one it is described as the confusion of the psychologist's own standpoint with that of the mental fact about which he is making his report. In another it is described as the assumption that the mental state studied must be conscious of itself as the psychologist is conscious of it.[41]

James's characteristic way of elaborating the fallacy is to draw attention

135

to a hierarchy of relations to an original mental state. Some person may *have* the experience and may at a higher level comment on and report it, while a psychologist may in turn comment on or report those first-order comments. Such hierarchies influence James in several of his arguments, for example, in his debate with Russell over truth. There the fallacy is associated also with the central error of what James calls 'vicious intellectualism', that is, the claim that objects can genuinely have only the properties which they are defined to have. James's general view, noted earlier, is that our theoretical constructs, however useful, nevertheless simplify and distort the experience on which they are based. If we are not sensitive to this, then we may define some item within our theory and overlook its additional features.

These are quite general heuristic guides, but James plainly thinks the danger especially serious in psychology itself. Two illustrations might be given from more recent discussions. In the first the suggestion is that if we can construct some model which achieves the same result as some human performance to be explained psychologically, then the latter must have been achieved in the same way. Suppose that we wish to explain how children learn to ride bicycles, and construct a machine which has the ability to learn this skill. It may be that the machine has to have built in to it some realisation of physical laws governing gravity and balancing on two wheels. We might say that the machine achieves its learning by applying those physical laws to its situation on the bicycle, working out theoretically the appropriate responses, and making those responses more and more quickly. It would be quite wrong, however, to suppose that this must be the way in which a child learns to ride a bicycle. There is a temptation to say that the child must also apply those physical laws to its situation, but that since it cannot express those laws they must be a part of its unconscious 'innate structure'.

An argument of this kind was considered in the debates over Chomsky's hypothesis about innate ideas in first language learning.[42] A suggestion was made that the child had an unconscious, innate, knowledge of certain general grammatical principles of a kind that would enable a machine to learn a first language in the same time as a child. James indicates two fallacies which such an argument commits. He would replace the appeal to unconscious knowledge by a physiological account, as in the other cases of claimed unconscious experience. He would also point out that the argument confuses knowledge *of* with knowledge *about*. The child undoubtedly has a knowledge of balance but it generally has no theoretical knowledge about it. James would not have wanted to say that such a model was useless, but only that its lessons should be carefully drawn. The model might guide us towards a better understanding of brain function and other mechanisms necessary for a child to learn to ride. But there is no direct inference from the model's success to an explanation of the procedure followed by the child. The psychologist's fallacy here is simply that of carelessly assuming that what is true of his theoretical construction must also be true of the original experience.

A second illustration might be given from recent anxieties over the ascription of propositional attitudes such as belief. It was noted earlier that when James identifies the neutral content of mental states in his doctrine of pure experience an ambiguity arose about the expression of such contents. For we might ascribe belief contents to some subject in terms which he would, or does, use to identify those contents, but we might also use terms which he either would, or does, not use. Such a distinction has been associated by Fodor, and others, with the contrast between 'de re' and 'de dicto' expressions of belief. The former would be an expression which, for example, referred to the items which the believer had in mind, but identified them in a way that he would not. The latter would identify those items in just the way the believer would.[43] The distinction seems associated with James's account of the psychologist's fallacy, since de re ascription of belief contents identifies them in the psychologist's terms and not in the subject's terms. In that earlier context it was suggested that the ambiguity presented no serious hazard to James's account of a neutral pure experience. If the association is plausible, then it appears that James even partially recognises some such distinction. The lesson from the fallacy, conceived in this way, would be simply to make sure that we recognise the dangers of such alternative ways of formulating belief contents. But it has also been suggested, by Fodor for example, that the distinction presents a serious problem for psychology as a whole.

In Fodor's account the problem arises out of a conflict between a 'naturalistic' and a 'solipsistic' psychology, defined respectively in terms of the 'de re' and 'de dicto' ascription of contents.[44] The suggestion is that the latter, which deals, as Fodor says, with 'states of the head, syntax, and computational models' is too restricted, while the former, which deals with 'real objects, wide mental states, and semantics' is in some way out of reach. Fodor presents the issue as an exclusive choice between these alternatives, neither of which seems palatable. The point might be especially damaging for James, since he, on one side, plainly advocates a 'naturalistic' psychology, and yet, on the other, stresses the phenomenological, subjective, experience which points towards a 'methodological solipsist' attitude. The psychologist's fallacy, interpreted in this way, admits the dangers, but assumes that they can be overcome with sufficient care. If Fodor's argument is correct, then the division presents a much more serious obstacle.

That argument is complex, and has been discussed in variant terms by numbers of other theorists. But one aspect of Fodor's case seems to be quite inadequate, and if that is so then James's attitude to the contrast may be defensible. For the initial reason which Fodor gives for the unattainability of a naturalistic psychology is that the de re reference to real objects is dependent upon a final explanatory account of nature from other sciences. Fodor says of that requirement that a naturalistic psychology cannot just wait patiently, but must wait forever. It is not just that natural science comes first and psychology second, but rather that psychology, if it has to wait for a complete explanatory account of nature, must come *nowhere*. The suggestion is that a naturalistic psychology is not a serious option at all.

If the argument rested solely on that point, however, it would have little force. The simplest way to see this would be to note that although the intention is clearly to *contrast* a natural science, like physics, with psychology the effect of the argument is to assimilate the two disciplines. Even physics must presumably also wait for a final explanatory account of nature. Moreover, if one takes James's view that we have no reason to suppose that such a final definitive account is possible, then even physicists will have to wait not just for a time, but for ever. In that case, however, naturalistic psychology is no worse off than physics, and I imagine that most psychologists would be happy to settle for that.

The argument has been elaborated in other more subtle ways. In one version the issue is whether psychologists can expect to formulate natural *laws*, in the way that physicists are supposed to. Arguments have been constructed to claim that there are no such psychological natural laws. It is not clear what James's view of such a position would be. On one side he clearly assumes that the formulation of laws should be the aim of psychologists; but he also expresses the view that no such laws have yet been formulated. James was not even prepared to accept the famous Weber-Fechner 'law', but he shows no sign of doubting generally whether any such laws could be found. In another version of the argument the debate has concentrated on the need to account for the meaning of the contents of propositional attitudes, and on the different, even conflicting, accounts of such a meaning given in the de re and de dicto modes of identifying such contents. James himself is not sensitive to those issues, though the pragmatic theories of Loar and Grice mentioned earlier may offer some resolution of them.

3   James's account of the emotions

James's account of the emotions has been widely discussed and criticised. Watson spoke of psychology's requiring a long time to recover from it,[45] and other psychologists have thought that it was empirically false.[46] It presents a good example of James's procedure in psychology, and an even better example of the confusion that can result from a failure to distinguish empirical from conceptual issues.

The account is set in the framework of James's previous discussion of instincts. Although James does not think that instincts and emotions are the same, he is nevertheless prepared to say 'The physiological plan and essence of the two classes is the same'[47] and this similarity clearly affects his discussion. What James mainly aims at is some guiding principle which would both outline the central character of emotions and provide criteria for distinguishing between the different emotions. Without what he calls a 'deductive or generative principle' the listing of emotions and their features strikes him as no more interesting than descriptions of rocks on a New Hampshire farm. In order to achieve this principle James adopts the strategy of separating the 'coarser' from the 'subtler' emotions, on the general ground that it should be easier to discover the mode of operation of the former, more obvious, cases. James offers no clear line of division between the two, but gives grief, fear, and rage as examples of the former and aesthetic responses and 'intellectual or moral rapture' as examples of the latter.

Once he has drawn that distinction he introduces a plausible common sense account of the emotions, which he intends to deny. According to that theory when we have an emotion we observe some object which excites the mental affection we call the emotion and which in turn produces certain characteristic bodily responses. We see a bear, are frightened, and flee; we detect the insult, are angry, and retaliate. James's own view is put by contrast in the following way: 'That the bodily changes follow directly the perception of the exciting fact, and that our feeling of the same changes as they occur IS the emotion.'[48] It appears that the opposition between the two theories is essentially one of the order in which certain events occur, and James reinforces this by characteristically reversing that common sense order. Where common sense is inclined to say that we cry or strike because we are sad or angry, James advocates as 'more rational' the claim that we are sad or angry because we cry or strike.[49] Although in many contexts, especially when he contrasts intellectual wisdom with common sense, James sides with common sense, it is clear that in this case he is quite prepared to correct it.

James has already prepared his readers for disbelief in the theory, but he thinks that the grounds for it are decisive. Two such grounds are offered. First he claims that previous arguments have shown that all our bodily changes are felt, obscurely or acutely, the moment they occur, and that objects excite bodily changes by what he calls a 'pre-organised mechanism'.[50] He does not make it clear whether he thinks such a claim is true of all bodily changes, but certainly such a claim would be false. There are bodily changes which are not felt, though they might be; and there are others, such as brain events, which simply cannot be felt. The phrase 'pre-organised mechanism' seems to make a reference back to instincts and the physiological mechanisms in which they function, but James is not claiming that emotions are instinctive rather than acquired, and he could allow that we may acquire or develop certain emotions. The subtler emotions will presumably often be of that developed kind. The idea is rather that whatever the provenance of the emotion it will have to be associated with those established physiological mechanisms.

This first point cannot in any case serve to distinguish the two theories. Even the common sense view could accept both claims. It could say, for example, that when we perceive some object the bodily changes due to that perceptual mechanism, or some of them, are experienced or felt the moment they occur. When the object additionally evokes an emotional response in us, which then produces a further bodily change, that change also is felt the moment it occurs. Such a common sense view, moreover, might readily accept that in all these cases the basic physiological mechanisms are 'pre-organised'. What it could not accept would be the identification of the two purported mechanisms. For with these assumptions if there were no difference between the perceptual and the emotional mechanisms, then certainly there would be no time gap between the perception of the exciting object and the bodily changes characteristic of an emotion. It might be thought that James himself assumed that the two processes, perceptual and emotional, were identical, and yet his own examples do not bear that out. The description of his emotional reaction to the horse's blood, for example, demonstrates a clear difference between the perception and the subsequent emotional reaction.[51] What is hinted at in such points is the empirical possibility of identifying different brain mechanisms, or routes, which underlie perception and emotional reactions based on it. Even then the empirical issue is not clear and does not involve a simple difference of time order.

This first point, then, is quite inconclusive between the two theories, though it appears that some possible empirical investigation of the brain, and even measurement of the order of events in the brain, might be relevant to the question. James himself recognises that the time order of these postulated occurrences would be extremely difficult to test, but though that is true there is a more serious obstacle to such an empirical resolution of the issue. For the difference between the two theories is not just a difference in the time of certain brain or bodily events, but a difference in the order in which these events are related to 'the emotion'. The common sense theory is represented as taking the view that the emotion occurs between the perception of the exciting object and the characteristic bodily changes. James's theory by contrast represents the emotion as simultaneous with the bodily changes. But this seems to assume that we already know what the emotion is and how it is to be related to certain physiological events.

Two difficulties of a non-empirical kind immediately arise. The first is that such an account seems to confuse physiological and psychological descriptions in a way which in other contexts James deplores. It is not obviously meaningful to ask when the emotion occurred in all these physiological events, for the emotion is not itself just another physiological event. It makes sense to raise questions about the time order of different physiological occurrences, though these might be difficult empirically to answer. It makes sense to ask how these physiological occurrences are related to what we mean by 'emotion', though that is no longer a matter of empirical physiology. But it does not seem to make sense to ask whether the emotion occurred before or after some bodily changes, as if the emotion itself were just another physiological event beside all the others. At this stage it remains unclear how emotions are to be understood. They might be treated as mental events distinct from physiological brain events; or they might be treated as something which involved the whole sequence of physiological events rather than some specific item in the sequence.

Once that point is reached a second difficulty arises. The whole issue arose because it was unclear what emotions were. The central question which James asks just is one about the nature of emotions. If the empirical attempt to date their occurrence already assumes that we know what they are, then it is difficult to see how such empirical factors could settle the prior issue. If we cannot identify emotions, then there is no prospect of an empirical test to determine their temporal location, and no hope of using some empirical measurements to settle the issue. The empirical temporal test presupposes a prior understanding of what an emotion is, and yet that is precisely what is at issue in the debate.

It seems clear that the debate is not just an empirical matter, and that the arguments which represent it in that way are seriously misleading. James in fact relies far more on the second argument, which he calls 'the vital part of my whole theory'.[52] He admits, however, that many have failed to grasp its significance, and this may be because its point is a logical or conceptual one rather than simply empirical. He says:

> If we fancy some strong emotion and then try to abstract from our consciousness of it all the feelings of its bodily symptoms we find we have nothing left behind . . . What kind of an emotion of fear would be left if the feeling neither of quickened heart-beats nor of shallow breathing . . . were present, it is quite impossible for me to think. . . . A purely disembodied human emotion is a nonentity. I do not say that it is a contradiction in the nature of things, or that pure spirits are necessarily condemned to cold intellectual lives: but I say that for *us* emotion dissociated from all bodily feeling is inconceivable.[53]

James concedes that a man might see a bear, judge it prudent to run, and run away without any of the usual bodily feelings of fear. In such a case, however, he would be inclined to say that the man was not frightened at all but was simply acting in a calm rational manner.

Two things serve to confuse the structure of James's argument. First is the point that the initial ground for his theory seemed to turn on a question of the empirical order of certain physiological events. It may reasonably be asked how the second point of logic could possibly determine the answer to such empirical questions. Second, however, is the point that James actually denies that his second argument is a matter of logic. He does not claim it is what he calls a 'contradiction in the nature of things',[54] and raises the issue whether pure spirits have emotions. It seems, however, that that latter issue is irrelevant. If we can conceive of creatures which have emotions but have none of the associated bodily feelings, or are even disembodied, then James's claim about the inconceivability of such a case cannot be sustained. If the claim can be sustained, then however such pure spirits operate they do not have emotions as we understand the term. James himself makes an appropriate qualification when he speaks of determining the conceivability of *human* emotions without these associated feelings.

Once the argument is understood in this conceptual way, then James's theory rests essentially on that clarification of the term 'emotion'. To say of humans that they have an emotion is necessarily to say that they have certain bodily responses and feelings. Construed in that way it is not clear that common sense would deny the claim, though it might regard it as so far somewhat uninformative. James, however, clearly hopes that once we accept such a framework we can distinguish different emotions by reference to the different bodily states with which they are associated. If anyone, however, took the view ascribed at the beginning to common sense, namely that the associated bodily feelings are subsequent to the emotion and causally connected to them, then James's view is opposed to that. For if the connection between the emotion and those bodily states is not causal but logical, then the view attributed to common sense cannot be correct. Its suggestion of a specific time order relating an emotion to those bodily states is wrong not because the temporal order is different, but because it makes no sense to speak of a temporal order between items which are logically connected. When James says that we are sad because we cry the term 'because' has to be construed as logical rather than causal. It would be like saying that Jones is a bachelor because he is unmarried, rather than that Jones is a bachelor because his parents divorced.

If James's theory is understood in this way it explains some of the otherwise puzzling aspects of his view. It still does not establish that the view is correct, and three major objections can still be raised against it. The first and most obvious is that the second argument does not establish an identity between the emotion and the relevant bodily feelings. Even if it is accepted it establishes only that the bodily features are necessary rather than sufficient conditions of the ascription of emotion. James is claiming that we cannot conceive someone's having an emotion without the relevant bodily feelings, but not that we cannot have those feelings without the emotion. Yet in his own account of the emotion he represents the connection between the bodily feelings and the emotion as one of identity. The argument does not warrant such a conclusion, and it seems independently unplausible.

The second difficulty arises from James's expectation that his account will provide some means of classifying specific emotions. If we suppose that at any time while we are awake and conscious we inevitably have certain bodily feelings, then the necessary connection between emotions and some bodily feelings or other seems quite trivial. James requires to be more specific about the link between particular emotions and bodily feelings, but he notes also how variable such feelings are. It is possible that some compromise might be achieved in which certain broad bodily factors characterise specific emotions, but the prospect does not look promising.

The third difficulty is associated with the incompleteness of his account, once it is construed as a statement of a necessary but not sufficient condition for emotions. Even if his weakened claim is granted we might ask for a more complete account, in which some other factor plays a part. Another factor which has been suggested, and which James gestures towards, is the idea of a cognitive element in emotions. The suggestion here is that when we are moved by some perceived object it is, or may be, as a result of certain background beliefs or evaluations with which we may approach the object. James talks about perceiving an exciting object as though objects are just exciting or not in their own right. Perhaps some are; but many are exciting to us because we hold certain beliefs about them. If we do not hold those beliefs, or do not recognise their application to what we are perceiving, then the emotion will not arise. James may have neglected this aspect of emotions because he wished to give an account of *basic* emotional reactions on which other more complex cases may build. The horse's blood case supports such a view. Elsewhere, in his radical empiricism James does draw attention to the class of 'appreciations'[55] which recognise something of this complex cognitive background to emotions, but in the *Principles* he overlooks this.

8

Meliorism, Morality, and Religion

James's philosophy not only covers issues in morality and religion, but was even dominated by them. His own personal struggle over the free-will problem, his serious commitment to religious belief, and the background of his father's Swedenborgian sympathies all underline the importance these problems had for him. His discussion of these non-cognitive issues, however, depends upon his epistemology; indeed it is not too much to say that his epistemology was in part constructed *for* these issues. James evidently wished to provide an empiricism which was not only rigorous and down to earth but also accommodated moral, religious, even super-natural beliefs. It was this wish which led him to mediate between the tough- and tender-minded philosophies and to envisage with characteristic cheerfulness a new dawn in which empiricism and religion were reconciled and co-operative.[1] He recognised, however, the difficulties of that recon-ciliation. Even in his own writings there are clear signs of conflict between, for example, the hostility expressed to supernatural belief and to 'trans-marginal' consciousness in the *Principles*[2] and the sympathetic attitude to these expressed in *A Pluralistic Universe* and his articles on psychic phenomena.

There are two clear points of contact between James's empiricism and his philosophy of religion and morality. In the first James draws a fundamental distinction between our experiences and the theoretical accounts we subsequently give of them. In his epistemology this led him to a distaste for 'metaphysics', to his corrective recognition of conjunctive relations, and to the special device of 'pure experience'. He took a parallel view of the distinction between religious experience on one side and the theoretical accounts of it given on the other by intellectual apologists such as theolo-gians. Just as psychologists might distort the experiences of their subjects in some theoretical construction, and even commit the psychologists' fallacy, so James thought that theologians were apt to become so absorbed

144

in their theories of religion that they too distorted the vital experience on which it rested.[3] James's wish in the moral and theological, as in the cognitive, contexts was to give as undistorted a description of the relevant experiences and beliefs as he could. He even envisaged a science based on ordinary reports of those experiences and beliefs, and used this as a guideline for his review of recorded mystical and religious experiences in *The Varieties of Religious Experience*.[4]

The second point of contact has to do more with his own theoretical accounts of moral and religious belief. For James believed that he had a key to the adequate unification of religious and scientific, affective and cognitive, belief, in his own pragmatic theory of truth. Since that theory was admitted by James to be both controversial and incomplete even in the cognitive sphere, his sanguine faith in its power to achieve this further goal is perhaps surprising. Yet it is evident that his pragmatic account of truth offers a natural prospect of such a reconciliation. For it rests the notion of truth, even in the cognitive realm, on the idea of the 'working of belief', and it seems natural to suppose that such operations exist even in the non-cognitive context. Given James's theory and the acceptance of the working of beliefs even in the non-cognitive realm the two kinds of belief might be assimilated under a general conception of truth. It remains to be seen how far James is entitled to make such an assimilation, or even how exactly he envisaged it. It is clear that he did not deny all significant differences between the two contexts. At its best his account would be designed to give an account of truth which could cover both kinds of belief while allowing for the appropriate differences between them.

This final section must, then, consider James's proposed extension for the notion of truth from the cognitive to the affective cases. But James also had other views about morality and religion. Foremost among these, both at a personal and an intellectual level, was his account of free-will and what he called 'novelty'. James considers this issue in his earliest works, such as the *Principles* and *The Will To Believe*, and in his latest, such as *Some Problems of Philosophy*.[5] It formed one of the central examples of pragmatic method in his lectures on pragmatism, where he describes a belief in free-will as a 'doctrine of relief'. I shall concentrate on his discussion in the early paper 'The Dilemma of Determinism'.[6]

In that paper and others James also outlined his views about morality. Of course he had his own specific first-order moral convictions to canvass, and he discusses some of these in such papers as 'The Moral Equivalent of War' and 'On a Certain Blindness'.[7] Those convictions appear strongly but on the periphery of his discussions in the references to Morrison Swift in *Pragmatism*[8] and to the thoughtlessness and hypocrisy of the fictional Russian aristocrat in the *Principles*.[9] They show James as a man with a tolerant and human moral temper not at all in tune with the prevailing social divisions and distress of nineteenth century life. They show also that like contemporary moral philosophers James was not afraid to engage in applied moral debate, even though he was typically modest about the role of philosophy in such a context. For together with his own applied moral convictions James also gives a brief account of the nature of morality.

What mainly interests him in that issue is the 'emergence' of moral, and other, values in the natural world, and the tests appropriate for moral beliefs. Although in *Pragmatism* he had associated his own philosophy loosely with utilitarianism, as with positivism, he is more critical of that moral philosophy in *The Will To Believe*. There he stresses the extent to which we may be 'creative' in constructing morality and religious faith, in a way which echoes the discussion of the hybrid case of 'appreciations' in his radical empiricism. In that discussion he suggested that we are able to 'project' our own responses and attitudes onto objects in a public world. In a similar way he believed that in matters of morality, religion, and inter-personal relationships we may create the very facts which our convictions are directed towards.[10] In this way he raises questions about the extent to which he accepted what might be called 'moral realism'.

That projective idea of morality, coupled with James's persistent claim that over such a matter as free-will we have a choice whether to accept or reject it, is part of an overall attitude to life which James held in contrast to optimism and pessimism. His own view was what he called 'meliorism', a gradualist policy of limited capability and realistic achievement. It was partly for this reason that James described a belief in free-will as a doctrine of relief. For his melioristic view at least frees us from the excessive demands of total responsibility, and the excessive frustrations of unachievable goals. James quoted with approval a line from R.L. Stevenson in which he wrote: 'Total failure is our lot; our business is to continue to fail in good spirits.'[11] Although the sentiment veers closer to pessimism than James would officially have approved, it nevertheless echoes James's own stress on the 'manly', 'robust' virtues of what he called the 'energetic' and 'strenuous' life.

These views, specific and general, about morality and faith are given support in James's doctrine of the will to believe. James himself subsequently said that the title should have been the *right* to believe,[12] and so indicated his recognition of the extent to which the chosen title had been misunderstood. It was widely thought, by Mussolini for example,[13] that James's doctrine allowed us to believe anything we wished, provided only that we could summon up the will to believe it. Such misconceptions led James ruefully to quote others' description of pragmatism as the 'go as you please' philosophy. The focus of his views is the debate with W.K. Clifford about the justification for religious belief. Clifford took the stern view that where there were no intellectual grounds for deciding between opposing beliefs it was simply immoral to accept either. The argument was not confined to the case of religious belief, but it was that latter case in which

James was especially interested. He believed that Clifford's view was wrong, and that its central error rested on an over-sharp distinction between cognitive and affective belief. James's own view of truth, and the proposed assimilation of cognitive and non-cognitive belief, form an important part of this debate. It can then serve as an introduction to James's extended account of truth and his attempt to assimilate the cognitive and affective cases.

James, of course, recognised that there are still significant differences between cognitive and non-cognitive belief, just as he recognised that his own doctrine of pure experience made room for an admissible distinction between the mental and the physical. Whatever the outcome of that proposed assimilation there still remains an issue about James's understanding of religious supernatural belief. Pragmatism and radical empiricism are clearly linked with an emphasis on immanence rather than transcendence. But it may be thought that in his later works, *The Varieties of Religious Experience* and *A Pluralistic Universe*, James goes too far towards a reference to a supernatural world. It is true that he wraps such beliefs in a firmly pragmatist methodology by concentrating on specific cases and reports of mystical experience.[14] It is also true that he regarded his own enquiry as part of a larger psychological science of religion which would stand to those experiences as optics stands to visual experience.[15] But these necessary provisos cannot blind readers to a difficulty for James over the *content* of, and *claims* for, those experiences. If a pragmatist account of meaning is essentially verificationist, as some recent commentators claim, then James ought to regard such supernatural beliefs with their contents as empty or meaningless. Yet James notoriously does not take such a view. It would be wrong at this stage to dismiss such ideas as an aberrant inconsistency on James's part, but it remains to be seen whether and how he might escape such a charge.

1 Free-will

In his discussion of free-will in the *Principles* James concentrates mainly on empirical features of human will. Here there is no doubt about the occurrence of choice or variation in that strength of commitment, effort, or persistence which we commonly associate with will power. Such a treatment is in line with James's view that a science such as psychology has to make certain assumptions which may nevertheless be queried by a more metaphysical approach. He notes the existence of a metaphysical issue about free-will, but regards it as beyond the scope of psychology. The metaphysical issue arises out of two conflicting postulates, one which governs science and is deterministic, and another which governs moral or legal operations, and allows free choice and personal responsibility.

Such a conflict of postulates between disciplines, or between science in general and other areas of life, cannot be settled by science. James unclearly suggests that psychology might contribute one relevant fact, namely whether effort is fixed or variable,[16] but since there is no way of measuring effort such an enquiry is a dead end. In that case, then, the preference for one or other postulate can be settled only by making a definite commitment to one side or the other. James believes that a choice is justifiable in such a case because it cannot be avoided. 'Since an objective choice is not to be had the only course is voluntary choice, for systematic scepticism is also voluntary choice'.[17] It is at this point that James expresses the claim, made in several contexts, that 'the first act of free-will should be to affirm its reality'.[18] James does not think such a choice quite arbitrary or irrational, but the grounds for it are primarily moral. That confirms him in his view that psychology cannot settle the issue.

The idea that we can settle the issue by making up our minds may be of practical value to one who, like James, suffered because of his doubts about free-will. One part of James's anti-intellectualism regarded that practical value as greater than any to be derived from a purely abstract intellectual debate, and he shows considerable impatience with the known ebbs and floods of philosophic argument in it. Still, if the issue is the intellectual one of finding a rational ground for the preference James's therapeutic advice seems weak. In his paper 'The Dilemma of Determinism' he attempts to meet that requirement.

In the paper James makes clear certain limits to his discussion. He tends, for example, to disparage what he calls a 'soft determinism' which he associates with Hume and his friend Shadworth Hodgson. What he explicitly objects to is Hodgson's unhappy description of his position as 'free-will determinism',[19] but James links this with any compatibilist position. James thought that the conflict between the two postulates, of determinist natural law and free-will, was a total opposition which left no room for their reconciliation. Compatibilism, or soft determinism, could be only shallow and unsuccessful. For that reason James prefers initially to express the conflict simply as one between determinism and indeterminism. The crucial question is whether there is room in the world for what James called 'genuine novelty' or real alternative possibilities.

> Indeterminism thus denies the world to be one unbending unit of fact
> . . . To that view actualities seem to float in a wider sea of possibilities,
> from out of which they are chosen, and *somewhere*, indeterminism
> says, such possibilities exist and form a part of truth.
>
> Determinism, on the contrary, says that they exist *nowhere*, and that
> necessity on the one hand and impossibility on the other are the sole
> categories of the real. Possibilities that fail to get realised are for
> determinism pure illusions; they never were possibilities at all.[20]

If we put the question in this way then there is no possibility of reconciliation between the two postulates. Determinism and indeterminism are contradictory.

James is, of course, entitled to set the limits to his own discussion but his dismissal of compatibilism is open to question. First his assumption that determinism can adequately be defined in terms of the necessity of natural laws might be queried. In James's own terms this might be done by rejecting the inference ascribed to the determinist from

(1) There are possibilities that fail to be realised

to

(2) These were never real possibilities at all.

For it seems absurd to make it a requirement of a real possibility that it *is* realised. No doubt a determinist might formulate his view to avoid this, but he would still need to give an account of what is meant by 'natural law' and by 'necessity'. Compatibilists such as Hume have used that query as a part of their attack on determinism, and James should have considered this if he wished to set compatibilism aside in a reasoned way. Though he discusses the issue, inconclusively, in *Some Problems of Philosophy* the present argument does not consider it.

The second query is more serious. The dispute, as James describes it between determinist and indeterminist, might arise without any reference to human action or choice. It might arise even with respect to the physical world. There the issue would be whether *every* circumstance is strictly governed or determined by physical laws, and the answer is by no means clear or obvious. James himself makes later use of the idea that laws might exist which enable us to predict with certainty the outcome of a game of chess,[21] and yet in which we could not predict the detailed moves in the game which led to that outcome. Something similar might be true of physical phenomena as well. We might be able to predict the overall size of the damage to be inflicted by a hurricane of a certain ferocity, and yet be quite unable to predict whether this cup or saucer in its path would be destroyed. A botanist might predict within certain limits the height or yield of a plant raised in a controlled environment and yet be quite unable to predict the angle of its leaves. It may still be said that if we only had more or better information even these details would be predictable with the same certainty, but this remains an article of faith. It is what James calls in the same context an 'altar to an unknown God'.[22]

Such issues can and should be raised independently of the issue about human choice and freedom. The further addition of the human factors raises another problem for James. For it is clear, despite his way of putting the issue, that he wishes to focus his discussion on human action and choice. It is all the more surprising, therefore, that he deliberately uses the term 'chance' to mark the feature which determinism denies and indeterminism requires. To speak of a 'chance' or 'random' event in the physical sphere might conflict with a determinist belief that every physical event is governed by law. But there is no reason to equate such chance events with what we ordinarily call 'free', 'voluntary' actions. This yields a fundamental ambiguity in James's discussion which he partially admits. For indeterminism might be formulated in at least two ways, either as

(3)   Some events have, or can be given only, a probability of occurrence which equals the probability of their non-occurrence.[23]

or as

(4)   Some events are governed by voluntary human choice.

(3) expresses an indeterminism which might be confined to the physical realm, while (4) canvasses such a doctrine restricted to the realm of human action. (3) and (4) are not even extensionally equivalent. The class of equi-probable events under (3) is not identical with the class of events governed by human choice under (4). Some of the former, a penny's falling heads or tails uppermost, are not matters of choice, and most of the latter are not equi-probable.

James never explicitly resolves this confusion in his discussion. He uses the term 'chance' sometimes to mean 'random probability', and sometimes to mean only the 'hope' of some desirable outcome, sometimes in accordance with (3) and sometimes in accordance with (4). He never considers the difficulty in his argument that 'random', or 'erratic', or 'unpredictable' behaviour on the part of some person, which might satisfy (3), is often a sign not of a free agent but of someone in the grip of some pathological condition which inhibits voluntary choice. He further underlines these difficulties by his use of the term 'novelty' and by saying such things as that the words that an author writes are 'novelties' in the sense that they surprise him.[24] Nevertheless James acknowledges the awkwardness in this terminology. He is throughout very defensive about his term 'chance', and says at one point;

> Well, I admit there may be just a dash of perversity in its choice. The
> spectacle of the mere word-grabbing game played by the soft
> determinists has perhaps driven me too violently the other way.[25]

It remains to be seen how this background difficulty affects his central argument, in which he retains the view that the dispute is theoretically insoluble. The arguments on both sides are not, as he says, coercive, and all that can be done is to 'deepen our theoretic sense of the difference'[26] acceptance of either postulate would make.

His elucidation of that difference turns on the notion of regret. He refers to the fact that we 'constantly have to make judgments of regret'. Some of these, he admits, may be foolish, but he cites a particularly brutal murder where such regret is both natural and 'not to be tampered with'.[27] Given such a fact James insists on a dilemma for the determinist. Such regret implies that the world ought to have been different, but the determinist denies officially that this is possible. Two different objections might be made here to the determinists' position, and James notes both. On one side it might be said that such a position is just incoherent, so that one or other of the conflicting beliefs would have to go. On the other side the position might be said to yield unwelcome consequences, since it naturally leads to a cosmic pessimism that the world should necessitate such horrible events.

A determinist might escape these objections by abandoning his judgments of regret. James initially considers only one way of doing this, namely by treating the regrettable event as a ground for optimism. The basis for such an unlikely manoeuvre is the idea that short-term disappointments or regrets sometimes are, as we say, 'for the best' in the long run. A faith of this kind which paints an optimistic wash over every regrettable event, however horrible, is associated with the fictional Dr. Pangloss in Voltaire's *Candide*. However feasible such a manoeuvre might be James believes that it is unjustified. One pragmatic objection would be that we have no ground to generalise from some regrets which turn out to be 'blessings in disguise' to the belief that all such disadvantages are for the best. But James objects primarily on the ground of a persistent conflict, which he thinks cannot be disguised by such an optimism, between our judgments of regret and that optimism. However much we may wish to accept the optimistic faith we cannot simply prevent ourselves feeling the initial regret.

James's argument is less than totally conclusive here. An improved version of Dr. Pangloss might find other positions to fall back to. He might say that we need only modify, rather than totally reverse, our judgments of regret. To this it might be countered that a world in which the longer-term benefits were obtained without even the short-term regrets would be still preferable, but a determinist might claim that the latter are strictly necessary for the former. He would then hold the view Bradley expressed in an aphorism which claimed: All is for the best in the best of all possible worlds, and everything in it is a necessary evil. The new Dr. Pangloss might even take a leaf out of James's Darwinian background to claim that the feelings of regret we have are no more than a biological residue, like the appendix, which has no real function. Such lines of defence may reinforce James's assumption that no argument is strictly coercive in this matter, but they seem either ill-grounded or thoroughly pessimistic.

James takes the argument through one further variation. He notes that the pessimistic implications of determinism might be avoided if we concede that the world has no final objective purpose to modify our short-term regrets, so long as there is a 'subjective' goal in view. Here the ultimate aim is not that of achieving paradise but only that of 'deepening the theoretic consciousness of what goodness and evil are'. The world may not end in some ultimately desirable state, but at least we may hope to realise fully our consciousness in a subjective recognition of its good or evil condition. James associates this view with soft determinism, and he thinks it is strongly supported by the intolerable boredom of standard descriptions of paradise. For if that objective goal is not worth striving for, then perhaps the aim should be only our own self realisation. James prefers subjectivism to pessimism, but since he rejects soft determinism anyway he thinks there is a better alternative.

The objections to subjectivism are, he says, 'frankly of a practical order'. They consist in the unwelcome psychological consequences of such a view.

> Everywhere it fosters the fatalistic mood of mind. It makes those who are already too inert more passive still; it renders wholly reckless those whose energy is already in excess.[28]

The only escape is by what he calls 'the practical way' illustrated by Carlyle when he wrote:

> Hang your sensibilities! Stop your snivelling complaints and your equally snivelling raptures. Leave off your general emotional tomfoolery and get to WORK like men.[29]

The essence of this 'old-fashioned', 'classical' morality, compared with its subjectivist rival, is the idea of limits to our understanding and our achievement. When we have fulfilled the limited responsibilities open to us at any time, then we feel at peace; until that point we are, as James says, 'restless'.[30] It is in this way that James sees the belief in freedom as a doctrine of relief. But once he has made these psychological points James returns to the more logical claim that determinism is incompatible with our ordinary feelings of regret.

> What interest, zest, or excitement can there be in achieving the right way, unless we are enabled to feel that the wrong way is also a possible and natural way . . . And what sense can there be in condemning ourselves for taking the wrong way, unless we need have done nothing of the sort, unless the right way was open as well . . . I cannot understand regret without the admission of real, genuine possibilities in the world.[31]

James persists in expressing this outcome in terms of 'chance', when, for example, he says: 'the chance that in moral respects the future may be other and better than the past has been . . . is the only chance we have any motive for supposing to exist'.[32] Here the term 'chance' means simply 'hope' or 'possibility' rather than 'probability'. For there is no reason, even in James's terms, to suppose that the probability of a better future is increased under indeterminism. Rather, because James rules out a compatibilist solution, indeterminism merely offers a possibility of that better future where determinism excludes all possibilities in favour of strict necessity. James's intention is surely to say that the future can be affected by our choices, and that possible futures of that sort may be superior to other possible futures to which our choices make no contribution. For the determinist strictly such talk of alternative possible futures is excluded. This is why James's unclarity over the term 'chance' is not in the end a serious hazard to his argument. He argues essentially for the minimal indeterminist position, that is one which allows for non-determinate futures, in the belief that this at least makes possible a human choice affecting those outcomes. He is not required to equate human choice with mere random occurrences, but only to hold that the denial of determinism allows for the possibility of human choice. His failure to take compatibilism seriously merely means that he fails to take advantage of another way of rejecting what determinism intends.

If we accept James's assumptions, that none of the arguments is coercive, and that compatibilism is not an option, then his position is reasonable. Both assumptions might be attacked, but the former is defensible and the latter is at least still controversial. We might, somewhat charitably, take him not to deny compatibilism so much as to seek a different defence of free-will. If it is thought that compatibilism provides a good defence, then at least to accept it will in that case strengthen rather than weaken James's hand. In any case the two central objections to determinism in James's defence are first that the doctrine commits an incoherence once we accept the fact of judgments of regret; second that the temperamental consequences of determinism are unwelcome.

The first objection is not coercive, since the determinist has other lines of defence, and may actually be more inclined to pessimism anyway. James generally takes the view that no amount of logic can dispossess such temperamental inclinations, though they may yield to a recognition of the unwelcome consequences implicit in the second objection. Certainly if we adopt a strict mechanistic determinism then the upshot is pessimistic and bleak. As we shall see later James reinforces this bleakness in his general account of morality. Nor are the alternatives open to a determinist, such as Panglossian optimism or Romantic subjectivism, much better. The former is absurd, and the latter at least uncomfortable for those who are not Romantics. The alternative James offers in terms of a limited, gradualistic, meliorism has patent advantages over the other possibilities. In the end this is what James seems mainly to insist on.

Two further questions might be raised about James's position, and both were considered by him in other essays in *The Will To Believe*. For we might ask what the moral objectives of meliorism are and how we might argue for or test their value. And we might ask whether there is any way of strengthening the motive for the choice in favour of free-will.

2 Meliorism and morality

According to James optimism holds that the best outcomes are necessary, pessimism that they are impossible and meliorism that they are at least possible. But he also provides a catalogue of ultimate attitudes open to us in matters of morality and religion which help to define meliorism. We may

(5) Follow intellectualist advice and wait for evidence
(6) Mistrust other powers and let the universe fail
(7) Trust them and do our best
(8) Flounder with inconsistent attitudes.[33]

He thinks that (6) and (8) are too feeble to be worthy of acceptance. (5) is a version of the doctrine held by Clifford about the immorality of holding unsupported beliefs, and will be examined in the next section. (7) is the only position left and well expresses James's meliorist view. He insists, of course, that we have a genuine choice between these alternatives and that even in the absence of an intellectual ground for the choice it may be entirely legitimate.

In considering the motives for such a choice we might raise two questions. We may ask *what* are the outcomes or objectives towards which we should strive, and *why* in any case we should strive for them. The first of these raises issues about morality and the criteria for right action, but even if they were answered we might still raise the second question. Even if we knew with complete certainty which goals we ought to aim at we may also think it futile to aim at them. If the pessimistic view of the universe were correct then there would be no possibility of making a difference to the outcome through our own efforts. James clearly associates a belief in free-will with the *hope* of making such a difference, but he recognises that that hope is quite fragile. We might ask, as James does, whether that hope might be bolstered by other considerations.

In his paper 'The Moral Philosopher and the Moral Life'[34] James offers answers to both questions. He discusses in relation to the former the nature and emergence of moral values and the past attempts of philosophers to provide tests for right action. His account of morality is severely critical of the efforts of philosophers to reduce the chaos of moral opinion to some unitary formula. Just as in epistemology he believed that there was no single foundation for knowledge, so in moral philosophy he held that no single formula could capture informatively all our moral requirements. Though pragmatism is loosely allied to utilitarianism James now endorses a standard objection to its formula, namely that it would be immoral to buy happiness for the majority at the expense of even one person's suffering. James nevertheless believes that utilitarians have come closest to the truth and he seeks to give his own version of that truth.

In relation to the latter question not of the *content* of our moral goals but of the *motivation* for them, James considers two possibilities. In one, humanism, the motive is simply the benefit for future generations; in the other, theism, it rests on a religious belief which holds that the future is somehow safeguarded, though not independently of our efforts. James

154

plainly wishes to endorse the second motive and so distances his own views still further from a secular utilitarianism.

James's account of the emergence of moral values is parallel to his account of the development of cognitive beliefs. Without any form of sentient life there could be no values, but with even one sentient creature its demands form the basis for a value system. With only one set of demands to be met the system will be excessively simple, enjoining the fulfilment of as many of its demands as possible. Two or more creatures, with their distinctive and conflicting demands, may produce a higher order demand for compromise and for some acceptable ranking of their requirements. At this point there may arise a philosophical search for a rational and decisive test to adjudicate between conflicting interests. James's attitude to this task is mixed. On one side he thinks it a mere superstition to suppose some abstract moral order existing independently of the creatures' feelings. The search for a rational test could not then be represented as an attempt to discover that underlying moral reality.[35] On the other side he wishes to avoid moral scepticism. As in epistemology James thinks the temptation to fall into scepticism about moral values is greatly strengthened by philosophers' inevitable failure to find any decisive test. His view is that the search for some over-arching moral principle is an illusion, though he concedes that philosophy may clarify what is at stake in moral debates. He thinks that the quest for a single moral principle might succeed if there were some 'common essence' in morally right acts, but he rejects the idea of such an essence.[36]

Paradoxically this does not deter James from formulating his own 'most universal principle', namely that 'the essence of good is simply to satisfy demand',[37] a principle he later qualifies, by writing:

> must not the guiding principle . . . be simply to satisfy at all times as *many demands as we can*? That act must be the best accordingly which makes for the best whole, in the sense of awakening the least sum of dissatisfactions. In the casuistic scale, therefore, those ideals must be written highest which *prevail at the least cost*, or by whose realisation the least possible number of other ideals are destroyed.[38]

James's position here looks highly vulnerable. On one side he rejects a common essence for good and on the other expresses just such an essence. He rejects the formulation of a single supreme principle of morality only to formulate one himself. But he plainly treats his principle as having only a limited value. It enjoins a certain tolerance and rejects the idea of a moral order existing independently of feelings or desires.

Beyond those limits the principle has no value as a specific measure of moral or social policy. It might still be argued, however, that James has not demonstrated the impossibility of such a general principle. It is true that he summarily rejects some candidate principles, and makes shrewd comments on them. He says, for example, that the principle of not harming people is open to exceptions; that the injunction to accept only universal laws overlooks the significance of exceptions; that the will of God is vague and unascertainable; while a basic goal, such as survival, is interpreted differently by different groups and individuals. None of these points suffice to show the impossiblity of formulating general moral principles. At most they show how difficult such a task is bound to be.

James's main interests, however, lie elsewhere, though he does add one further point to indicate not the impossibility so much as the futility of formulating moral principles. His main task is to clarify the nature and basis of moral values, but he wants also to contrast the philosophers' search for a rational test with the practical decision procedures which are in fact employed. The test, according to James, is simply that of historical success. The practical operations of social, political, and personal networks determine moral decisions at any particular point in time. Such a decision procedure is defeasible, like any other, and may be erroneous, argued against, and ultimately revised. But the suggestion is that it alone provides a practical resolution of conflicts, and that its power is vastly at odds with the 'closet philosopher's' rational arguments. James is, typically, scornful of intellectualist pretensions here:

> Better chaos forever than an order based on any closet philosopher's rule, even though he were the most enlightened possible member of his tribe. No! If the philosopher is to keep his judicial position, he must never become one of the parties to the fray.[39]

James acknowledges that philosophers may contribute to moral decisions by clarifying the issues, and even constructing ideal moral worlds to guide us in revising current views. But such ideal intellectualist constructions lose importance and practical value when contrasted with the practical decisions of social or moral life. Philosophical arguments, according to James, must always for this reason wait upon the facts. James is not, however, saying that historical decisions are always the right or best outcomes. They are, however, inevitable and respond at least as much to people's feelings and desires as to rational argument.

This picture of morality is offered as a basis for James's account of the relevance of religion to morality. Much of what he says, and particularly his account of a practical historical decision procedure, seems to make no room for religious belief. This is further reinforced by his claim that humanism provides as good a basis for ethics as religion.

> Whether a God exist, or whether no God exist . . . we form at any rate an ethical republic here below. And the first reflection which this leads to is that ethics have as genuine and real a foothold in a universe where the highest consciousness is human as in a universe where there is a

God as well. 'The religion of humanity' affords a basis for ethics as well as theism does. Whether the purely human system can satisfy the philosopher's demand as well as the other is a different question.[40]

In answering this question James appeals to another set of 'facts'. 'The chief of all reasons why concrete ethics cannot be final is that they have to wait on metaphysical and theological beliefs.'[41] This is so, James thinks, because our own natures impose demands on us which we cannot ignore. The deepest contrast in our moral life is that between the 'easy-going' and the 'strenuous' mood. The former inclines us to avoid present ills even where they lead to future benefits; the latter encourages us to accept them at least where the future benefits are sufficiently strong. It is James's view that in this situation a belief in God provides the maximum incentive to the strenuous life. He does not deny that humanism may provide some motivation. We may be encouraged to deprive ourselves for the sake of future generations, but James is cynical about the strength of such a motive. He says, rather tartly, 'We do not love these men of the future keenly enough.'[42]

For these reasons James thinks that even in the absence of any metaphysical grounds for believing in God we would still postulate Him 'simply as a pretext for living hard'. 'For this reason the strenuous type of character will on the battlefield of human history always outwear the easy-going type, and religion will drive irreligion to the wall.'[43] James admits that the postulate of God's existence may be quite unclear, but it will still have its psychological function.

> In the interests of our own ideal of systematically unified moral truth therefore we as would-be philosophers must postulate a divine thinker and pray for the victory of the religious cause. Meanwhile exactly what the thought of the infinite thinker may be is hidden from us even were we sure of His existence; so that our postulation of Him serves only to let loose in us the strenuous mood.[44]

Much of what James says here will not readily commend itself to moral philosophers. The characteristic criticisms of intellectualist moral philosophy may arouse hostility, and James's interests may seem peripheral to present-day philosophers. The attitudes of cosmic pessimism and optimism are less apparent nowadays, perhaps because of the greater separation of moral and religious beliefs. Questions of motives and temperamental attitudes which give James's discussion a psychological flavour, are less discussed now than questions of reasons or justification for moral claims. Beyond these divergences objections may be raised to James's account of the emergence of moral values, to his acceptance of a historical test for moral claims, and to his defence of the role of religious belief.

Few will disagree with the claim that values, and moral values, arise only where there is sentient life. Though James does not go into detail about the diverse factors in that life which contribute to the emergence of value, it seems clear that he would want to include simple pleasures and pains, feelings of attraction and repulsion, desires and the pursuit and recognition of goals. His view seems to be that moral values emerge out of such natural factors as these, so that the moral order is neither simply co-ordinate with the natural order nor simply reducible to it. The term 'emergence' in this context, fashionable at the time James wrote, is a precursor of the current relation of 'supervenience'. Though James sometimes uses the latter term he never offers a clear definition of it.

It would be natural to object to James's account that his principle of tolerance, especially when coupled with his insistence on the historical test, is far too generous. To suggest that every demand deserves to be met draws no distinction between legitimate and illegitimate desires, or good and evil demands. But this is to misunderstand James's position. There is no reason why such a distinction could not be drawn in James's scheme; indeed it will naturally arise just at the point where it is necessary to reconcile conflicting demands. James's primary purpose, however, is only to show how values arise on the basis of such demands and not to adjudicate between those that are acceptable and those that are not. Such contrasts will be made in the light of the historic decision-making process. James does not claim that the process will produce solutions which are the best or even admirable. It is part of his meliorist view that we may hope gradually to improve the situation, but not that we necessarily start from a state of innocence or develop into a state of harmony and reason.

Viewed in this way James's account is undeniably bleak and pessimistic. Even if we suppose that philosophers have reason on their side there can be no assurance that the processes of history will conform to the reasonable view. Some may react to this situation by seeking to justify the extreme optimism which James decried. His own view was that we should recognise the bleak outlook and do our best to improve it. We should, as he says, simply *take* our moral holidays rather than attempt the futile task of guaranteeing them.

It is this pessimistic outlook which, however, calls for religious belief in order to 'let loose the strenuous mood'. Such a claim may seem both weak and objectionable. It may be said to be weak on the ground that other, secular, beliefs might be at least as effective, perhaps even more effective, in stimulating such a mood. It may be thought objectionable in that the appeal to God, vague and ill-understood as it is admitted by James to be, has no role of the envisaged kind to play.

In one way James admits that the religious mood is not the only one with this function. If we *are* Romantics, then the subjectivist attitude may motivate us in a similar way. James implies that it is unlikely to be so effective as religious belief and claims that it will certainly not work for everyone. But it may be replied that the same will be true of religious belief. Not everyone will respond to those beliefs or respond to them with the same degree of commitment. Similar points might be made in relation to political beliefs. James evidently believes that political motivation is weak on the ground that we do not care enough for the welfare of future generations, but many political activists would say that James was just mistaken about such a point of fact.

James puts his points generally in terms of the *strengths* of the various motives, but he might do better to distinguish between different *kinds* of motive. There is a contrast, for example, between the motives supplied respectively by subjective Romanticism and personal benefit. To advise someone to do something because they will then benefit might be said to be a basic or intrinsic motive for the action. To advise someone to do something not because they will benefit but because they will then understand better is not in this way basic or intrinsic. To say 'You will be better off, but that's no reason to do X' is absurd; to say 'You will be no better off, but you will understand better; but that's no reason to do X' is not absurd. Someone, of course, might be motivated by the wish to understand better, and so come to see that outcome both as a part of being better off and as a reason for doing X. But there is no necessity to take that view, and others might be quite indifferent to such a motive. Someone who claimed to be indifferent to the motive of being better off is, however, much less easy to comprehend. Such a difference holds also between what I have called a basic or intrinsic motive and the motive of benefiting future generations. It is not absurd to reject that latter motive in the way in which it is absurd to reject the former. Such a contrast might also be expressed in terms of the strength of motives, but it is not then just an empirical difference of degree.

Such a distinction perhaps does something to support James's rejection of the purely political motive of benefiting future generations, but it does nothing to support the idea that religious motives are themselves basic, intrinsic, or even unique. James, of course, is not prepared to endorse such a role for *every* belief in God. Such a belief of the optimistic kind is decisively rejected to him on the ground that it inclines one to fatalism, but he does not make clear what sort of religious belief he would endorse. Nor is it clear that there is any version of such a religious belief which would meet the requirements for both a basic and an unique motive. The only suggestion I can find in James is that the idea of God is to be that of an ultimate 'fall-back' or safeguard, in place to remedy our failures if it should be necessary. It is the kind of belief that might be expressed as 'The cause is not necessarily lost, even if we lose'. This may encourage us to worry less about the outcome and so to get on with our own best efforts to succeed. It would be a doctrine of relief in its recognition that some of, but not all, the responsibility is ours.

Two final comments might be made on such a position. Plainly such an account does not differentiate religious from political beliefs. Secular political faiths also generate the same sense of relief,[45] not by appealing to a transcendent being but rather by appealing to fellow workers in the field. An individual may fail, but the official consolation is that the group will continue and may ultimately succeed. James is surely right to recognise the importance of such motives. They define an essential part of what we mean by 'faith', whether religious or secular. But they do not serve to differentiate religious from secular faiths. James's account does something, but less than he would claim.

A more serious hazard arises from the content and grounds for a religious belief. In one obvious way the solidarity of a political faith in ones fellow workers is a more naturally pragmatic or pluralist conviction than a faith in a transcendent being. Whatever the strengths of these alternative motives may be, the secular has a clear content and, if the motive of future benefit is accepted, a clear supporting ground. James admits that the content of the religious belief is obscure, and the consequent support for it must be no less dubious. It remains questionable, therefore, whether James is even entitled to appeal to such beliefs, and this was the issue which he debated with Clifford.

9

Voluntarily Adopted Faiths

1   The debate with Clifford

James represents the central issue of free-will as a choice between alternative postulates where there is no coercive intellectual argument or decisive empirical evidence on either side. In his account of morality and religion he similarly represents a belief in God as beneficial but not grounded in any intellectual way. Both kinds of case are examples of what he calls 'the lawfulness of voluntarily adopted faith',[1] and both raise the issue of the legitimacy of such faiths. In 1877 W.K. Clifford published his paper on 'The Ethics of Belief',[2] in which he argued that there could be no justification for holding a belief without sufficient evidence or intellectual warrant. James felt obliged to defend his view of lawfully adopted faiths and did so in the essay which gave its title to the collection *The Will to Believe*.

Clifford's claim was based firmly on a moral argument. To hold a belief merely, as he says, 'for the solace and private pleasure of the believer'[3] without adequate evidence, proof, or even perhaps enquiry was for Clifford simply immoral. Even in such cases as those of religious belief where evidence, proof or enquiry may have no place the suggestion was that we ought to suspend belief rather than choose a view which appeals to, or comforts, us. Clifford took a very high moral line in the matter, claiming, for example, that even where such a belief did no direct or perceptible harm the immorality of holding it remained. For we may thereby be encouraged to hold other beliefs on such an inadequate basis, and this will lead to disadvantageous consequences in the long run both for the licentious believer and for humanity in general. According to Clifford such a procedure is

sinful, because it is stolen in defiance of our duty to mankind. That

161

duty is to guard ourselves from such beliefs as from a pestilence which may shortly master our own body and then spread to the rest of the town. It is wrong always, everywhere and for everyone to believe anything upon insufficient evidence.[4]

James had no wish to dispute every aspect of Clifford's thesis. Though he rightly complains of Clifford's strident yet querulous tone,[5] he nevertheless also referred to some aspects of his view as 'healthy' and would have echoed it for most cases of belief. James would not have wished to query the thesis that wherever possible we should proportion our beliefs to the available evidence. But he also thought that there were legitimate exceptions to Clifford's universal condemnation to be found among moral and religious belief. Even in that context James did not think that all beliefs of these kinds were legitimate exceptions. His concern was principally to identify as clearly as possible the conditions under which such exceptions could be validated. But he also thought that Clifford's view rested on a general misconception about the nature of belief. In particular it rested on a failure to appreciate the overlap which James had stressed in the *Principles* between belief, volition, and attention.

The central inadequacy of which James complained in Clifford's account was the latter's refusal to allow any interest other than the intellectual in the acceptance of belief. For James all our beliefs, whether factual, moral, or religious are held on the basis of what he called 'passional' as well as 'intellectual' interests. Among the former James includes not only our consciously recognised hopes, wishes, fears or comforts, but also the often unacknowledged assumptions, prejudices and partisanship which result from our social, historical or temperamental conditions. Such a view is in line with the claims noted earlier that most of our beliefs are held on trust as an unexamined credit balance. 'Our faith,' he now adds, 'is faith in someone else's faith and in the greatest matters this is most the case.'[6] He thinks that even our regard for truth as something desirable includes a passional interest, and is indeed 'but a passionate affirmation of desire in which our social system backs us up'.[7]

James contrasts two different attitudes to the acceptance of belief exemplified respectively by himself and Clifford. In his own we adopt as a guide

(1)   Discover the truth,

while in the other, Clifford's, we adopt the more cautious

(2)   Avoid error.

The difference here is like that in a battle between the aim of winning a victory as opposed to that of at least avoiding defeat, or in a chess game between playing for the win or only for the draw. The first attitude in each case is bold, and aggressive, but also vulnerable or even dangerous, while the second is cautious, even timid, but correspondingly less risky. James admits that temperamentally he is drawn to the bolder attitudes, while he thinks that Clifford clearly illustrates the more cautious. Whether that is so or not, however, James believes that we will always have some such general attitudes towards belief so that it cannot be totally divorced from these passional or temperamental interests.

James also concedes that in some areas, particularly science, the more cautious attitude may be the right one to adopt, and he associates Clifford's own view with such a scientific background. He regards institutional science as having been successfully erected on such careful attitudes.

> Science has organised this nervousness into a regular *technique*, her so-called method of verification. . . . But in our dealings with objective nature we obviously are recorders, not makers, of the truth; and decisions for the mere sake of deciding promptly and getting on to the next business would be wholly out of place. Throughout the breadth of physical nature facts are what they are quite independently of us.[8]

James makes two points about the restricted scope of such a model for belief. In the scientific and dispassionate avoidance of error there is no particular urgency. It is always possible for us to withhold judgment and suspend belief until adequate evidence has appeared. Such issues he describes for this reason as 'trivial' rather than 'momentous'. They are also, James thinks, for most people who are not scientific experts 'dead' rather than 'live' issues.

These descriptions form part of the specific conditions under which James allows exceptions to Clifford's view. They are expressed in three contrasts between options which are
(3)   Live rather than dead
(4)   Forced rather than avoidable
(5)   Momentous rather than trivial.[9]
Where an option is of the first kind in each pair, that is, live, forced, and momentous James calls it a 'genuine' option, and it is only among such genuine options that he believes legitimate exceptions to Clifford's view are to be found. James adds one further final proviso, namely that we may hold such beliefs without adequate evidence only where a decision cannot be made on intellectual grounds. James believes that when all these conditions are met we not only may but positively *must* make a decision on grounds other than the intellectual, where inevitably on Clifford's view the evidence will be insufficient.

James's argument has two parts, and each is open to objection. In the first part where he charges Clifford with an inadequate conception of belief it may be objected that James's account is no better. In the second where he defends his exceptions against Clifford's thesis it may be argued that the defence is mistaken or inadequate.

Perhaps the strongest case that could be made against James's conception of belief would be to show that there is no room for the will, or for any passional interest, in the matter of belief. An argument of this kind, which might be used to defend Clifford against James, has been provided by Bernard Williams.[10] His view is that it is a necessary condition for belief that beliefs cannot be 'acquired at will'. Although Williams does not refer to either Clifford or James and may not have envisaged a use for his argument in defending the former, still it seems to offer such a defence. If the defence were to succeed then James's specific account of the exceptions to Clifford's principle would be untenable.

Williams's argument turns on a claimed connection between belief and truth. Unlike Clifford, who took the view that it is possible but immoral to acquire a belief at will, Williams argues that it is logically impossible to do so. His argument is neatly summarised in the following passage.

> If I could acquire a belief at will I could acquire it whether it was true or not; moreover I would know that I could acquire it whether it was true or not. If in full consciousness I could will to acquire a belief irrespective of its truth, it is unclear that before the event I could seriously think of it as a belief, i.e. as something purporting to represent reality. At the very least there must be a restriction on what is the case after the event, since I could not then in full consciousness regard this as a belief of mine, i.e. as something I take to be true, and also know that I acquired it at will. With regard to no belief could I know – or if all this is done in full consciousness even suspect – that I had acquired it at will.[11]

Two difficulties arise if such an argument is used to defend or strengthen Clifford's case. The first is that Williams assumes that the beliefs in question can be characterised as true or false, in terms of some accessible evidence, and can further be said when true to represent some reality. The case is more complicated if we allow, for example, that there are moral or religious beliefs, correctly so called, where the issue of truth or falsity does not arise, or where, if it does arise, the ascription does not turn simply on an appeal to accessible evidence. There is a still further complication which would arise if we allow the ascription of truth or falsity to such beliefs but in a way which does not entitle us to infer directly to a corresponding reality.[12] In that latter case, for example, it is far from obvious that where there is no question of a correspondence with some accessible reality there is any objection to our acquiring beliefs at will. James's own position turns on just such cases, for he is inclined to say of moral or religious beliefs that they are genuine beliefs, that they can be characterised as true or false, but that their truth or falsity is not just a matter of correspondence with some independent reality. The effect of Williams's assumptions here is to restrict his case to beliefs which are not at the centre of James's concern. The issues which such a point raises, though, will be considered in the next section.

For the present, then, I simply accept the implied restriction.

For there is a second difficulty in the argument, even with this restriction, which turns on an ambiguity. The argument rests essentially on the ideas of 'acquiring a belief at will' and 'acquiring a belief whether it is true or not'. It seeks to establish that I cannot acquire a belief whether it is true or not, on the ground that it would then not be, or be able to be thought to be, a *belief*, that is something which purports to represent reality. But if we ask what it is to 'acquire a belief whether it is true or not' then two possibilities arise. In the first it means 'acquiring a belief even if it is known to be false', or perhaps 'acquiring a belief in total disregard of available evidence'. In the second it means 'acquiring a belief when it is not known to be true' or perhaps 'acquiring a belief where the evidence is inconclusive'. The first, strong, case is where someone is prepared to flout or violate the connection between belief and truth by choosing to 'believe' without regard for the known truth or evidence. The second, weak, case is that of someone who holds a belief not in violation of the truth but in ignorance of it.

Now Williams is surely right to say of beliefs to which truth and falsity can be ascribed and which purport to represent reality that someone who acquires beliefs at will in the first sense is simply at odds with our conception of such beliefs. The case is less clear for other beliefs where truth or falsity might not be at issue, or where, though they are at issue, nevertheless there is no corresponding reality. But it is also clear that this prohibition is not even faintly true of the second weak sense of 'acquiring a belief at will'. For most of us, most of the time, are forced to believe, and act in the belief, that things are thus and so whether they are or not. In such cases it surely must sometimes be legitimate to 'acquire a belief whether it is true or not', or to 'acquire a belief at will'. Indeed it might be said that it is another required feature of *belief*, as opposed to *knowledge*, that we sometimes hold, and have to hold, beliefs in such a state of ignorance.

That weak sense in which belief and will are legitimately connected is, of course, just the kind of case James is concerned with. If that is so, then the argument cannot damage James's position. What it succeeds in pointing to, though, is the nature of the specific case James has in mind. For that case is one not merely where we lack evidence or knowledge which is in principle available, but where there is no such evidence available in principle. It might, of course, be argued that in such cases the notion of belief is changed, or even inapplicable, but that was not the form of the original objection.

It might still be objected that James misrepresents the role of the will in belief in other ways. For he suggests sometimes that by an exercise of the will we may actually make the belief true, or create the circumstances which will in some way verify it. A different view might be that the will may be useful in overcoming an intellectual paralysis in which by default one of the options available comes into play simply because no choice has been genuinely exercised. On such a view it would be quite wrong to think of a choice between options as somehow creating the truth of the belief. James has two clear replies to such an objection. First he would be inclined to say that a choice between options does not determine *the* truth of the belief, any more than the current acceptance of a belief determines its continued acceptance in the future. Second, although James does talk in this context of 'creating truth', he does not conceive it in this mistaken way.

James imagines situations in which a commitment may bring about the relevant benefit, when that benefit may simply be lost through inaction or paralysis of the will. He talks of a tacit trust between colleagues which may help actually to foster trustworthiness; of a decision to express affection for someone which may stimulate a reciprocal feeling; or of a decision to marry which may help a relationship to flourish.[13] The relevance of such cases for James is that without such decisions the potential benefits will remain untested and lost. In such cases James represents agnosticism or inaction as taking one of the options in the matter rather than simply remaining neutral between them. If I consider marrying someone but remain agnostic about its feasibility to the point of inaction, then, according to James, I am in effect choosing not to marry. There is no suggestion here that the benefits of exercising a choice are in any way guaranteed, but only that if there are benefits then both agnosticism and a negative choice rule them out. As in the case of free-will James thinks that a decision in favour of free-will leaves open chances of improvement; but meliorism differs from optimism precisely in its recognition of the possibility of failure.

These cases in which we are forced to act or else, through inaction, simply exclude a potential benefit seem to leave no room for a third agnostic possibility. It may finally be objected to James that his central cases of voluntarily adopted faith, the religious cases, are not of this kind. If choices between options are not urgent or momentous in science, as James claims, then it may seem quite unplausible to suppose them urgent or momentous in religion. Such an objection may rest in part on the peculiarities of James's vocabulary. There is infelicity in his suggestion that scientific decisions are 'trivial' rather than 'momentous', and in his use of the term 'genuine' only to describe options which are live, forced, and momentous. It is easy to imagine decisions in science which are in the ordinary sense both genuine and momentous.

These semantic points show some weakness in James's account, but they can be guarded against by treating his vocabulary here as technical and distinct from our ordinary usage. James would not deny that some scientific options are non-trivial, but he insists that in their case a commitment to such an option should wait upon the appropriate evidence. He is inclined to agree with Clifford that in such a context agnosticism or suspension of belief is the rational attitude to adopt. In the contrast between scientific and religious belief it is not so much that the former are never urgent while the latter always are, but rather that in the former case it makes sense to wait for further resolution of the issue where in the latter it does not. In the case of religious belief to wait for further evidence is to wait forever, and to wait forever is to lose whatever benefits such beliefs may confer. It was no doubt for this reason that in his discussion of materialism James had spoken of enjoying the benefits of a belief in God in advance of an ultimate decision between it and spiritualism.

A more serious hazard arises from the thought that James is surely wrong to exclude an agnostic attitude towards religious belief. James ascribes to Clifford the motive of sheltering atheism under the guise of agnosticism, because he believes that to be an agnostic in such matters is to lose the potential benefits of the belief. But it is not easy to see why we may suspend judgment in science but cannot do so in religion without losing potential benefits. James's response would presumably be to point to the requirement that the option be forced rather than avoidable, and further that if the difference between the alternatives is not to be idle or empty there must be some difference between the attitudes and behaviour appropriate to such alternatives. Both points should be queried. It remains unclear why such choices in religion are forced; and it is doubtful whether there has to be some difference in the relevant behaviour.

In the case of urgent action in the face of some danger the options may naturally be presented as an exhaustive and exclusive choice. If there is but one possible line of escape, itself extremely hazardous, then we may be faced with an urgent decision between attempting the escape or doing nothing. In such a case to take no decision at all is simply to do nothing, to lose the potential benefits of the escape attempt and to reap whatever are the disastrous consequences of not escaping. But a choice between religious beliefs, however momentous, may not be of this kind. It may be suggested that the description of optional choices as forced or avoidable is not necessarily determined by the nature of the options but rather by the way in which those options are presented.

Suppose, for example, that I am a scientist wrestling with the decision whether to accept Snell's law. I may represent this as a choice between
(6)   Believing Snell's law
and
(7)   Not believing Snell's law.
To represent the choice in this way is to represent it as 'forced' for there is no third option. But the choice could also be represented in the following different way between
(8)   Believing Snell's law
(9)   Believing some other law-like relation between the phenomena
and

167

(10) Suspending judgment between (8) and (9).

In this case there is room for agnosticism. Both James and Clifford agree that where the evidence for (8) and (9) is insufficient, then (10) is the only rational and moral attitude to adopt.

It is difficult to see, however, why the same variations in the presentation of choice cannot be provided in the religious sphere. Consider, for example, the difference between

(11) Believing in God's existence

and

(12) Not believing in God's existence.

In such a case we have a parallel with (6) and (7) and apparently a forced choice between the options, for even to suspend judgment is to satisfy (12). (12), we might say, like (7), really covers the two cases where we believe God does not exist and where we do not form any belief one way or the other. This may lead us to represent the situation more subtly by separating

(13) Believing in God's non-existence

from

(14) Suspending judgment between (11) and (13).

Clifford might fairly say that the 'forced' nature of the choice between (11) and (12) is misleading. He might add that James's argument appears in danger of fallaciously identifying (12) and (13) or even (13) and (14).

James's reply to this is to insist that if there is to be a genuine difference between (11) and (12), then it must issue in some difference of behaviour between the believer and the non-believer. If this were so, then it would justify the assimilation, in point of the subsequent behaviour, of (13) and (14). The suggestion is that someone who accepts (12) by endorsing (14) rather than (13) will nevertheless behave in the same way as one who accepts both (12) and (13). As in the cases of mutual trust to be agnostic is, on this view, to leave untested whatever benefits (11) might confer and so to lose them. Otherwise the supposed difference between (11) and (12) will be idle.[14]

Clifford should reply to this that the argument is simply fallacious. Of course there must be some difference between (11) and (12) if the dispute between them is not to be idle, but it does not follow, and is in any case false, that that difference has to be a difference of behaviour. The fallacy might be argued for by querying the pragmatic theory of meaning on which James bases his view, but this would be a long and complex exchange. It is simpler to demonstrate the fallacy by contrasting what can be called the 'extensional' and 'intensional' aspects of the various injunctions associated with these beliefs.

Consider the two injunctions

(15) Do X

(16) Do not do X,

and contrast them with

(17)   Do X *as* a religious conviction

and

(18)   Do not do X *as* a religious conviction.

Clearly the two members of each pair oppose each other. Equally clearly (18) is compatible with (15), for I may choose to do X and yet not choose it *as* a religious conviction. Someone in Clifford's position, therefore, might accept (18) and reject (17) but need not in so doing accept (16) or reject (15). So the difference between a religious believer and Clifford does not have to be one in which their conduct differs. It could be one in which their conduct is the same but their conception of it, as required or not by some religious faith, is different. There is room for debate as to whether we should accept criteria which determine that their conduct or behaviour is then different. But it suffices to bring out the fallacy in James's argument that there is at least one conception of 'same behaviour' for which his argument fails.

James can be faulted for not clarifying these points, but a central strand of his argument remains intact. Even if we were to admit that the behaviour of an agnostic might be extensionally indistinguishable from that of a believer he has still two points to make. First he might recall his earlier claim that a religious faith provides the best motive for a 'strenuous' mood. If we accept that claim then the argument is not so much that the believer's and agnostic's behaviour are always different as that the former's motive for continuing in such behaviour is stronger. It was suggested earlier, however, that the claim could not simply be accepted, on the grounds that such religious faith provided no stronger a motive than other secular beliefs. Second, however, James might say that all he needs to do to repudiate Clifford's universal prohibition on such religious beliefs is to establish just one case where that motive is stronger. On straightforward empirical grounds it seems highly plausible to suppose that such cases exist, that is, people who would be unmotivated to a strenuous mood and life if they were unable to accept religious beliefs. Clifford is committed to denying the morality of any such case, but the opposing view rests on a moral argument at least as strong as Clifford's. Clifford represents such beliefs as functioning solely for the private solace of individuals, but James's case rests on his belief that they may have a wider and more valuable role. It is undeniable that they may have such a wider role for some people; to complain that they achieve this partly through the solace they provide looks priggish.

James, however, makes a slightly different point when he says

> I therefore for one cannot see my way to accepting the agnostic's rules for truth-seeking, or wilfully agree to keep my willing nature out of the game. I cannot do so for the plain reason that a rule of thinking which would absolutely prevent me from acknowledging certain kinds of

truth if those kinds of truth were really there would be an irrational rule.[15]

Such a position stresses not the moral benefits of religious beliefs but rather their simple truth. It echoes Pascal's wager in its suggestion that even though such truths and such a reality may be quite hidden from us, still if there are truths and benefits there it is irrational to exclude our recognising them. In this way James raises the final set of issues to be considered about moral and religious realism.

2 Moral and religious realism

When James's account of moral and religious belief is set against his epistemology and his pragmatism a number of related issues arise. The most general, but rather uninformative, way of putting these is to query the success of the project to reconcile the tender- and tough-minded philosophies. We might ask whether the envisaged new dawn in which religion and empiricism are to co-operate is not, after all, a false dawn. The most general issue can, however, usefully be split into these more specific problems.

(1) Can the notion of truth be used to cover both cognitive and non-cognitive belief?

(2) Is there a moral or supernatural reality? Have we any reason to believe in such realities?

(3) In what way can moral or religious beliefs have a legitimate role? How are such beliefs related to experiencable phenomena?

(4) How can we account for the meaning of moral or religious beliefs? *Can* James satisfactorily account for them?

It is important to note that the issues about moral belief will be different from those about religious supernatural belief, for while the former may be tied in some way to natural phenomena the latter seem to go beyond such phenomena. The first two issues naturally go together, as do the second two; and I discuss them roughly in that order.

The questions are, however, complex and the relations between them still unclear even nowadays. An affirmative answer to (1), for example, does not entail an affirmative answer to (2). There may be sufficient similarity between cognitive and non-cognitive beliefs to support the use of '. . . is true' in both cases, and yet enough dissimilarity between the two cases to justify a negative answer to (2). At the most general level such a point shows that if we start by determining the use of the truth predicate we need a further principle to determine the metaphysical consequences of this for (2). We need a criterion for what is to count as reality, and no such clear or agreed criterion is available. Less generally the point indicates a degree of confusion about the truth predicate and its relation to the notion of reality which would need to be resolved before final answers could be given to either (1) or (2).

It might, however, be useful at this stage to scotch one sensational but inaccurate version of James's view of these questions. For it might be claimed that James actually *reverses* our intuitions about reality by denying it in the cognitive realm but affirming it in the non-cognitive. It is easy to see how this might come about. For his pragmatic theory of truth might be classed as a 'coherence' theory which rejects the idea of any independent reality corresponding to our true beliefs. It might also be thought that by allowing the ascription of truth to non-cognitive beliefs James is simply affirming the existence of a reality 'in itself' wholly independent of our experience. In this way James would attract the same fate as Kant who is sometimes taken to accept the reality of things in themselves, totally independent of our experiences, and so to regard the course of those experiences as purely subjective or even illusory. In both cases, however, such accounts, spectacular as they seem, are naive and incorrect. The argument as presented is also quite incoherent. For if the ascription of truth in the cognitive case is non-realist there is no reason why it should be realist in the non-cognitive case.

We have seen that James's pragmatic theory of truth did not *exclude* the idea of a corresponding reality, though it did *limit* that idea to certain basic cases. Other cognitive beliefs, of a theoretical or ejective kind, had no such correspondence with reality, even though their functions within some holistic theory allowed the ascription of truth or falsity to them. To *assume* that any account of truth, such as James's, must give a simple 'Yes or no' answer to such a question as 'Do truths correspond to reality?' is to succumb to a naive and objectionable craving for generality. On the other side of the ascription of truth to non-cognitive beliefs the account fares no better. James makes many provisos about the legitimate ascription of truth to such beliefs. In the moral sphere, for example, he explicitly rejects as a mere superstition a naive realism in which a distinct moral order is supposed to co-exist with the natural order. For James moral values emerge from a natural order which includes sentient creatures with their natural demands. The moral order is not distinct from the natural order but depends upon it. In the realm of supernatural or mystical beliefs James contends for their meaning and value, but he also concedes that any corresponding reality is not directly accessible to us. This raises problems for him under (3) and (4), but not the supposed problem of defending a supernatural reality at the expense of the natural order.

James does not state quite explicitly that moral and religious beliefs attract the predicate '. . . is true', but he gives clear indications that he does believe this.[16] His own pragmatic account of truth, moreover, naturally opens the way for such a view. If James had held a simple correspondence theory, had regarded moral beliefs as about a different subject-matter from

171

factual beliefs, and had also denied a co-ordinate moral reality, then his position would have been difficult to rescue from inconsistency. If the ascription of truth turns on the working of beliefs, then the task is at least much easier. For it is difficult to deny that moral and religious convictions can be called beliefs, or that they operate in ways similar to those of cognitive beliefs.

Three aspects of such a similarity of operation can be summarily noted. First it is undeniable that we speak of moral and religious views in terms of 'belief', and that we sometimes characterise those beliefs as true or false. Such a point is, however, quite inconclusive with regard to James's intended assimilation of the two cases. It might, for example, be said that the term 'belief' in at least one of its uses is more at home in religious or moral contexts than it is in the factual or cognitive contexts. This might lead to the view that there is no unitary phenomenon called 'belief', but at least two different uses of the term, in one of which it might be replaced by the term 'faith'. It might be replied to this that even if there are two such uses of the term there are still sufficient similarities to justify the use of the same term in both cases.

Both of these linguistic practices might be simply mistaken or careless. There are uses of '. . . is true', for example, which indicate primarily an illocutionary force of expressing agreement, making concessions, and so on. It could be argued that when we ascribe the predicate to non-cognitive belief all that is preserved is such illocutionary force and not literal sense. This point too is quite inconclusive. It would be just absurd to deny that we assess moral beliefs, revise, reconsider them, argue for or against their acceptance or rejection, offer reasons, grounds, and support for them. In all this, no doubt, the operations in which they figure show some differences from the parallel operations of cognitive belief. The strict question, however, is whether we are entitled to mark these similarities by the parallel use of '. . . is true'.

Second it has long been noted that moral or religious beliefs work logically in similar ways to cognitive beliefs. We draw valid or invalid inferences in which moral and religious beliefs figure, and in many of these the moral and the cognitive beliefs work alongside each other without obvious strain. Just as we may reject a mathematical assumption by drawing validly from it, in conjunction with other true premises, conclusions which are absurd or impossible; so we may seek to refute a moral claim by drawing validly from it, in conjunction with other acceptable premises, conclusions which are blatantly, even admittedly, unacceptable.

Even this point is not decisive in showing that truth has the same role in both moral and non-moral contexts. For it may be that we could appeal to other notions than truth or falsity in explaining the validity of arguments. Instead of defining validity in terms of joint combinations of truth or falsity, we might define it in terms of joint combinations of acceptability or unacceptability.[17] In one way such an account conforms well to James's own position. For his pragmatic account of truth puts the ideas of acceptance or rejection of belief at the forefront of his picture. But we might draw an un-Jamesian conclusion from this. For we might decide to confine the predicate '. . . is true' to the cognitive realm and see it as one species of the generic notion of acceptance. James's own proposal is that that generic notion *is* the notion of truth, so that if we wished to isolate the purely cognitive branch we would have to find some other term. It is easy to see how such issues may become little more than questions of verbal policy.

There is a third similarity between the two broad areas, namely that in both we make, and sometimes have to make, decisions about acceptance. To hold a belief, in either sphere, is to decide about its acceptance within the repertoires of individual and social enquiry, though not, of course, in a way which excludes later revision. James sometimes uses the term 'verification' to stand generally for such repertoires, whichever specific context they concern, though sometimes he uses the term more narrowly only for the scientific or cognitive case. His vocabulary can be faulted here, as in the parallel fault in which 'satisfaction' is sometimes used for overall acceptance and sometimes for affective satisfaction. Both faults, however, clearly reflect his general wish to assimilate the cognitive and the affective cases under some generic notion of truth related to the acceptance and rejection of belief.

In this third context, too, the considerations are quite indecisive. For there are, and are admitted by James to be, serious dissimilarities also between the cognitive and non-cognitive cases. As a radical empiricist James treats cognitive beliefs as based ultimately upon an enriched, conjunctive, sensory experience. At a more sophisticated level there will also be a contribution from theoretical or ejective concepts. But moral beliefs are not, for James, similarly based on empirical observations and coupled with a theoretical apparatus to record nature. In the moral sphere we are makers as well as recorders of truth. It is true that basic feelings of attraction or repulsion, and simple pleasure or pain, play a basic part in our moral attitudes, but so also do our more developed preferences, our biological goals and needs, and the practical operations of public approval or disapproval which are used to settle conflicts. Of course parallels might be found even here with the development, testing, and acceptance or rejection of theories, but the search for such parallels can easily become absurdly strained.[18] In morality what are important are the conflicts between policy and individuals' demands; in science what are important are the conflicts between our beliefs and some independent reality. The idea of a moral policy or a theoretical belief working successfully can be employed in both contexts, though there will be differences between them. James wished to insist on the basic similarity, but he certainly did not wish to deny all differences between the two contexts of cognitive and non-cognitive belief.

Because of this indecisiveness it is best, in response to (1), to accept the boring truth that there are both similarities and differences between the cognitive and non-cognitive cases, and to treat the ascription of truth to both simply as a record of the parallels between them. There is a substantive issue here lying behind that purely verbal policy, namely that of mapping the similarities and dissimilarities. Such a task gives substance to the traditional and confused debate about the 'subjectivity' or 'objectivity' of values. For even a cursory glance at the two contexts shows that it will be quite misleading to regard either factual or moral contexts as purely subjective or purely objective. James's 'export' of truth from the cognitive to the non-cognitive realm is, so far, no more than a marker for that programme.

It may be thought that a further substantive issue has been evaded with regard to question (2). Here, however, James is more sensitive to the differences between the two areas. He identifies a certain kind of naive moral realism, but only immediately to reject it.

> Our ordinary attitude of regarding ourselves as subject to an over-arching system of moral relations, true 'in themselves', is therefore either an out-and-out superstition or else it must be treated as a mere provisional abstraction.[19]

For James, as we have seen, moral values 'emerge' from our demands, from their more sophisticated developments and from the conflicts these inevitably produce. The idea of a moral reality existing in isolation from those demands is consequently absurd. James nevertheless appears to speak approvingly of a 'system of unified moral truth' which we might at least hope to formulate. In other passages, despite the fact that he likens the historical decision procedures of morality to scientific experiments, he nevertheless denies that moral features are just like natural features, such as the aurora borealis or a magnetic field whose effects are observable in the movements of a compass needle.[20]

To clarify James's answers to (2) we need to separate the moral from the supernatural case. In the former James is clearly a naturalist of some kind. This might be inferred from his sympathy for utilitarianism, despite his reservations about that theory. It appears even more clearly in his view of the emergence of moral values from the natural phenomena of sentient creatures' demands. These natural phenomena provide a definite but complex natural base for moral values and beliefs. But in the supernatural case it seems scarcely possible to make a comparable claim. Although James wishes to tie supernatural beliefs to the natural phenomena of the believers' easy-going or strenuous motives, these appear more as consequences of, rather than bases for, the beliefs.

174

Though James does not pursue these issues far it is feasible to begin to outline positions which he rejects in the moral case. For he certainly wishes to reject the idea of a realm of values existing independently of and co-ordinate with the natural world. Less clearly he seems also to reject the idea that moral values just are straightforward features of the natural world. This is a consequence of the complexity of the natural features on which moral values are based, and of the imperatival or prescriptive character of those values and the demands from which they arise. It seems consequently that James would reject an analytic reduction of moral beliefs to claims about natural phenomena. James's characteristic ideas of 'emergence' and of 'novelty' imply that some new item arises in such cases. This is certainly true of the way in which he envisages the emergence of consciousness from the material organisation of the brain. It fits in well, too, with James's generally holistic and non-reductionist attitudes.

If those denials are part of James's view then he holds that moral terms do not name distinct non-natural phenomena, and do not name simple or complex natural phenomena either. Those requirements, however, are compatible with a number of different views. If we think of the function of moral utterances, for example, then they might be met by an 'expressive' theory. According to such a view moral utterances do not describe or report such things as emotions or subjective demands, but express or evince such emotional responses. James would probably not want to deny such a function, though he plainly thinks moral beliefs more complex than this, but he could not have regarded it as the whole story. For an expressive theory on its own could not treat such utterances as straightforward beliefs, and still less as beliefs with a truth value. James, therefore, might have agreed that moral utterances are not mere reports or descriptions of emotional states, but he would not have wanted to deny them the status of belief or a truth value.

For that reason James is committed to an account of the logical relations between moral beliefs and the corresponding claims about the relevant, complex, natural phenomena. If James were an analytic reductionist then those relations would amount to synonymy or two-way entailment; if he is not a reductionist then some weaker relation is required. James talks extensively of 'emergence' and occasionally of 'supervenience'[21] in this context, but he does not make clear how he would define this relation. One possibility would be to weaken a mutual entailment between moral and natural beliefs in favour of only a one-way entailment. Another would be to replace an intensional with an extensional relation. A further possibility would be to use some of the accounts of 'supervenience' which have been canvassed recently. Some of these features fit reasonably into James's own account. He would certainly claim that moral values depend upon natural features rather than the other way round. He would probably have accepted the view that any moral value ascribed to some given natural situation must be ascribed also to any other situation of that kind. What he would almost certainly, though, have wanted to stress is that there is a distinction to be drawn between natural phenomena which are independent of sentient creatures' demands and those demands themselves. One creature might legitimately ascribe a moral value to the former natural phenomena which another such creature might equally legitimately withhold. For the ascription of such values is dependent upon the creature's own demands which will vary from creature to creature.

Such incomplete accounts of moral beliefs and values indicate in general terms James's answers to questions (3) and (4) for those moral items. But questions (2), (3), and (4) for supernatural or mystical belief are more difficult to resolve. There James certainly insists on some tie between the beliefs and phenomena such as motives and subsequent conduct, but such a tie seems different from that in the moral case and is both unclear and dubious. In this context the question arises whether his view of supernatural beliefs can be reconciled with his pragmatic principles, but it is important to notice that James's own attitude to such beliefs is ambiguous. Sometimes he adopts a very cautious approach to them, but on other occasions commits himself to them in a stronger way.

In his more cautious vein James refers only to the bare logical possibility of a supernatural realm of which a glimpse might be given in the 'margins' of consciousness. In this context James stresses rather the need to keep an open mind and the inconclusiveness of the case against such possibilities than any positive grounds for the actual existence of a supernatural reality. He says, for example,

> The lower manifestations of the subliminal, indeed, fall within the resources of the personal subject; his ordinary sense-material, inattentively taken in and subconsciously remembered and combined, will account for all the usual automatisms. But just as our primary wide-awake consciousness throws open our senses to the touch of things material, so it is logically conceivable that *if there be* higher spiritual agencies that can directly touch us, the psychological condition of their doing so *might be* our possession of a subconscious region which alone should yield access to them.[22]

In talking in *The Varieties of Religious Experience* of nitrous oxide intoxication[23] and its peculiar effects, akin to mystical experience, he says:

> One conclusion was forced upon my mind . . . It is that our normal waking consciousness . . . is but one special type . . . whilst all about it . . . there lie potential forms of consciousness entirely different . . . No account of the universe in its totality can be final which leaves these other forms of consciousness quite disregarded . . . How to regard them is the question – . . . At any rate they forbid a premature closing of our accounts with reality.[24]

When James collects his overall views about mystical experience he makes these points. First he says that mystical experiences 'usually are, and have the right to be, authoritative' to the mystic himself; second that their authority cannot extend to outsiders; and third that they 'open out the possibility of other orders of truth in which, so far as anything in us vitally responds to them, we may freely continue to have faith'.[25] Such claims are modest in their insistence on the bare possibilities of a supernatural reality, and on the relative positions and rights of believer and non-believer. The non-believer may have no right to deny or reject such beliefs; but the believer equally has no ground or right to export his claimed authority to others.

In other contexts, however, James appears to go further. Of the 'mind-cure' religion he says:

> The mind-cure gospel thus once more appears to us as having dignity and importance. We have seen it to be a genuine religion and no mere silly appeal to imagination to cure disease. We have seen its method of experimental verification to be not unlike the method of science, and now we find mind-cure as the champion of a perfectly definite conception of the metaphysical structure of the world.[26]

Elsewhere he says:

> we have in the fact that the conscious person is continuous with a wider self through which saving experiences come, a positive content of religious experience which, it seems to me, is literally and objectively true as far as it goes.[27]

James speaks of religion, too, not merely as 'an illuminator of facts already given elsewhere', but as a 'postulator of *new* facts as well'.[28] Such a claim might be compatible with an account in which religious beliefs, like moral beliefs, supervene in some way on the natural world. But James makes it clear that he is here thinking of a new realm of facts altogether.

> I believe the pragmatic way of taking religion to be the deeper way. It gives it body as well as soul, it makes it claim, as everything must claim, some characteristic realm of fact of its own. What the more characteristically divine facts are, apart from the actual inflow of energy in the faith-state and the prayer-state I know not.[29]

Finally in a postscript to *The Varieties of Religious Experience* James faces directly the issue of his commitment to supernaturalism and distinguishes between what he calls 'refined' and 'crass' supernaturalists. The former are associated with most philosophers of James's day, but James prefers to classify his own view as of the latter 'crass' type. Such a one accepts some causal link between supernatural reality and the natural world, while the 'refined' theorists deny this. He sums up his position in the following way.

177

Both instinctively and for logical reasons I find it hard to believe that principles can exist which make no difference in facts. . . . In spite of its being so shocking to the reigning intellectual tastes, I believe that a candid consideration of piecemeal supernaturalism and a complete discussion of all its metaphysical bearings will show it to be the hypothesis by which the largest number of legitimate requirements are met.[30]

Though there seems to be a difference between a weak and a strong commitment to supernaturalism in these passages the outcome is not wholly clear. Someone who accepts the weak claim that a supernatural reality is at least not logically impossible does not strengthen his commitment merely by adding further logically possible descriptions of such a reality. If James's 'crass' supernaturalism accepted a causal link only within the framework of a logically possible supernatural reality, it would still not amount to a strong commitment to a supernatural reality. Similarly the 'mind-cure' cases, and the appeal to 'margins' of consciousness, might not commit James to more than the weak claim, so long as the supernatural reality was supposed to be no more than logically possible. The stronger claim would arise, however, if James thought not only that such a belief was logically possible but that there was some evidence to be adduced for its truth. James sometimes seems to take that further step.

Even the weaker supernaturalist thesis is vulnerable to some objections. If James's account of meaning were verificationist in the way that the logical positivists' account was, and could admit as meaningful only verifiable or analytic claims, then supernatural beliefs would have to be classed as meaningless. This is to put in the starkest form the conflict James recognised between empiricism and religion. That objection can, however, be answered. For James is not a verificationist of that kind. He tends to take a holistic rather than an atomist view of belief, truth, and meaning, even though he has no clear development of such a holistic theory of meaning to offer. Indeed the main objections to the positivists' verificationism came from holistic considerations,[31] and James would have had more sympathy with them than with the positivist view itself.

Moreover, although the term 'verification' is used by James in his account of truth it was noted earlier that his use of it is ambiguous. If it is used, as the positivists used it, in a narrow sense in which it applies only to the empirical claims of science and other cognitive disciplines, then James's theory is not verificationist. It explicitly allows for the acceptance and rejection of non-cognitive beliefs in terms of their overall 'satisfaction'. For James there is no sharp line of division between the cognitive and non-cognitive cases. Moral claims, for example, have their acceptability determined in part by certain facts, such as the natural conditions from which they emerge, and only in part by the personal satisfaction which they yield.

But supernatural beliefs seem to occupy one extreme end of the spectrum between narrow verification and personal satisfaction. They appear to acquire their meaning *only* in relation to that latter end.

In this way the weaker thesis, which claims only logical conceivability for supernatural beliefs, might be guarded against the most obvious objections. They would be associated with acceptance conditions and their meaning could be explained in terms of the differences which such acceptance would make. But it was noted earlier that two general problems still arise, and in a particularly serious form for such supernatural claims. On one side the benefits, or satisfaction, arise from the acceptance of such beliefs, but then it seems that the beliefs must already have some content apart from those satisfactions. If, however, they occupy the extreme emotional end of the acceptability spectrum, then it is difficult to see how they could have any other content.[32] On the other side their acceptance may vary from individual to individual, and then the notion of a public meaning for such contents may seem to disappear.

The first of these problems might be elaborated in two different ways. Clearly if we think of emotional responses to some belief as only causally connected to that belief, then those responses cannot be counted as part of the meaning of the belief. On the other hand we do conceive of certain emotional responses as being more closely tied to the meanings of certain words. The attitudes of approval or disapproval which we link with certain moral terms, for example, might with some reservations be counted as part of their meanings. James might argue that the same is true of the supernatural beliefs he has in mind. It is plausible to associate those supernatural beliefs with certain pessimistic or optimistic attitudes, and these could provide some emotional content for them. James would mainly have to be careful that he did not allow all such emotional responses to be counted as part of the meaning of any expression which elicited such a response.

A second, more difficult, objection arises once we accept the possible inclusion of emotional features in the meaning of supernatural beliefs. For if those features are only part of the meaning of such beliefs, as the affective account is only a part of the meaning of moral terms, then some explanation is required for the other part of their meaning. James is particularly required to offer some such explanation. For if these affective responses were *all* that could be said of the meaning of such beliefs, then he might be forced to admit that their content was not supernatural at all. For if those emotional responses exhausted their meaning, then we would be tempted to translate such beliefs into statements about those emotional responses. In this case, too, it would not be much better to consider an 'expressive' theory for such beliefs. For what is expressed would still be something natural rather than supernatural, namely individuals' emotional responses. A holistic theory of meaning might claim that piecemeal translation of such expressions was not possible, but that is a highly dubious claim to make in

179

the absence of a developed holistic account of meaning.

James does not squarely face these difficulties, and offers no definite response to them. He takes for granted that supernatural religious beliefs have a content which may include, but is not exhausted by, the references to strenuous moods or personal satisfaction.[33] Lines of defence are available in principle, but they remain unclear. James might appeal, for example, to the idea of 'extending' analogous natural beliefs beyond the natural realm. Claims about God use, inevitably, a vocabulary which has its primary application in the natural realm. The difficulty is to understand how such a primary use might, without loss of meaning, be extended so far beyond that primary use. James is quite candid about the indeterminacy of concepts of God and of the supernatural. He recognises both that different people or faiths may have quite different conceptions of such things and that their application is, as he says, unascertainable. He seems to envisage only a common element in such apparent references to something indeterminate in a supernatural order, which may bring about changes in the natural world and be beneficent. Even that minimal claim, though, still faces the challenge to explain how our natural use of such expressions might meaningfully extend to the supernatural.

Here, too, James might appeal to other authorities. He might refer to the Kantian idea that if we characterise limits to our knowledge and understanding, then we must be able to make some meaningful reference to what lies outside those limits. Kant's recommendation was that we allow a meaning to such references but strictly recognise the cognitive limits which that meaning sets. James is, in any case, committed to some such account of other concepts than the religious, such as those of 'truth' itself or 'freewill'. For he conceives of these, in some of their uses, as 'recognition-transcendent'.[34] We never will, or conceivably could, come face to face with a final Truth. James is in no doubt that we have such a conception which may have a heuristic value as well as mislead us. Perhaps he could simply make it a *requirement* of any adequate account of meaning that it should allow just such transcendence, though this is bound to seem a problematic guide in the absence of any developed theory of meaning.

So far, however, only the weak claim for supernatural beliefs has been considered, namely that they are at least logically conceivable. In the stronger thesis, however, the suggestion is that we actually have some cognitive ground for supporting such claims. James indicates two ways in which such support might be offered. In the first the support is only of that consequential kind which belongs also to moral beliefs. He says, for example, 'The uses of religion, its uses to the individual who has it, and the uses of the individual himself to the world are the best argument that truth is in it. . . . The true is what works well on the whole.'[35] This adds nothing to what has been said already of such support for moral beliefs. In particular it poses no distinctive problems about the supernatural realm.

The benefits which provide the test for our ascription of truth to such beliefs belong to the immanent world of the ethical republic and not to any supposed supernatural realm.

In the second of these suggestions James assimilates these non-cognitive beliefs more closely to the cognitive, and represents religious belief as a kind of theory for which there is, or may be, some empirical support. The support James envisages is primarily that from mystical, or trans-marginal, experience in which it may at least be imagined that we have some access to what James calls 'the unseen order'.[36] This second idea clearly gets closer to the strong commitment to a supernatural realm, though even here James makes innumerable provisos. The basic evidence from mystical experience is not, after all, authoritative to outsiders as it is to the mystic himself. The analogies with scientific theorising are recognised by James to be strained and misleading. In the comparable area of psychical research James condemned those scientists who simply dismissed the phenomena, the 'evidence', as spurious without any serious consideration. But he was not himself prepared actually to endorse any such claims. He occupied the uncomfortable, though tenable, position of one who pleads for the case to be made but did not believe that anything had been established. It is not even clear that his envisaged 'science' of religion could offer any help in such a context. For it might simply explain the occurrence of mystical, transcendent, experiences rather than elucidate or support their content.

James really has no ground for that stronger thesis, and might in any case be better to stress the differences rather than the similarities between religion and science. For certainly what he mainly insists on is the strength of the personal experience and the personal faith which that confers.[37] If it can be supposed that the content of such a faith has meaning in some way then James is characteristically unmoved by intellectual arguments against it.

> I need not discredit philosophy by laborious criticism of its arguments. It will suffice if I show that as a matter of history it fails to prove its pretension to be 'objectively' convincing. In fact it does so fail. I believe that the logical reason of man operates in this field of divinity exactly as it has always operated in love, or in patriotism, or in politics, or in any other of the wider affairs of life, in which our passions or our mystical intuitions fix our beliefs beforehand. It finds arguments for our convictions, for it *has* to find them. It amplifies and defines our faith, and dignifies it, and lends it words and plausibility. It hardly ever engenders it; it cannot now secure it.[38]

James is talking here of the failure of the intellectualist attempt to found religion on reason, but he would have taken the same view of its failure to deny religion by reason.

10

Pragmatism and Systematic Philosophy

It was suggested earlier that pragmatism was partially eclipsed behind such movements as logical positivism in philosophy and behaviourism in psychology. Even among pragmatists James himself has sometimes been thought to be over-shadowed by Peirce. For Peirce based his ideas more solidly on logic and language than did James. One commentator, a psychologist, has even said that although James was a first-rate psychologist, he was not in the same class as a philosopher. He is described as 'at best little more than a brilliant and slightly irresponsible amateur'.[1] A similar, but more revealing, judgment was expressed by Russell in an obituary notice when he wrote:

> When full allowance has been made for his healthy and human reversal of the tone and methods of philosophy it will appear even more regrettable that the actual system (or denial of system) with which Professor James later associated his name was of the insufficient sort that it was.[2]

The suggestion is that James's pragmatism, like political pragmatism in general, may be healthy in its critical aspect but has no adequate positive or systematic philosophy to offer.

It is true that pragmatism, and its natural associate empiricism, are often thought to be radically insufficient or incomplete. They often appear to give us less than we originally expected. Hume's discussion of causality, for example, has often been regarded as patently inadequate just because it replaces the ideas of causal power or efficacy with those of a mere constant conjunction and a subjective habit. Of course, merely to insist on this is just to beg the question against Hume, since he offers extended argument to show that there *is* nothing else. In a similar way James's account of truth may seem to focus on our ways of ascribing truth rather than on truth itself. His account of personal identity may seem to concern our ways of determining that identity instead of what constitutes it. Moreover, as Russell's comment indicates, James's view of philosophy itself may seem insufficient both in giving it a role subservient to other disciplines and in its lack, or even denial, of a philosophical system. These natural objections give the impression that James's pragmatism is off-target. It misses the real point.

This would be a serious objection if James were either unaware of such criticisms or incapable of answering them. Russell, in the light of his criticism of James's account of truth, probably believed that that disjunction was true. But it has been noted already that in some contexts James was both aware of, and attempted to rebut, just such objections. He himself stressed the inadequacy of traditional empiricism and the unwelcome consequences of that inadequacy in leading on one side to scepticism, and on the other to transcendentalism. Radical empiricism, with its conjunctive relations and its holism, was specifically designed to make good those traditional defects. James noted also the contrast between how truth is arrived at and what it is, and acknowledged the objection that he had concentrated on the former and missed the point of the latter. But he believed he had answered that objection by saying that his account of truth covered *both* and by stressing that the former was, logically and ontologically, prior to the latter. Similar points might be made about his treatment of the self and of philosophy. In all these cases James's defence, like Hume's, against the charge that he has missed the point, or left something vital out, is that there *is* no further point, and that nothing *has* been left out.

It may nevertheless be said that although James recognised these problems, and offered responses to them, he did not satisfactorily resolve them. I therefore take the opportunity in this final section to pull some threads together by examining summarily three of these contentious issues. These are, first James's improved, radical, empiricism; second, his account of truth; and third, his view of philosophy itself.

1   Radical empiricism

James's radical empiricism provides an interesting criticism of, and alternative to, traditional empiricist ideas. In recent years, in part under a renewed Kantian influence, it has sometimes been supposed that if empiricism is insufficient then it needs to be supplemented with resources of a non-empirical, a priori, kind. To take such a view is to approach the transcendentalism which James believed to be mistaken. He preferred instead to argue for an enrichment of the basic empirical resources of experience. In this way radical empiricism offers in principle to retain the spirit of the traditional doctrine while avoiding its disadvantageous consequences.

Two obstacles, however, stand in the way of accepting James's view. Both have to do with the criterion for separating what is given from what is not, in order to identify those enriched empirical resources. The first objection claims that any such view, like traditional empiricism itself, founders on Wittgenstein's private language argument. For that argument, construed in *one* way, claims that no public language could be based simply on an individual's private experience.[3] If, as the argument suggests, there is no sense in identifying such private resources, then there can be no serious question whether those resources are rich or poor. If it is impossible to characterise them at all then it makes no sense to ask whether they should be characterised in 'conjunctive' or 'atomist' terms.

The second objection arises out of that initial problem. For what we count as basic may vary according to the role we envisage for it. If the task is to show how complex concepts or propositions might have their meanings, or their truth-conditions, elucidated by reference to simpler concepts and propositions, then the simple elements will already form part of a public language. If the task is to show how such items, even the simplest, might be learned from sensory experience, then that latter experience needs to be characterised in some way. The problem then is to justify James's conviction that it should be characterised as 'conjunctive' rather than as 'atomist'.[4]

Wittgenstein's private language argument, in one version, turns on the claimed incommunicability of supposed private sensory experiences. We saw earlier that James, in his account of 'pure experience', refers to the 'speechlessness' of that experience, and to its particularity as a 'this' or 'that' without any further official classification. Yet James is inevitably forced to provide some further account of such an experience, and he does so in his appeal to conjunctive relations and to the neutrally construed intentional contents of that experience. But this apparent conflict may seem only to reinforce the private language argument's insistence on the incoherence of such a view.

Wittgenstein's main line of argument begins with the supposition that a private linguist might give meaning to the terms of his language by associating them with his immediate, private, experience. Given the privacy of that experience the language will then be intelligible to only one person. If it is further supposed that our own language has to be based on such private operations then the outcome will be a scepticism about the communicability and intelligibility of our language. Wittgenstein's claim is that, with certain other assumptions, the initial supposition of such a private language is incoherent, and the language will be incomprehensible not only to outside observers of the private linguist but to the private linguist himself. For if others cannot understand the supposed language, why should the private linguist be able to grasp it? One obvious answer is that he, and only he, can remember its rules and conventions but, as is well known, Wittgenstein argues that such memory claims can be no better founded than the original supposition itself. This is so, not just because memory is fallible,[5] but because in such a case there is in principle no way of checking the correctness of the memory, that is, no way of determining whether or when it *is* fallible. In such circumstances, Wittgenstein argues, whatever seems right to the linguist will be right, that is, the contrast between correctness and incorrectness breaks down. It is a further assumption, perhaps confusedly shared with the opposition, that such a breakdown excludes the possibility of a genuine language.

It was suggested earlier that Wittgenstein was not rejecting an ordinary conception of private experience, but only a conception distorted by certain erroneous assumptions. The argument has nevertheless implications for our understanding of private experience, since the rejection of the distortions enables us to see more clearly what a private experience is. Among the assumptions which define that distorted view are:

(i)   That memory has no need to be independently checkable.

(ii)   That words have a meaning in virtue of their naming objects.

(iii)   That linguistic conventions need make no room for a contrast between correct and incorrect application.

(iv)   That a person's sensory experiences are inaccessible to others.

There is no reason to doubt that James would have agreed with Wittgenstein over (i) and (iii). He, like Wittgenstein, would have rejected both of those assumptions. We saw earlier that James, at one point, got close to accepting (ii), although later he, like Wittgenstein, explicitly rejects it. But James's radical empiricism also rejects (iv), since the account of 'intersections' between experiences makes room for a literally shared, common, but personal experience. The immediate consequence of these attitudes is that James agrees with Wittgenstein in rejecting the assumptions responsible for the distorted conception of a private experience. James is no more liable to that distortion than was Wittgenstein.

Still it may be said that although James is not vulnerable to Wittgenstein's argument he nevertheless differs from Wittgenstein in rejecting (iv). That claim is not obviously correct, but whether it is or not there is a further problem for James about the identification of pure experience. The reason for doubting whether James and Wittgenstein differ even over (iv) is that once the distorted conception of a private experience is rejected, then this makes room for our ordinary conception of a shared experience. Both James and Wittgenstein would agree that the only way to identify experiences is through their intentional contents, and this inevitably involves the apparatus of a public, shared, language. But James, in rejecting (iv), seems to wish to go further. It is his view that the sharing of experiences is actually given to us in the conjunctive relations which link us with a spatial world and its other inhabitants. The publicity of experience, in its reference both to a common physical world and a shared experience of it, belongs to the enriched basic resources of radical empiricism.

If such a view were to be accepted it would have to explain how to identify such given, conjunctive, experiences even where they were not accompanied by any linguistic resource. It would have, further, to explain how more complex aptitudes, including relevant linguistic abilities, might develop. In the former basic case the linguistic resource has to be supplied by the observer, and theoriser, of such experience, but is not matched by a comparable skill on the part of the experiencer. James's distinction between having an experience and reporting it, and the consequent errors of the psychologist's fallacy, make it plain that he had some apparatus to meet these requirements. In a particular case, such as the experience of space, what would be needed is a means of distinguishing between creatures which occupy and function in space, those which additionally recognise a three-dimensional, 'voluminous', context but have no further developed spatial or linguistic aptitudes, and those which, like ourselves, have further developed complex metrical and formal ways of elucidating and exploiting that basic experience. For James the 'voluminousness' of space is given; the feeling of distance, as he says, is 'nothing if it is not a feeling'.[6] But the complex, articulate, further devices, such as accurate measurement or the elaboration of formal geometries, are not given and are not part of the basic conjunctive experience.

What is plainly necessary in drawing these distinctions is some reference both to behavioural operation and physiological apparatus. An entity which operates within a three-dimensional background but has no evident means of experiencing it could not qualify for the ascription of such conjunctive relations. One which additionally had some requisite sensory apparatus but showed no ability to make fine discriminations, and had no language, might qualify for the ascription of such relations, but not for the more developed metrical or linguistic skills that we possess. There may be difficulties in pursuing such distinctions, but it is hard to believe that they cannot be made. James's own account of cognitive development in the *Principles* relies on just such discrimination. It is also true that such an account puts less emphasis on linguistic aptitude than philosophers commonly do, but it is part of James's psychological background to note degrees of ability in dealing with spatial and other matters which are not necessarily tied to language. As we saw earlier James believed that the appeal to language was essential in the theory of such experience, but he did not think that it was correct to infer from features of such a theoretical language to corresponding features of the experience itself. When Davidson, for example, infers from the 'interpretative' context of a language for describing beliefs that such a feature belongs also to the believers' experience he commits what James would regard as a fallacious step. James clearly believed language to be of great importance, but he did not believe that it was the only, or even the most important, aptitude in an account of cognitive development.

If we give such an account of James's radical empiricist views, then we clearly put him close to developmental psychology, and to learning theory. This may finally encourage the suggestion that his interests remain peripheral to epistemology; that here, too, he has missed the point. The challenge must then be to find some role for epistemology which James makes no room for. There is, of course, room for theories of meaning, but James has made some allowance for this. There is room for theories of language learning, but there is no reason to doubt that James could accommodate these too. What seems most obviously missing is any reference to that traditional response to scepticism which tries to provide, and then build upon, indubitable foundations for knowledge. James does not overlook such a project, but he clearly thinks it worthless. This is, first, because there are no such indubitable foundations; and, second, because scepticism is ultimately a temperamental attitude not susceptible of intellectual treatment. We are left with a position which fits naturally into what Wittgenstein said of epistemology in the *Tractatus*: 'Theory of knowledge is the philosophy of psychology'.[7] If James's radical empiricism misses the point of traditional epistemology in this way, it may be because he saw more clearly than other philosophers the weaknesses of that traditional enquiry.

2   The theory of truth

In outlining James's theory of truth I noted that James was, or intended to be, by his own lights a realist; that he did not exclude processes we normally call scientific verification or testing; that he was prepared to concede a reference to absolute truth as a regulative marker for the defeasibility of our ordinary truth ascriptions; that he then thought such a marker depended upon the latter operations rather than the other way round; and that he admitted a distinction between 'how truth was arrived at' and 'what truth is' but claimed that his theory dealt with *both* within the framework of that earlier priority. He conceded also that the 'logic of science', and so any account of the working of our beliefs, was as yet incomplete; but he looked to his own programme for the completion of that task rather than to any traditional enquiries. The problem here, too, is whether James has really missed the target, left out of account, or misplaced, some key element in the concept of truth. We can envisage a strong and a weak set of complaints against James's theory. According to the former the account omits some factor in what constitutes truth; according to the latter nothing may have been left out but the pieces are assembled in the wrong order.

Two initial points might be made. James was, of course, opposing the conceptions of truth familiar to him, and in particular that monistic conception of an absolute, final, definitive truth which he associated with Bradley. It was noted earlier that James saw no reason to think that there was any such unique, final truth, and in this he sides with Quine against his fellow pragmatist Peirce. But apart from that consideration James also held that the notion of a definitive truth was of minimal importance beside the everyday decisions and actions, governed rationally by the working of our beliefs, which provide the basis for our ascription of truth. James's pragmatism, rightly, saw the absolutist conception as a marker for the defeasibility of our practical acknowledgment of truths in the plural. The question is whether such a notion has any other value or importance.

James's own terminology, secondly, has already been admitted to be confused in the assimilation of cognitive and affective beliefs. The term 'satisfaction' is used sometimes in a narrow sense to signify the emotional appeal characteristically attached to affective beliefs; but it is also some-times used in a wider sense to stand for that overall acceptance of beliefs which balances narrow satisfaction against other considerations. 'Verifi-cation' is used most often in a conventional sense in which it indicates the characteristic testing operations on which the acceptance of scientific, cognitive, beliefs depends. But if James wishes to use 'true' to stand for what was called overall acceptance, then the cognate term 'verification' should also be used for the acceptance determining operations of affective beliefs, as for the narrower emotional factors in the acceptance of any belief, whether cognitive or affective. The most natural way to clear up such terms would be to use 'acceptance' for wide 'satisfaction' and to restrict 'verification', as we normally do, to the narrow, cognitive, case. But it may then be argued that the central fault in James's account stands out quite clearly. James is interested in what I have called 'acceptance', which includes but goes beyond the confines of truth. His theory is not a theory of *truth*, but of that wider notion of acceptance. Perhaps he has not totally missed the target, but he scores an outer rather than a bull.

If we ask what the cash-value of that point is, then one answer is obvious. It is that what is true, strictly speaking, corresponds to reality, and that it is only cognitive beliefs which correspond to reality when they are true. Since, on such a view, non-cognitive beliefs have no such correspondence, whether we accept them or not, it is simply mistaken to assimilate the two broad kinds of belief under the umbrella of truth. Such a view is a natural response to James's account, but it suffers from three major defects.

First James, as we saw, was quite prepared to admit the notions of a reality, and of correspondence with reality, but only within the framework of the general working of our beliefs. It is, therefore, just a mistake to suppose that James excludes any such reference. Second, James rightly notes that even within the cognitive context the notion of correspondence with reality needs to be qualified for 'ejective' or theoretical beliefs. The question of deciding, even within this cognitive sphere, which beliefs correspond to reality when true is, for James, the question of marking the functions of the relevant concepts in those beliefs, and ordering the

188

priorities among them. Once those priorities are clear we may choose to draw a line between certain 'basic' beliefs and others so that only the former strictly correspond to reality.

James's own tolerant ontology, like Grice's, and his holistic tendencies are admittedly hostile to such a division. His suggestion seems to be that once we show the order of priorities there is no merit in devising some criterion which distinguishes between beliefs which do and those which do not correspond to reality. At the very least, though, some such criterion is needed, and it remains quite unclear what that criterion should be. Third, such a programme of demonstrating the priorities among beliefs was also envisaged by James for non-cognitive beliefs as well. It was such a programme towards which he gestures in his accounts of moral beliefs and their 'emergence' from certain natural phenomena. In this case, too, James indicates no preference for drawing a line between those beliefs which do and those which do not correspond to reality. It is true that James does not pursue this programme in detail, but the general task is outlined. It is also true that the programmatic nature of his idea makes it difficult to test whether there is any *other* consideration which James has left out.

One answer which it is initially natural to give in the light of recent ideas turns on the development of a formal truth condition theory. Within such a theory, it may be said, the orders of priority and dependence among concepts and propositions will be exhibited in a systematic way. James certainly lacks any overt recognition of such a theory, but it would surely be wrong to think that he can make no room for it. Indeed, if the characterisation of such a theory is fair, then it might meet the requirements of the programme James himself envisages. There is plainly some difference between the style of such a formal theory and what James describes as the working of our beliefs, but it would be natural to regard such a truth condition theory as a formal representation of that working. James had no reason to reject the idea of a formal theory of truth, any more than he would have had reason to reject the idea of a formal economic theory. In both cases, however, he would have insisted that the formal theories be developed in the light of, and be answerable to, the practical operations in question. In the former case these will be the practical operations in which we accept or reject, challenge, modify, or test our beliefs; in the latter case they will be the ordinary practical transactions of our economic life. It is for this reason that he insists on the logical and ontological priority of those practical affairs over the formal theories.

In recent philosophy debates about realism and anti-realism have turned not only on the development of such formal theories of truth, but also on the alternative logics which might be employed in them. In particular realists have been associated with the use of classical two-valued logic, while anti-realists have been associated with the use of non-classical systems such as intuitionistic logic, where the principle of bivalence does not hold. The suggestion has been that the former suppose a determinacy in our view of reality which the latter lack.[8] Although James knew nothing of such debates, and envisaged no such choice between logics or associated truth condition theories, his own view of these issues is not difficult to reconstruct. In so far as such theories have a function and work in relation to some set of beliefs James would presumably be ready to admit their value. In particular if such theories have an application to the semantics of natural language, then he would have treated alternative theories as rival hypotheses between which linguists and others have to choose. But he would have been inclined to question the use of such distinctions as a criterion for determining what is real and what is not. He would, at least, have wanted some assurance that there was a genuine cash-value in such disputes about reality, in case they are independent of any testable hypothesis. Without some clear and agreed criterion for what is real there is a danger that such disputes might trespass on the ground of idle metaphysics. James's pragmatic attitude is sensitive to that danger and offers guidance in avoiding it. In so doing his philosophy at least does not carelessly overlook or arbitrarily dismiss those issues.

3 Pragmatism and systematic philosophy

In the cases so far considered James's philosophy is not incomplete or deficient simply through oversights. The alleged gaps, and the supposedly missed targets, face a deliberate pragmatic challenge to find some clear function for the missing items. It is not at all clear that such a challenge can be met; but it is even less clear that the challenge itself is inappropriate or unjustified. That latter claim might be made out if James had simply misunderstood the nature of philosophy itself, and that is indeed suggested by Russell's complaint that pragmatism is unsystematic. For if it turned out that philosophy itself had some distinctive subject-matter about which it could be systematic, then James's conception of philosophy would be incomplete.

In one way it is surprising that Russell should have made such a complaint. For his own view of the relation between philosophy and other disciplines, expressed in his accounts of logical atomism, is very like that of James himself. The principal difference between them lies in Russell's recognition of formal logic as the principal tool of philosophy. But we should distinguish between philosophy's having a distinctive method, in logic, and its having a distinctive subject-matter. Perhaps Russell's complaint derived mainly from his logical atomist conviction that the methods of logic could also yield an adequate metaphysics. Certainly James's lack of logic prevented him from recognising the importance of that formal method, and his pragmatic conception of philosophy questioned the development of a distinctively philosophical or systematic metaphysics. As a matter of history Russell's attempt in that period to construct such a metaphysics, however, has not been generally accepted; and Wittgenstein's apparent later repudiation of such a systematic approach led, indeed, to a conception of philosophy which is more like James's pragmatism than Russell's atomist metaphysics.

Recently, however, that more pragmatist conception has been challenged in a paper of Michael Dummett's, 'Can Analytical Philosophy Be Systematic and Should it Be?'. Dummett rests his case on the distinction, noted above, between two ways of being systematic. To be systematic (1) is to 'issue in an articulated theory', while to be systematic (2) is to 'have agreed methods'. Dummett believes that philosophy can and should be systematic in both ways, and he criticises both Austin and Wittgenstein for their rejection of such a view. Since both Austin and Wittgenstein share the pragmatist view with James, Dummett's criticisms can readily be seen as objections to James's account.

Dummett believes that not all disciplines have been, or have claimed to be, systematic in both ways. Philosophy itself has often claimed to be systematic (1), in its construction of metaphysical systems, but it has not, until recently, been able to claim plausibly that it is also systematic (2). History, by contrast, is systematic (2), but not systematic (1), since there is no evident room for a distinctively historical theory. That latter claim does not deny that historians may appeal to theories in explaining their historical data; it does deny the suggestion that those theories are specifically 'historical' rather than, say, economic, or sociological. Dummett thinks it surprising that philosophy has not yet become systematic in *both* ways, though he believes that it has now the ability to achieve this. He says:

> If philosophy is regarded as one, perhaps the most important, sector in the quest for truth . . . it is amazing that it should not yet have established a generally accepted methodology, generally accepted criteria of success, and therefore a body of definitively achieved results.[9]

In order to defend his view Dummett appeals to the development of philosophy since Frege in order to show the importance of the theory of meaning as the central topic of philosophy. Such a topic has lent itself to formal logical treatment, and Dummett evidently regards Frege's interest in that topic and his use of those methods as a signpost to a systematic philosophy in *both* senses. He cites in opposition to such a view Austin's piecemeal efforts at linguistic clarification, and Wittgenstein's official ban on any role for philosophy other than that of an ad hoc therapy. Neither of these philosophers believed in the development of a distinctively *philosophical* system. Both Austin and Wittgenstein, like James and even in some respects Russell, thought that philosophical clarification might be a preliminary to systematic development in other disciplines. They did not envisage any such systematic development within philosophy itself.

Much of what Dummett says of the importance of Frege's work, and of the development of philosophy after Frege, is scarcely questionable. His claim that philosophy of language is *the* central branch of philosophy has been questioned, but I shall not query that claim. For the attempt to allocate such priorities to different branches or topics in philosophy seems to me largely futile, and such a dispute in any case conceals the central thesis in Dummett's paper. For that thesis says that philosophy should be systematic in both senses, and this might be so, even if it was thought that philosophy of language was not the only, or the most important, branch of the subject. Opposed to that central thesis are the views of Austin, Wittgenstein, and James, for whom there is no distinctively philosophical subject-matter for the discipline to be systematic about. For them the central role of philosophy was to prepare confused or unclear thoughts for transmission to other disciplines which might then systematically develop them on a clear basis. For them the best that philosophy can achieve is to hand over relevant ideas in a clear and testable shape. The belief that there is some topic in which philosophy itself has a distinctive or unique interest, and which it might develop systematically is, on such a view, just an illusion. Indeed, Wittgenstein goes further in suggesting that such a 'scientific' pretension is one of the deepest illusions of traditional philosophy. Dummett recognises that the perennial drive for system in philosophy has been regarded as illusory, and he responds in the end by saying only that 'Time will tell'. He has, however, probably made out the best case for a systematic philosophy, and if it were accepted, then James's conception of the subject would be seriously incomplete. As in the other cases, however, it may be doubted whether Dummett's view is correct.

There is one centrally weak part of Dummett's argument. It was no part of Wittgenstein's, or Austin's, or James's view to deny that the topics considered by philosophers were capable of systematic development. All believed that these topics might be systematically developed by non-philosophers. What they thought was impossible and illusory was the idea that some such topic might belong distinctively or uniquely to philosophy, so that no other discipline could be involved in its development. The suggestion is that philosophy has no subject-matter of its own. Its concerns, if they are legitimate, overlap with those of other disciplines in such a way that it is their role systematically to develop the theories in that area. The point can be made very plainly in relation to theories of meaning, for these naturally belong to linguistics rather than to philosophy itself. That is not to say that philosophers may not contribute to such theories, as Frege and Dummett himself have. But it does not follow from such a contribution that the topic belongs distinctively to philosophy, and such a claim is in any case independently unplausible. It is a remarkable gap in Dummett's argument that he makes no concession to this aspect of the development of theories of language.

Such a weakness may seem to reveal only a curious fact about the development of philosophy and its interest in language. Dummett's suggestion that time will tell offers the hope that perhaps philosophy has changed, and that its future development will make apparent that it is now on the path of a science of the kind Dummett envisages. But it can be argued that James's view is not just a contingent limitation on the scope and development of philosophy so much as an integral part of the conception of the subject. On this view there could no more be a systematic distinctive philosophy than there could be a distinctively historical theory. In the case of history Dummett seems to concede that that denial is not just a curious fact about the subject's development, but a central part of the conception of the discipline. If we accept in this way that there is no room for a distinctively historical theory, then it is an illusion to expect that future contingencies may show otherwise. The difficulty is that the same view might be taken of the limitations of philosophy itself. The very conception of these disciplines may impose restrictions on their scope which exclude the idea of a distinctively philosophical subject-matter, or a distinctively historical law. It might be replied that to conceive these disciplines in such a restrictive way is to beg the question against Dummett. That such a conception is at least not arbitrary or just question-begging can be seen from the fact that Dummett's own preferred subject-matter, the theory of meaning, belongs at least as much to linguistics as to philosophy.

If we view James's pragmatic conception of philosophy in this way, then on this final point his position is neither indefensible nor even plainly wrong. Once again there is a characteristic response to be made on James's behalf against the claim that something vital has been left out. It is that despite the naturalness of such an objection what is supposed to have been omitted is at least contentious and vulnerable to a pragmatic challenge. That challenge shows at least that the alleged gap is not simply obvious. It may even be able to demonstrate that it is an illusion.

Notes

Books of James's referred to in notes

P	*The Principles of Psychology* 2 Vols. Macmillan 1918.
Ps	*Psychology: A Briefer Course.* Macmillan 1908.
APU	*A Pluralistic Universe.* Longmans Green 1909.
TWB	*The Will To Believe.* Longmans Green 1899.
ERE	*Essays in Radical Empiricism.* Longmans Green 1912.
VRE	*The Varieties of Religious Experience.* Longmans Green 1902.
Prag	*Pragmatism.* Harvard University Press 1978.
TMOT	*The Meaning of Truth.* Harvard University Press 1978.
SPP	*Some Problems of Philosophy.* Greenwood Press 1968.

Unpublished manuscripts in the James Archive, Houghton Library, Harvard have the general number b.Ms. Am.1092. The correspondence is prefixed by A and other manuscripts by B. I have then given the item numbers after these prefixes. Unpublished material from the James archive is quoted here by permission of the Houghton Library and of Alexander James.

1 Introduction

1 *Writings of William James*, ed. J.J. McDermott, New York, 3–9.

2 A questionnaire sent by Pratt to James drew from him the comment that he believed in God, 'but *emphatically* not from any argument. Rather because I need it, so it must be true'. B 4474. Elsewhere James described what he called a 'faith-ladder' which had the following steps: 'It is fit to be true; it would be well if it were true; it might be true; it may be true; it ought to be true; it must be true; it shall be true.' B 4542.

3 James, however, described his Americanism as a 'tender plant'. In a letter to Stumpf, December, 1895, he wrote: 'It unsettles my Americanism (that tender plant) to go too often abroad.' A 3778–3811. His attitude, though, still differed significantly from that of his brother Henry.

4 *La Personnalité de W. James*, M. Le Breton, Paris, 1929. Quoted in Perry, *Thought and Character of William James, (TCWJ)* Cambridge, 1935, Vol.1 383.

5 Perry, op.cit., Vol. 1, 233. See Ch. XII and XIII.

6 Letter to Münsterberg, 1891. James archive, Harvard, A 3263-3305.

7 M. Knight, *William James*, London, 1950, 30.

8 J.W. Anderson, 'The Worst Sort of Melancholy', *Harvard Library Bulletin*, October, 1982.

9 *Ps* Preface iii.

10 In a letter to Münsterberg, in 1897, he wrote, 'I see that my future interests will lie with philosophy'. A 3263–3305.

11 Perry, op. cit. Vol. 1, 338.

12 Hartshorne and Weiss, *Collected Papers of C.S. Peirce*, Vol. V. Harvard, 1934, 223 note.

13 *P* Vol. 1, 421.

14 Perry, op. cit., Vol. 2, 583.

15 I use the terms 'cognitive' and 'non-cognitive' (or 'affective') to stand only for an intuitive distinction between, for example, factual and moral or religious (evaluative) beliefs. The terms are not ideal, since James wishes ultimately to assimilate the two classes, while the natural vocabulary tends to separate them.

16 James claimed to connect his own term 'pragmatism' with Kant's account of 'pragmatic belief', *Critique of Pure Reason*, B 852.

17 James's official distaste for Hegel and later Hegelian writers was expressed forcibly in 'On Some Hegelisms' in *TWB*. Unofficially he suggested to the editor of *Mind*, Croom Robertson, the following mischievous idea. 'Why don't you have a special neo-Hegelian department in *Mind*, like the agricultural department or the childrens' department in our newspapers, which educated readers skip?' Letters to Hodgson, A 969–998. James contrasted Hegel unfavourably with Bergson, whom he calls a 'magician'. See also James's treatment of Bergson in *APU*.

18 'Philosophical Conceptions and Practical Results', in McDermott, op. cit. 361–2.

19 Claparède, *Archives de Psychologie*, Vol. X, No. 37, Sept. 1910, 99.

20 J.B. Watson, *Behaviourism*, New York, 1924, 110. Watson had other damning comments to make. E.g. 'Nearly everyone is familiar with James's classic chapter on the stream of consciousness. We have all loved that chapter. Today it seems as much out of touch with modern psychology as the stage-coach would be on New York's Fifth Avenue.' *Behaviourism*, 137. And on page 140: 'Nearly forty years ago James gave to the psychology of the emotions (a theory) from which it has only recently begun to recover.'

21 Russell, *The Analysis of Mind*, Allen and Unwin, 1921, Lecture I, and in *The Philosophy of Logical Atomism*.

22 Levinson, *Science, Metaphysics, and the Chance of Salvation*. Scholars Press, 1978, introduction.

23 James's public adherence to pragmatism is sometimes dated from his 1898 Berkeley address 'Philosophical Conceptions and Practical Results', though both the *Principles* and *The Will To Believe* were published before that.

24 *APU* 311 ff.

25 Russell associates James with 'neutral monism' both in *The Analysis of Mind* and *The Philosophy of Logical Atomism*, though James does not himself use the term.

26 Milek Capek, 'The Reappearance of the Self in the Last Philosophy of William James', *Philosophical Review*, 1953.

27 A.J. Ayer, *The Origins of Pragmatism*, Macmillan, 1968, 290. *SPP*, 106.

28 *Prag* 106.

29 *Prag* 13. Ayer, op. cit., 192.

30 James wrote of Myers's 'investigation of the subliminal' that it was 'the most important definite investigation opened of late in psychology', but I cannot date that comment.

31 J. Barzun, *A Stroll with William James*, Harper and Row, 1983.

32 *TWB*, 319.

33 B. Wilshire, *William James and Phenomenology*, Indiana, 1968; Ayer, op. cit.; M. Ford, *William James's Philosophy*, Amherst, 1982.

34 Examples of James's lack of pomposity are not difficult to find. It formed part of that 'unstiffening' process with which he believed pragmatism confronted the fashionable monist absolutism of Bradley and Royce. It is an interesting measure of the task James faced that in *The Times* obituary his style was said to be 'disfigured at times by a crassness of metaphor and the intrusion of slang'. On his election to the Académie des Sciences Morales et Politiques he wrote in a letter to Peirce: 'La renommée vient à ceux qui ont la patience de vivre, et s'accroît à raison de leur imbécilité.' (Fame comes to those who have the patience to survive; and it grows in proportion to their imbecility.) A 3370–3427.

35 *TMOT* 247; *P* II, 9.

36 Perry quotes from a letter to Schiller in which 'technical philosophy' is described by James as 'a crime against the human race'. *TCWJ*. Vol. 2, 287.

2 Pragmatic Method

1 *Prag* 37.

2 *TMOT* 172–3.

3 *Prag* 6.

4 *TMOT* 172–3.

5 In a letter James also underlined the close link between pragmatism and radical empiricism, when he wrote: 'I am sure that, be it in the end judged true or false, it is essential to the evolution of clearness in philosophic thought that *someone* should defend a pluralistic empiricism radically.' *Letters of William James*, ed. Henry James, Vol. II, 203–4. Quoted in J.J. MacDermott, *The Writings of William James*.

6 *VRE* 444.

7 *Prag* 29; *VRE* 444–5. James formulates the same principle differently in other places. In *SPP* 60, for example, he wrote 'The meaning of a concept may always be found if not in some sensible particulars which it directly designates, then in some particular difference in the course of human experience which its being true will make.'

8 *Prag* 31–2.

9 *Prag* 32. 'Pragmatism agrees with positivism in its disdain for verbal solutions, useless questions, and metaphysical abstractions.'

10 *Prag* 31; *SPP* 100–1. At *Prag* 52 he says: 'In every metaphysical dispute some practical issue is involved.'

11 *Prag* 28.

12 James invokes the notions of immanence and transcendence at various places, e.g. *ERE* 224, *TMOT* 234–5.

13 *Prag* 32.

14 *Prag* 28.

15 *TMOT* 204; *Prag* 14.

16 *TMOT* 273–4.

17 James says of the traditional candidates for foundations: 'To hold any of them as if it should never be re-interpretable or corrigible I believe to be a tremendously mistaken attitude.' *TWB* 14.

18 *TMOT* 238.

19 Such imagery is to be found, for example, at *ERE* 52, 86 and *Prag* 46.

20 *ERE* 3.

21 *ERE* 136. At *ERE* 70 James says: 'Conceptions, kinds, are teleological instruments.' At *P* 2, 461 he treats what he calls 'conceptions' as functions. James does not make quite clear what he means by a function, but seems to conceive it in an epistemological or psychological way. I have found no references to Frege in James's writings, though he discusses Cantor in *SPP*, but there is some connection between James's idea and Frege's treatment of concepts and functions.

22 *P* I, Ch. VII. See Chapter 7 below.

23 *Prag* 27–8.

24 *Prag* 29–30.

25 H.S. Thayer, *Meaning and Action*, Indianapolis, 1968. Ch. 2.

26 *Prag* 27–29, 61. 'The pragmatic method . . . is to try to interpret each notion by tracing its respective practical consequences.'

27 One of the issues arising from Quine's 'Two Dogmas of Empiricism' turns on the question whether we should accept our intuitive distinction between analytic and synthetic truth and base a linguistic theory on that distinction; or whether we should abandon the distinction if, as Quine believed, no linguistic theory could accommodate it.

28 G.E. Moore, 'A Proof of an External World', and 'Refutation of Idealism', in *Philosophical Papers*, London, 1959. In other respects James is more like Quine than Moore. For he accorded a priority to common sense over metaphysics, but a priority to science over common sense. *Prag.* Lecture VIII.

29 *TMOT* 269. James actually has 'automatic sweetheart'.

30 *Prag* 54–56.

31 In Chapter 9.

32 Wittgenstein, *Philosophical Investigations*.

33 Russell, 'Logical Atomism' in *Logic and Knowledge*, ed. Marsh, 339 and 341. And *The Philosophy of Logical Atomism*, in *Logic and Knowledge*, ed. Marsh, 281. Russell puts the point succinctly in the latter passage. 'I believe the only difference between science and philosophy is that science is what you more or less know and philosophy is what you do not know. Philosophy is that part of science which at present people choose to have opinions about. Therefore every advance in knowledge robs philosophy of some problems. . . .' Russell

leaves something out, namely the idea that some simply factual advances may have no bearing on any philosophical issue, though this might be qualified by a Quinean holism. But the conviction that the two sets of disciplines *overlap* is common to Russell and James. Austin, *Philosophical Papers*, 'If's and Can's', outlines a similar view. See Chapter 10.

34 H.P. Grice, 'Meaning', *Philosophical Review*, 1957. See also papers in *Philosophy of Language*, ed. J. Searle, OUP, 1969.

35 Wittgenstein, *Philosophical Investigations*, 43. Wittgenstein makes many references, direct and indirect, to James's psychology both in *Philosophical Investigations*, and in his *Remarks in the Philosophy of Psychology*.

36 At *P* 1, 275.

37 At *SPP* 59 James specifically allows for the inclusion of deliberative consequences. 'These (consequences) may lie either in the way of making us think or in the way of making us act.'

38 F.P. Ramsey, 'Facts and Propositions', in *Foundations*, ed. D.H. Mellor, 57.

39 The purist view is that Wittgenstein himself canvassed no positive theory of meaning, in line with his ban on confusing philosophy with other disciplines. This would make his therapy and James's very similar at the weakest end of the spectrum.

40 Quine, op. cit., argued for this generally on the grounds that ordinary meaning was 'intensional' while the appropriate theory to account for it was standard 'extensional' logic.

3 The Theory of Truth

1 R. Walker in *Mind*, January 1985 draws some distinction between a criterion for truth, and what truth 'consists in', but he does not make clear what the latter amounts to. It was a natural objection to James's account that he dealt more with how we arrive at truth than with what truth is, but he noted, and attempted to answer this in *TMOT*, Ch. VIII, where he says that the pragmatic theory deals with *both*, but treats the former as prior to the latter. 'Intellectualist truth is only pragmatic truth in posse. Truth in posse means only truths in act . . . and these latter take precedence in the order of logic as well as in that of being.' *TMOT* 277. A similar distinction between 'how we determine personal identity' and what it 'consists in' is appealed to by Parfit, *Reasons and Persons*. See Chapter 5.

2 Tarski, *Logic, Semantics, and Metamathematics*, OUP, 1956. Austin, *Philosophical Papers*, 'Truth', 'Unfair to Facts'. There is controversy about treating Tarski's account as a 'correspondence' theory, and this reflects the wide variety of theories, semantic, epistemological, ontological, that might be included under such a vague title.

3 G.E. Moore, *Proceedings of the Aristotelian Society*, 1907–8; Russell, *Albany Review*, January 1908, *Edinburgh Review*, April, 1909.

4 *TMOT* 313.

5 *Prag* 110.

6 *Prag* 110.

7 *Prag* 107. In a letter to Bradley of July 16, 1904, J. Kenna 'Ten Unpublished Letters from James to Bradley' *Mind* July, 1966, James speaks of a reconcilia-

tion between his humanism and the absolute. 'Nothing debars you from believing in our humanism bag and baggage – you need only throw your absolute round it . . .' He uses the same image at *TMOT* 210. On the same track in a letter to Royce, in 1908, James wrote: 'I'm sorry you say that we don't see truth in the same light, for the only thing we see differently is the absolute, and surely such a trifle as that is not a thing for two gentlemen to be parted by.' A 3594–3641.

8 *Prag* 106.

9 *TWB* 76.

10 Of a discussion with Holt on truth James wrote: 'For the pragmatist there is an ultimate reality concerning which the truth is to be obtained. He *assumes* the truth is there. But what is the use of talking of ultimate truth? It is such a purely abstract ideal that it serves only as a vanishing point.' B 4461–4464.

11 *Prag* 100.

12 W.K. Clifford, *Lectures and Essays*, Macmillan, 1879, 72–3, seems to have invented the term, which James took over. *ERE* 68, 73, 83. James sometimes distinguishes between 'ejects' and 'unobservables'.

13 *Prag* 103.

14 Quine himself puts the point in this way. 'A theory will imply a lot of observation-conditionals . . . each of which says that if certain observable conditions are met, then a certain observable event will occur. But, as Duhem has emphasised, these observation conditionals are implied by the theory as a whole. If any of them proves false, then the theory is false, but on the face of it there is no saying which of the component sentences of the theory is to blame.' 'The Pragmatists' Place in Empiricism'. This consideration was important in arguments rejecting the logical positivists' verification theory of meaning. See note 31, Chapter 9. James refers to Duhem at *SPP* 90, note.

15 *Prag* 99–100.

16 *Prag* 104.

17 *Prag* 38–39.

18 *Prag* 97–99.

19 It was, no doubt, this kind of consideration which attracted James's attention to the passage quoted at the start of the book from Montaigne's 'L'Apologie de Raymond Sebond'.

20 James makes this point quite explicitly in a letter to Perry, in 1907, when he says that *both* intellectual *and* emotional satisfactions count for truth. A 3429–3472.

21 *Prag* 97–98.

22 Ayer, op. cit., 201.

23 In a letter to Royce, in 1910, James wrote: 'I'm glad it's up to you now to defend my doctrine against the stupidity of others. I don't believe the fault has been with the inconceivable obscurity of my exposition. I see more and more that it lies with the unfamiliarity to readers of the genuinely concrete way of looking at things.' A 3594–3641.

24 Russell, *History of Western Philosophy*, 845. 'Transatlantic Truth', *Albany Review* January, 1908, 400, quoted *TMOT* 312. 'Pragmatism'. *Edinburgh Review*, April, 1909.

25 *TMOT* 220.

26 It has been argued that even synonyms may not always be substituted 'salva veritate' in belief contexts. If that case can be made out, then even with Russell's assumption about the synonymy of the two expressions the inference would be invalid and James's position defensible. But I do not think that James was defending his case in that way.

27 *TMOT* 315.

28 *TMOT* 318.

29 Russell, *TMOT 318*; Pratt, *TMOT* 258–9; Taylor, *Prag* 109; Rickert, *Prag* 109; Bradley, *TMOT* 210.

4   Extended Truth

1 *TMOT 189.*

2 *P 2* 551.

3 *TWB* 114. James also characteristically calls beliefs 'rules for action' *VRE* 444, *Prag* 28–9.

4 Perry, op. cit., 1 475.

5 *TWB* 29 note.

6 Though the slogan has been influential in this way, it is still ambiguous.

7 D. Davidson, 'Thought and Talk', in *Mind and Language*, ed. S. Guttenplan, OUP, 1975, 12. Also in *Inquiries into Truth and Interpretation*.

8 Ibid. 22.

9 This is a version from James's unpublished manuscripts in the Houghton Library, Harvard, B 4572. Other versions are given in *P* 1, 196–7.

10 I make only a weak claim here, that the argument presented is not compelling. Davidson outlines other ideas in *Truth and Interpretation* which might be used to support his conclusion. But if they are needed for that support, then the argument as presented is inconclusive. The argument has also recently been criticised by H.A. Lewis, 'Content and Community'. *Proceedings of the Aristotelian Society*, Supp. Vol. 1985.

11 H.P. Grice, 'Method in Philosophical Psychology'. *Proceedings of the American Philosophical Association*, 1975.

12 Ibid. 25.

13 Ibid. 39. There are other striking links between Grice's position in this paper, and James's own attitude, although Grice does not mention James. Both have a tolerant ontology, for example, which James expresses by saying, *SPP*, 101, 'Anything is real of which we find ourselves obliged to take account in any way whatsoever'; and which Grice endorses by keeping 'open house' for 'all sorts and conditions of entities'. He adds: 'Provided I can see them at work . . . I do not find them queer or mysterious at all . . . To fangle a new ontological Marxism . . . they work, therefore they exist.'

14 Russell, *The Analysis of Mind*, 65, 75–6.

15 G.P. Baker and P.M.S. Hacker, *Scepticism, Rules, and Language*. Oxford, 1985, 108.

16 Ibid. 108–9.

17 H.P. Grice, see previous reference Chapter 2 note 28.

18 James endorses this view of Santayana's in several places, e.g. *ERE* 218.

19 B. Loar, *Mind and Meaning*, CUP 1981; and 'Ramsey's Theory of Belief and

Truth' in *Prospects for Pragmatism*, ed. D.H. Mellor, CUP, 1980.

20 *Prospects for Pragmatism* 50.

21 Ibid. 55.

22 It would certainly be premature to think that James's 'extended' view has been established by these later theorists. Still the important point is that James's theory has this form, and that the resulting programme is not simply vulnerable to the conventional disparity between 'true' and 'expedient'.

5 Radical Empiricism

1 *TMOT* 172–3.

2 *P* 2, Ch. XXVIII.

3 *Prag* 52.

4 James identifies one difference between empiricism and rationalism in terms of the former's emphasis on parts of experience and the latter's emphasis on experience as a whole. *ERE* 52. But the difference was one of degree of emphasis, and it was plainly not James's intention to forbid empiricists to place an emphasis on the whole of experience. Indeed his own holism was specifically designed to rectify such a distortion in traditional atomist empiricism.

5 These principles might be applied in several related, but different, ways. They might be used to build a formal learning theory, or a theory of meaning, or a theory of the type outlined by Grice in his paper on philosophical psychology.

6 Russell makes such appeals in his lectures on logical atomism, as does James, e.g. in *P* 1, 453.

7 Kant's requirement was not merely that something other than sensory particulars was required, for that would be compatible with the claim that some concepts are also required, though the concepts themselves might be derivable from the sensory experience. The requirement was that some elements, concepts and intuitions, were required which were not derivable from that sensory experience.

8 This is a term used in L. Stevenson, *The Metaphysics of Experience*, OUP, 1984.

9 Kant might be viewed differently as one who adds extra synthetic material to the basic content of empirical experience, and he will then look quite like James. The obvious drawback here is that Kant's extra material is a priori even though synthetic. James would not have accepted this, so it is probably better to indicate Kant's view as I have in the text.

10 *P* 1, 243ff., *SPP* 200, and in many other places.

11 Ayer, op. cit. 225f., ascribes an extreme form of empiricism to James.

12 *P* 1, 245 note.

13 *ERE* 103.

14 *P* 1, 245.

15 On the 'great continua' *ERE* 94; Space *P* 2, 135-6, Time, *P* 1, 605-7; elsewhere, *ERE* 44–5, 108, *SPP* 85ff.

16 *SPP* 101.

17 *P* 2, Chapter XX.

18 Ayer, op. cit., 229, ascribes a straightforward analytic reductionism to James, even for 'ejects', such as theoretical terms. But James's view of the latter was

rather that their meaning arises through the role or function they have in some theory, and not that they can be simply eliminated in favour of observables. Doubt about this case, and the appeal to 'functions', make it doubtful also whether James envisaged a phenomenalistic reductionism.

19 The notion of 'reduction' is now regarded as ambiguous. A first move must be to distinguish 'analytic' from 'ontological' reduction. In the former some item of type B is supposed to be replaceable by some complex arrangement of other items of type A. In the latter this may not be so even though in some way B-type things owe their existence, or provenance, to A-type things, rather than the other way round. Further points might distinguish between types and tokens. James's general appeal to 'functional' analysis, as in the 'extended' account of truth, is closer to the latter than to the former. Even here, though, the suggestion must be qualified by reference to James's tolerant ontology, cited above. (Note 16)

20 *P* 2, 5.

21 *P* 2, 9.

22 *P* 1, 231.

23 *P* 1, 232–3.

24 Flanagan, in his chapter on James in *The Science of the Mind*, takes a different view.

25 *P* 1, Chapter on Mind-Dust Theory. Cf. Chapter 7 below.

26 *P* 1, 236.

27 *APU* 278. There is also a revealing claim at 279 on 'Green's intellectualism'.

28 Ayer, op. cit. 305–8, identifies certain basic 'E-statements' (statements of basic experience) as those which 'fit the data' but 'do not go beyond the data'. James's rejection of such an 'intellectualist' atomism makes it unlikely that he had Ayer's aim in view.

29 *P* 1, 237.

30 *SPP* 199. James's conviction goes with his emphasis on what he called 'overtones', 'haloes', or 'fringes' of experienced items, e.g. at *P* 1,281,1,472–3, 1,477, *TMOT* 234-5. James thought that the doctrine of such fringes could resolve the traditional problem of universals, and it was, perhaps, for this reason, and in connection with his own account of 'family resemblance', that Wittgenstein shows such interest in it. Wittgenstein, however, probably thought James's account of understanding in these terms was too psychological. The two doctrines have this in common, that they both allow for vagueness in the ascription of terms.

31 *P* 1, 242–4.

32 *P* 1, 336.

33 *P* 1, 365.

34 *P* 1, 401.

35 I offer some explanation of this view in Chapter 7.

36 *P* 1 292.

37 David Hume, *Treatise*, ed. Selby-Bigge, OUP, 255–262.

38 Ibid. 255.

39 *P* 1, 400–1.

40 *P* 1, 340–1.

41 *P* 1, 340–1.

42 *ERE* 37.

43 *P* 1, 342.

44 *P* 1, 337.

45 *P* 1, 338.

46 *P* 1, 339.

47 *P* 1, 340.

48 This is not the only, or even the most important, difference between James and Hume. James thought that the reassurance could be adequately provided by the recognition of the conjunctive relation of appropriation, which Hume's atomist account could not accommodate.

49 *P* 1, 373. 'Alterations of memory are either losses or false recollections. In either case the *me* is changed . . . These losses of memory are a normal incident of extreme old age and the person's *me* shrinks in the ratio of the facts that have disappeared.'

50 Ayer, *The Origins of Pragmatism*, 268.

51 Ibid., 280–281.

52 *P* 1, 331–2.

53 *P* 1, 330.

54 *P* 1, 340–1.

55 *P* 1, 336. 'There is no other identity than this in the stream of subjective consciousness . . . Its parts differ . . . but they are knit in these two ways; if either way of knitting disappears the *sense* of unity departs.' (My emphasis). See also *P* 1 334.

56 *P* 1 292.

57 D Parfit, *Reasons and Persons*. OUP, 1984, Part III, Chs. 10 and 11.

58 Ibid. 206.

59 There is, however, some doubt about the kind of reductionist Parfit is. It seems likely that he is a weak, ontological, reductionist rather than a strong, analytic, reductionist, but his discussion of these positions is not clear. One difficulty is that some weak forms of reductionism may be quite compatible with common sense views, although Parfit gives the impression that he rejects some such views. Moreover he links reductionism with possible indeterminacies in our ascription of personal identity, even though a common sense account might also acknowledge such indeterminacy without necessarily endorsing reductionism. James's view, as I have outlined it, seems custom built to allow some indeterminacy, but he seems not to have wanted to reject common sense or to endorse strong reductionism. See note 62.

60 Ibid. Introduction x.

61 Ibid. 206.

62 This may be one respect in which Perfect differs from Parfit. S. Shoemaker in his review of Parfit's book, *Mind* July 1985 makes the point that Parfit does not make a clear distinction between conceptual and metaphysical necessity, but may intend to use the latter rather than the former.

63 Ibid. 199ff.

64 It may reasonably be asked how such considerations could settle the issue. But it is not my intention to claim that appeal to facts just dissolves or settles the issue, only that we would have a clearer picture of this case if more information was available. James would, I think, take the pragmatic line he takes elsewhere,

and argue that in such a case it is no use pretending that an appeal to some non-factual necessity is any more likely to settle such a problem. James's own account of a basic feature on which our sense of identity, and derivatively our third-person ascription of identity to others, rests is plainly not addressing such an issue.

65 Ibid. 200.

6 Pure Experience

1 *ERE* 60.
2 *ERE* 12, 126; *TMOT* 202.
3 *ERE* 17–18, 21.
4 Russell, *The Analysis of Mind*, 10.
5 In *Prag* 66 James says of his discussion of monism: 'Monism is vague, but pragmatically treated we pass from the vague to the definite, from the abstract to the concrete.' He also says of more mystical expressions of monism: 'We all have some ear for this monistic music.' *Prag* 74–6.
6 *ERE* 94.
7 *ERE* 4, 233, 137.
8 *ERE* 34ff.
9 *ERE* 152, 154.
10 *ERE* 3–4.
11 *ERE* 233.
12 *ERE* 233, 4.
13 *ERE* 26.
14 *ERE* 123, 93, 23.
15 *ERE* 94.
16 *ERE* 11–12.
17 *ERE* 76.
18 *ERE* 77.
19 *ERE* 8–9.
20 *ERE* 197, 198.
21 *ERE* 21, 23.
22 *ERE* 31, 33. At *ERE* 31 James writes: '"Intentionally" at any rate, and when the mental state is a vivid image, hotness and wetness are in it just as much as they are in the physical experience.'
23 *ERE* 78.
24 *ERE* 79, 81.
25 *ERE* 78.
26 *ERE* 84.
27 *ERE* 85.
28 Ayer, op. cit., 232.
29 James is rejecting two kinds of dualism. First he rejects Cartesian dualism, that is, a philosophical account of a strict heterogeneity between the mental and the physical, which, according to James, creates an unbridgeable chasm in standard 'representative' theories of perception. Second, in relation to 'pure experience', he rejects common sense, dualistic, ways of describing it, for it is to be understood as 'neutral' between the two categories. In the end this claim

turns the appeal to pure experience into a device in which, while inevitably using ordinary committed language, we nevertheless understand it non-committally. Ayer's interpretation, however, assumes that we may describe pure experience in the ordinary, committed, ways. See *ERE* 137.

30 *TMOT* 180. See also *TMOT* 202, note 5. 'The reader will observe that the text is written from the point of view of naif realism or common sense, and avoids raising the idealist controversy.' *TMOT* 200: 'In all this there is no self-transcendency in our mental images *taken by themselves*. They are one phenomenal fact; the tigers are another; and their pointing to the tigers is a perfectly commonplace intra-experiential relation, if you once grant a connecting world to be there.' These passages are taken from James's 1895 Presidential Address to the American Psychological Association, published in the *Psychological Review* as 'The Knowing of Things Together'. James later considerably abbreviated it for inclusion in *TMOT*, as 'The Tigers in India'. It was of the original address that James later said, in *APU*, that he there retracted his attack on 'mental chemistry' and 'fusing without a medium'. See Chapter 7 note 20.

31 This account of James's argument is supported by an unpublished note in the Houghton Library, B 4424, where James says: 'Pragmatically we both "mean" objects in the same place; and the only difficulty in accepting this which I can think of arises from the introjective prejudice that the world of each one of us is in his own skull. Why may the space I mean *not* be the space you mean? The burden of proof is on the denier'. Here James plainly uses the argument to put the onus on the philosophical sceptics. In 'The Thing and its Relations', *ERE*, James tackles what he takes to be the central argument against him, deriving from Bradley's view of relations in *Appearance and Reality*. The central claim, which James convicts of vicious abstractionism, is the idea that no single thing can enter into two different relations.

32 *ERE* 132.

33 *TMOT* 192 note 8, *ERE* 6–8.

34 *ERE* 133.

35 *P* 1 226.

36 Wittgenstein, *Philosophical Investigations*, 304.

37 *TMOT* 183–5. *APU* 229.

38 *ERE* 58, 67.

39 *TMOT* 199-200. *ERE* 28, 62ff. *TMOT* 179ff.

40 *ERE* 61. See also on 'substitute theorising' *P* 1 Chapter XII.

41 *APU* 216–220. James did not wish to replace an exclusive stress on abstract concepts with an exclusive stress on sense experience. Like Kant he recognised the need for both, for example in the claim noted earlier that the marriage of fact and theory was endlessly fertile. In another passage, *SPP* 74, James wrote: 'Perception is solely of the here and now, conception is of the like and unlike, of the future and of the past . . . But this map of what surrounds the present, like all maps, is only a surface; its features are but abstract signs and symbols of things that are in themselves concrete bits of sensible experience. We see that for some purposes the one, and for some purposes the other, has the higher value. Who can decide off-hand which is absolutely better, to live or to understand life? We must do both alternately and a man can no more limit

himself to either than a pair of scissors can cut with a single one of its blades.'
This is James's version of Kant's more concise 'Thoughts without content are
empty; intuitions without concepts are blind.' *Critique of Pure Reason*, B 76.

42 *ERE* 70.

43 James comments in this way on 'mirroring' at *P* 2, 618. We are perhaps not
inclined to treat a computer simulation of a hurricane as somehow more real
than, or a competitor to, the hurricane itself.

44 *ERE* 153.

45 *TMOT* 193–4.

46 *TMOT* 190.

47 *TMOT* 198.

48 *TMOT* 186.

49 See also *P* 1 221.

50 *TMOT* 185 note.

51 James considers this argument in connection with Mill at *P* 1 471.

52 *ERE* 223.

53 This is James's extended polemic against Bradley in 'The Thing and its
Relations', *ERE*. James summarises the attack later in *APU* 220, where he says:
'In Mr. Bradley's difficulty in seeing how sugar can be sweet intellectualism
outstrips itself and becomes openly a sort of verbalism. Sugar is just sugar and
sweet is just sweet; neither is the other; nor can the word "is" ever be
understood to join any subject to its predicate rationally. Nothing "between"
things can connect them, for "between" is just that third thing "between", and
would need itself to be connected to the first and second things by two still
finer betweens, and so on ad infinitum.'

54 Ayer, op. cit., 302–3. The grounds I offer for querying Ayer's phenomenalistic
account of James's 'pure experience' may have been anticipated by Chakrabarti and Madden, in their paper in the *Peirce Society Transactions*, but I have
been unable to find a copy of their paper.

55 R. Walker 'Gassendi and Scepticism', in *The Skeptical Tradition*, ed. Myles
Burnyeat, 334, says, 'the perceptual judgments that the ordinary man makes
about the stick or the tower are bound to be true, if they accord with the
majority, or with the claims of normal people under normal circumstances (or
something of the kind; the details of this phenomenalistic aspect of his thought
are not worked out).'

7   *Philosophical Psychology*

1 *P* 2, 212ff.

2 *P* Preface v–vi.

3 *P* 1, 184–5.

4 *P* 1, 218–220.

5 *P* 1, 185.

6 *P* 1, 180.

7 *SPP* Ch. 1, 100–101, *Prag* 52, *Ps* 461.

8 *P* Preface vi.

9 James discusses and criticises the Weber-Fechner 'law' in *P* 1, 533ff.

10 *Ps* 467–8.

11 *P* 1, 4.

12 *P* 1, 216.

13 *P* 1, 1.

14 *ERE* 36. In a manuscript version of his talks to teachers James says: 'I have taken the modern standpoint of psychology and regarded man as a machine; for this science that is the most fruitful point of view, but I don't believe it is all. It must be supplemented by metaphysics. Unite (this method) with love for the machine and you get a perfect teacher.' B 4537.

15 *P* 1, 130-2.

16 Russell, *The Analysis of Mind*, 27.

17 These related notions of 'emergence', of 'novelty', and of 'chance' formed the essence of what James called 'tychism', a term he took from Peirce. Later he indicated a preference for a doctrine he called 'synechism', which he took from Bergson. James was not very precise about these doctrines, and I have preferred to concentrate on their cash-value, in such discussions as those of free-will. James admitted differences between his own understanding of tychism and that of Peirce, saying that the latter had to do with the logic of probability and statistics, while his own version simply provided a niche for moral freedom. He thought that synechism provided a better way of 'saving novelty' and identified it, obscurely, as the claim that 'the flux of reality escapes the logic of identity'. The claim has, however, an obvious reference to James's 'conjunctive relations' and his rejection of Bradley's 'intellectualist logic'. See *APU* appendix, and Perry *TCWJ*.

18 See references in Chapter 6.

19 *Ps* 279.

20 *Psychological Review*, 1895; *APU* 184ff., 286ff. The Psychological Review article, 'The Knowing of Things Together', is important in the light of James's later apparent recantation of his attack on 'psychic chemistry'. But in that article James is less than decisive in any rejection of the earlier attack, and the same is true also of his provisos about the earlier position in *APU*. In the article James relates that issue to the wider question whether you can keep metaphysics and epistemology out of psychology. He implies that he took this view in the *Principles* but no longer does. He goes on: 'That we do know things singly and together: That states of consciousness are the vehicles of that knowledge; and depend on brain-states. . . . I thought that a natural science of psychology might legitimately confine itself to tracing the functional relations of these three sorts of facts, and ascertaining what sorts of bodily states are the condition when the states of mind know determinate things and groups of things. Most states of mind can be designated only by what they are thoughts of . . .'. This shows the importance attached to brain-states in explaining mental phenomena, and a beginning recognition of 'intentional' factors in identifying psychological states. James shows a puzzlement about the conflicts in these factors, for example, that the former seem to involve physical causal mechanisms while the latter do not. He further indicates this puzzlement in the conclusion: 'Not till you have dropped the old phrases, so absurd or so empty, of ideas 'self-compounding' or 'united by a spiritual principle' . . . not till you have in your turn succeeded in some such long enquiry into conditions as the one I have just failed in; not till you have laid bare more of the nature of that

altogether unique kind of complexity in unity which mental states involve, not till then . . . will psychology reach any real benefit from the conciliatory spirit of which I have done what I can to set an example.' All of this was excised from the later version in *TMOT*. I do not think that such claims are a rejection of his earlier views so much as an expression of bewilderment and a challenge to find some alternative account. The argument in *APU* is more obscure, for James is there concerned not so much with psychology as with the religious belief that our individual minds might form part of some collective, absolute, mind. He thinks that his earlier attack on the compounding of mental states presents an obstacle to that religious view, and so seeks to qualify its implications. Despite that intention, however, he rehearses the earlier, familiar, objections to psychic chemistry with considerable force. In the end the suggestion is like that made in *VRE* that we cannot *exclude* such religious ideas, any more than we can finally reject appeals to a supernatural, 'unseen order'. See Chapter 9.

21 *APU* 288ff.; *VRE* 230ff, 477ff.
22 *P* 1, 162.
23 *APU* 189.
24 James refers to such triggering mechanisms at *P* 2, 529, for example.
25 *P* 1, 158–9.
26 This is another respect in which James's views match those of Grice in 'Method in Philosophical Psychology'. For Grice also takes the view that mental terms should be viewed as theoretical rather than observational terms. Grice, however, makes his view of theoretical terms clearer by appealing to Ramsey sentences to introduce them.
27 *P* 1, 157, 160.
28 In Ryle's *The Concept of Mind*, London, 1949.
29 *P* 2, 112–3.
30 *P* 1, 5, 129.
31 *P* 2, 232–3.
32 *P* 1, 177.
33 *P* 1, 178.
34 *P* 1, 181.
35 *P* 1, 182.
36 *P* 1, 182.
37 *P* 1, 401.
38 *P* 1, 185ff.
39 *P* 1, 189.
40 Wittgenstein, *Philosophical Investigations*, 104.
41 *P* 1, 196–7.
42 See Chomsky, Goodman, and Putnam in J. Searle ed. *Philosophy of Language*, OUP, 1968.
43 The contrast between 'de re' and 'de dicto' ways of identifying belief contents has been made in a number of different ways. See A. Woodfield ed. *Thought and Object*.
44 J. Fodor, 'Methodological Solipsism considered as a Research Strategy in Cognitive Psychology', *Behavioural and Brain Sciences* 3. See also A. Woodfield, op. cit.
45 Watson, op. cit., 140.

46 See W. Lyons, *Emotion*, CUP, 1980.

47 *P* 2, 442.

48 *P* 2, 449.

49 *P* 2, 449–50.

50 *P* 2, 450–1.

51 The case is one in which James as a child saw a horse bled and played with the blood in a bucket until suddenly overcome by an 'emotional' reaction.

52 *P* 2, 451–2.

53 *P* 2, 451–2.

54 *P* 2, 452.

55 *ERE* 34ff.

8 Meliorism, Morality, and Religion

1 *APU* 313–4.

2 James is not totally hostile even in the *Principles*. Cf. *P* 2, 291–2. Also *P* 2, 625.

3 *VRE* 446–7.

4 *VRE* 455–6. See also 'The Energies of Men' in McDermott, op. cit., 638.

5 *P* 2 Ch. XXVI; *SPP* Ch. IX–XIII.

6 *TWB* 145ff.

7 Both in 'On a Certain Blindness' and 'What Makes a Life Significant?' James pleads for a certain relativity and tolerance with respect to others' beliefs, on the ground that what gives these their 'zest' and 'significance' may easily elude the uninitiated onlooker. The former takes its cue from an R.L. Stevenson story 'The Lantern Bearers', from *Across the Plains*, in which a ritual, carrying a bull's eye lantern, is invested with a special significance in a Scottish childhood. James talks of the 'stupidity and injustice of our opinions so far as they deal with the significance of alien lives'. Of what he calls a 'mystic sense of hidden meaning' he says 'It absolutely forbids us to be forward in pronouncing on the meaninglessness of forms of existence other than our own; and it commands us to tolerate, respect, and indulge those whom we see harmlessly interested and happy in their own ways, however unintelligible these may be to us.' There is a strand of relativism in James's views, though not one incompatible with a robust realism. In *TMOT* 196 he quotes with approval Thackeray's remark 'My friend, two different universes walk about under your hat and mine.' But he was also highly critical of Rickert's philosophical relativism, *Prag* 113 note 1.

8 *Prag* 20–22.

9 *P* 1 125.

10 *TWB* 25. 'Faith in a fact can help create the fact'.

11 *VRE* 138.

12 James wrote this in a letter to Bradley of July 16, 1904, published in *Mind* July, 1966. J. Kenna 'Ten Unpublished Letters from James to Bradley'.

13 Mussolini was reported in the Boston Evening Globe, April 25, 1926, as saying: 'James taught me that action should be judged by results rather than by its doctrinary basis. I learned from James that faith in action and that ardent will to live and fight to which Fascism owes a large part of its success'. James came third to Sorel and Nietzsche in Mussolini's ranking.

14 *VRE* 18, 444–6, 502f.

15 See note 4 above.

16 *P* 2 571f.

17 *P* 2 573.

18 *P* 2 573. Freedom's first deed should be to affirm itself.

19 *TWB* 149.

20 *TWB* 151. Elsewhere James speaks of 'absolute novelties, unmediated begin-
nings, gifts, chance, freedom, acts of faith', *SPP* 156, to characterise indeterminism. It is in these terms that he tends to describe his 'tychism'. See note 17,
Chapter 7.

21 *TWB* 181.

22 *TWB* 147.

23 Randomness might be expressed in other ways. James does not specify exactly
what he means, and equi-probability is the simplest case.

24 *SPP* 213.

25 *TWB* 179.

26 *TWB* 159.

27 *TWB* 160–1, 178.

28 *TWB* 171.

29 *TWB* 174.

30 *TWB* 174–5. James, like Peirce, often contrasted 'restlessness' with a certain
'fixity' or 'stability' of belief.

31 *TWB* 175.

32 *TWB* 179.

33 Unpublished material from the James archives, Houghton Library, Harvard.
B 4469–70.

34 *TWB* 184.

35 *TWB* 197. 'They ("good", "bad" etc) mean no absolute natures independent
of personal support – no foothold or anchorage in Being apart from the
existence of actually living minds.' *TWB* 193. 'The real superiority or authority
postulated by the philosopher to reside in some of the opinions cannot be
explained by any abstract 'nature of things' existing independently to the
concrete thinkers themselves with their ideals'.

36 *TWB* 199–201.

37 *TWB* 200.

38 *TWB* 205.

39 *TWB* 204.

40 *TWB* 198.

41 *TWB* 210.

42 *TWB* 213.

43 *TWB* 212.

44 *TWB* 214.

45 *VRE* 360. James there admits that utopian socialists might generate a similar
motivation.

9 *Voluntarily Adopted Faiths*

1 *TWB* 2.
2 W.K. Clifford, *Lectures and Essays*, Macmillan, 1879, 177.
3 Ibid. 183.
4 Ibid. 184.
5 *TWB* 'robustious pathos' is what James calls it.
6 *TWB* 9.
7 *TWB* 18.
8 *TWB* 20–1. It is worth noting the realism implicit in James's remark here.
9 *TWB* 3.
10 B. Williams, *Problems of the Self*, CUP, 1973, 'Deciding to Believe'.
11 Ibid. 148.
12 James's provisos about the relation between moral beliefs and some corresponding reality were noted in the previous Chapter. Note 35.
13 *TWB* 23–5.
14 *TWB* 29 and note.
15 *TWB* 28.
16 *Prag* 40, *APU* 248, *VRE* 122, 377, 334.
17 Acceptability would have to be defined otherwise than as 'acceptability as true'. S. Blackburn, *Spreading the Word*, Chs 5 and 6, OUP, 1985, comments on this in a Jamesian way.
18 *TWB* 208, and 210.
19 *TWB* 194, 197.
20 *TWB* 195, 199, 213.
21 *P* 2 638. See R.M. Hare, 'Supervenience', and J. Kim, 'Weak Supervenience' for examples of recent use of the term.
22 *VRE* 242.
23 James frequently likened the excesses of metaphysical thinking to nitrous oxide intoxication. An unusual acquaintance called Benjamin Paul Blood drew his attention to the similarity.
24 *VRE* 388. Since James's pragmatic view of truth in any case forbids a premature closing of our accounts with reality this claim might be taken to add little to that view.
25 *VRE* 422–3.
26 *VRE* 118–225.
27 *VRE* 515.
28 *VRE* 518.
29 *VRE* 519.
30 *VRE* 523.
31 See, for example, Hempel, *Aspects of Scientific Explanation*, 101ff. and Quine, 'Two Dogmas of Empiricism'. The controversy goes back to Ayer's formulation of a verification criterion for meaning in *Language, Truth, and Logic*, and Church's criticism of it.
32 Later, in *SPP* 58–65, James makes an explicit distinction between the 'content' and the 'function' of thoughts. Some such distinction would be useful in *VRE*.

33 James gives a definition of religion which includes a supernatural reference intentionally in its content at *VRE* 31. '. . . the feelings, acts, and experiences of individual men in their solitude so far as they apprehend themselves to stand in relation to whatever they may consider to be divine'.

34 I use this term with reluctance, although it has become widely used. One difficulty with it is that it covers so many different kinds of case which are not usually distinguished under the general title of 'undecidability'. In this context, however, it is used to indicate just one kind of undecidability, namely that which attends supernatural claims.

35 *VRE* 458.

36 James makes such references to an unseen order at *VRE* 53, 485, 576, for example. 'Were one asked to characterise the life of religion in the broadest terms possible one might say that it consists of the belief that there is an unseen order, and that our supreme good lies in adjusting ourselves harmoniously thereto'.

37 At *VRE* 498–9 James says: 'Private and personal phenomena are realities. . . . Religion is individualistic and so treated . . .' See also note 32 above.

38 *VRE* 436.

10   Pragmatism and Systematic Philosophy

1 M. Knight, *William James*, Introduction 50.

2 *The Nation*, September 3, 1910.

3 Wittgenstein's argument is in *Philosophical Investigations* paragraph 202, and 243ff. A different interpretation of the argument has been recently provided by Saul Kripke, *Wittgenstein on Rules and Private Language*, but Baker and Hacker, *Scepticism, Rules and Language* have argued convincingly that Kripke's account distorts Wittgenstein's own views.

4 See Chapter 5.

5 If this point is not made then Wittgenstein may be represented as canvassing a scepticism about memory in general, when it seems clear that he did not intend this.

6 See also the references to Grice's philosophical psychology in Chapter 4. James says this in a letter to Stumpf in the James archive, A 3778–3811.

7 Wittgenstein, *Tractatus Logico-Philosophicus* 4, 1121.

8 Dummett has been the primary source of these views. See his *Truth and Other Enigmas*.

9 Dummett, *Truth and Other Enigmas*, 455.

Bibliography

Allen, G.W., *William James: a Biography*. New York, 1967.

Altshuler, B., 'Peirce's Theory of Truth and the Revolt against Realism'. *Transactions of the Peirce Society*, Winter 1981.

Anderson, A.J., 'The Worst Kind of Melancholy'. *Harvard Library Bulletin*. October, 1982.

Austin, J.L., *Philosophical Papers*. Oxford, 1961.

Ayer, A.J., *The Origins of Pragmatism: Studies in the Philosophy of Charles Sanders Peirce, and William James*. London, 1968.

Baker, G.P. and Hacker, P.M.S., *Language, Sense, and Nonsense*. Oxford, 1985.

Baker, G.P. and Hacker, P.M.S., *Scepticism, Rules, and Language*. Oxford, 1985.

Barzun, J., *A Stroll with William James*. New York, 1983.

Beard, R.W., 'The Will to Believe Revisited'. *Ratio*, December, 1966.

Blackburn, S., *Spreading the Word*. Oxford, 1984.

Bradley, *Appearance and Reality*. Oxford, 1893.

Brennan, B.P., *The Ethics of William James*. New York, 1961.

Brodsky, G.M., 'The Pragmatic Movement'. *Review of Metaphysics*. December, 1971.

Burch, R., 'James and the "New" Theory of Reference'. *Transactions of the Peirce Society*. Fall, 1979.

Capek, M., 'The Reappearance of the Self in the last Philosophy of William James'. *Philosophical Review*, 1953.

Chakrabarti, C. and Madden, E.H., 'James's "Pure Experience" versus Ayer's "Weak Phenomenalism" '. *Transactions of the Peirce Society*. Winter, 1976.

Chatterjee, S.C., 'The Pragmatist Theory of Truth and Error'. *Philosophical Quarterly of India*. Vol. 19.

Chomsky, N., *Selected Readings*, ed. J.P.B. Allen and P. Van Buren. Oxford, 1971.

Clifford, W.K., *Lectures and Essays*. London, 1879.

Davidson, D., *Inquiries into Truth and Interpretation*. Oxford, 1984.

Davis, S.T., 'Wishful Thinking and "The Will To Believe" '. *Transactions of the Peirce Society*. Fall, 1972.

Dooley, P.K., 'The Nature of Belief: The Proper Context for James's "The Will to

Believe" '. *Transactions of the Peirce Society*. Summer, 1972.

Dooley, P.K., *Pragmatism as Humanism: The Philosophy of William James*. Chicago, 1974.

Dummett, M., *Frege: Philosophy of Language*. London, 1975.

Dummett, M., *Truth and Other Enigmas*. London, 1978.

Field, H., 'Logic, Meaning, and Conceptual Role'. *Journal of Philosophy*, 1977.

Field, H., 'Mental Representation'. *Erkenntniss*. Vol. 13, 1978.

Fisch, M.H., 'Alexander Bain and the Genealogy of Pragmatism'. *Journal of the History of Ideas*, 1954.

Fisch, M.H., 'Was There a Metaphysical Club in Cambridge: A Postscript'. *Transactions of the Peirce Society*. Spring, 1981.

Flanagan, O.J., *The Science of the Mind*. Cambridge, 1984.

Flournoy, T., *The Philosophy of William James*. New York, 1917.

Fodor, J., 'Methodological Solipsism considered as a Research Strategy in Cognitive Psychology'. *Behavioural and Brain Sciences*. Vol. 3, 1980.

Ford, M.P., 'A Realistic Understanding of James's Theory of Truth'. *Transactions of the Peirce Society*. Winter, 1980.

Ford, M.P., *William James's Philosophy: A New Perspective*. Amherst, 1982.

Gellner, E., 'Pragmatism and the Importance of being Earnest'. In *Pragmatism Its Sources and Prospects*, ed. P.M. Zeltner. South Carolina, 1981.

Gochet, P., *Quine en Perspective*. Paris, 1978.

Gotlind, E., *Three Theories of Emotion: Some Views on Philosophical Method*. Lund, 1958.

Gould, J.A., 'R.B. Perry on the Origin of American and European Pragmatism'. *Journal of the History of Philosophy*. October, 1970.

Grice, H.P., 'Meaning'. *Philosophical Review*. July, 1957.

Grice, H.P., 'Utterer's Meaning, Sentence-meaning, and Word-meaning'. *Foundations of Language*. Vol. 4, 1968.

Grice, H.P., 'Method in Philosophical Psychology'. *Proceedings of the American Philosophical Association*, 1975.

Guttenplan, S. (ed.), *Mind and Language*. Oxford, 1975.

Haack, S., 'The Pragmatist Theory of Truth'. *British Journal for the Philosophy of Science*. Vol. 27, 1976.

Haack, S., 'Pragmatism and Ontology: Peirce and James'. *Revue Internationale de Philosophie*. Vol 31, 1977.

Hare, R.M., 'Supervenience'. *Proceedings of the Aristotelian Society*. Supplementary Volume, 1984.

Hare, P.H. and Kauber, P., 'The Right and Duty to Will to Believe'. *Canadian Journal of Philosophy*. December, 1974.

Hare, P.H. and Madden, E.H., 'William James, Dickinson Miller and C.J. Ducasse on the Ethics of Belief'. *Transactions of the Peirce Society*. Fall, 1968.

Hartshorne, C., 'James's Empirical Pragmatism'. *American Journal of Theology and Philosophy*. Vol. 1, 1980.

Hertz, R.A., 'James and Moore: Two Perspectives on Truth'. *Journal of the History of Philosophy*. April, 1971.

Hookway, C., *Peirce*. London, 1985.

Johanson, A.E., ' "The Will to Believe" and the Ethics of Belief'. *Transactions of the Peirce Society*. Summer, 1975.

Jubin, B., ' "The Spatial Quale": A Corrective to James's Radical Empiricism'. *Journal of the History of Philosophy*. April, 1977.

Kauber, P., 'The Foundations of James's Ethics of Belief'. *Ethics*. January, 1974.

Kaufman, M.R., 'William James's Letters to a Young Pragmatist'. *Journal of the History of Ideas*. July, 1963.

Kenna, J.C., 'Ten Unpublished Letters from James to Bradley'. *Mind*. July, 1966.

Kennedy, G., 'Pragmatism, Pragmaticism, and the Will to Believe – a Reconsideration'. *Journal of Philosophy*. July, 1958.

Kim, J., 'Weak Supervenience'. *American Philosophical Quarterly*, 1982.

Knight, M. (ed.), *William James*. London. 1950.

Lee, H.N., 'Pragmatism and a Behavioural Theory of Meaning'. *Journal of the History of Philosophy*. October, 1976.

Levinson, H.S., *Science, Metaphysics, and the Chance of Salvation: An Interpretation of the Thought of William James*. Missoula, 1978.

Levinson, H.S., *The Religious Investigations of William James*. North Carolina, 1981.

Levinson, R.B., 'Sigwart's "Logik" and William James'. *Journal of the History of Ideas*. October, 1947.

Lewis, H.A., 'Content and Community'. *Proceedings of the Aristotelian Society, Supplementary Volume*, 1985.

Loar, B., 'Ramsey's Theory of Belief and Truth'. In *Prospects for Pragmatism*, ed. D.H. Mellor. Cambridge, 1980.

Loar, B., *Mind and Meaning*. Cambridge, 1981.

Long, D.A., 'Kant's Pragmatic Horizon'. *American Philosophical Quarterly*. October, 1982.

Lovejoy, A.O., *The Thirteen Pragmatisms, and Other Essays*. London, 1963.

Lyons, W., *Emotion*. Cambridge, 1980.

MacDermott, J.J. (ed.), *The Writings of William James*. New York, 1967.

Macleod, W.J., 'James's Will to Believe Revisited'. *Personalist*. April, 1967.

Mavrodes, G.I., 'James and Clifford on "The Will to Believe" '. *Personalist*. April, 1963.

Mellor, D.H. (ed.), *Prospects for Pragmatism*. Cambridge, 1980.

Meyers, R.G., 'Meaning and Metaphysics in James'. *Philosophy and Phenomenological Research*. March, 1971.

Meyers, R.G., 'Ayer on Pragmatism'. *Metaphilosophy*. January, 1975.

Miller, D.S., 'James's Doctrine of "The Right to Believe" '. *Philosophical Review*. November, 1942.

Miller, D.S. and Moore, J.S., 'James's Doctrine of "The Right to Believe" '. *Philosophical Review*. January, 1943.

Moore, E.C., *William James*. New York, 1965.

Moore, G.E., *Philosophical Papers*. London, 1959.

Morris, C.W., *The Pragmatic Movement in American Philosophy*. New York, 1970.

Mulvaney, R.J. and Zeltner, P.M. (eds), *Pragmatism its Sources and Prospects*. South Carolina, 1981.

Murphey, M.G., 'Kant's Children: The Cambridge Pragmatists'. *Transactions of the Peirce Society*. Winter, 1968.

Myers, G.E., 'William James on Time Perception'. *Philosophy of Science*. Summer, 1971.

Nathanson, S.L., 'Nonevidential Reasons for Belief: A Jamesian View'. *Philosophy and Phenomenological Research*. June, 1982.

Newman, J., 'The Faith of Pragmatists'. *Sophia*. April, 1974.

Pancheri, L.U., 'James, Lewis, and the Pragmatic A Priori'. *Transactions of the Peirce Society*. Summer, 1971.

Parfit, D., *Reasons and Persons*. Oxford, 1984.

Parry, W.T., 'Are Things what they are Known As?'. *Philosophy and Phenomenological Research*. December, 1955.

Peirce, C.S., *Collected Papers*. ed. C. Hartshorne and P. Weiss. Cambridge, 1934.

Perkins, M., 'Notes on the Pragmatic Theory of Truth'. *Journal of Philosophy*. August, 1952.

Perry, R.B., *The Thought and Character of William James*. 2 Vols. Cambridge, 1935.

Perry, R.B., *The Thought and Character of William James: Briefer Version*. Cambridge, 1948.

Quine, W.V.O., *From a Logical Point of View*. Cambridge, 1953.

Quine, W.V.O., *Word and Object*. Cambridge, 1960.

Quine, W.V.O., 'The Pragmatist's Place in Empiricism', in M. Philip (ed.), *Pragmatism, Its Sources, and Prospects,* South Carolina, 1981.

Ramsey, F.P., *Foundations,* ed. D.H. Mellor. London, 1978.

Rorty, R., *The Consequences of Pragmatism*. Brighton, 1982.

Rosenthal, S.B., 'Recent Perspectives on American Pragmatism: Parts I and II'. *Transactions of the Peirce Society*. Spring and Summer, 1974.

Roth, J.K., 'Freedom and the Moral Life: The Ethics of William James'. *Philosophy*, 1969.

Russell, B., 'Transatlantic Truth'. *Albany Review*. January, 1908.

Russell, B., 'Pragmatism'. *Edinburgh Review*. April, 1909.

Russell, B., *The Analysis of Mind*. London 1921.

Russell, B., *Logic and Knowledge*, ed. R.C. Marsh. London, 1956.

Ryle, G., *The Concept of Mind*. London, 1949.

Scheffler, I., *Four Pragmatists*. New York, 1974.

Schwehn, M.R., 'James and the Life of the Mind'. *Harvard Library Bulletin*. October, 1982.

Scott, F.D., 'Peirce and Schiller and their Correspondence'. *Journal of the History of Philosophy*. July, 1973.

Shouse, J.B., 'William James and David Hume: A Comparison'. *Journal of the History of Ideas*. October, 1952.

Singer, M.G., 'The Pragmatic Use of Language and The Will to Believe'. *American Philosophical Quarterly*. January, 1971.

Smith, J.E., *The Spirit of American Philosophy*. New York, 1963.

Smith, J.E., 'Radical Empiricism'. *Proceedings of the Aristotelian Society*, 1965.

Smith, J.E. *Purpose and Thought*. New Haven, 1978.

Smith, J.W., 'Pragmatism, Realism, and Positivism in the United States'. *Mind*. April, 1952.

Sprigge, T.L.S., 'James, Santayana, Tarski, and Pragmatism'. In *Pragmatism and Purpose,* ed. L.W. Sumner. Toronto, 1981.

Suckiel, E.K., 'Adequate Evidence and "The Will to Believe" '. *Transactions of the Peirce Society*. Fall, 1979.

Suckiel, E.K., *The Pragmatic Philosophy of William James*. Notre Dame, 1982.

Taylor, E., 'James on Psycho-pathology'. *Harvard Library Bulletin*. October, 1982.

Thayer, H.S., *Meaning and Action: A Critical History of Pragmatism*. Indianapolis, 1968.

Thayer, H.S., 'James and the Theory of Truth'. *Transactions of the Peirce Society*. Winter, 1980.

Tibbetts, P., 'The Philosophy of Science of William James'. *Personalist*. Summer, 1971.

Wernham, J.C.S., 'Did James have an Ethic of Belief'. *Canadian Journal of Philosophy*. June, 1976.

Wernham, J.C.S., 'Ayer's James'. *Religious Studies*. Summer, 1976.

Wiener, P., *Evolution and the Founders of Pragmatism*. Cambridge, 1949.

Wild, J.D., *The Radical Empiricism of James*. New York, 1969.

Wilkins, B.T., 'James, Dewey, and Hegelian Idealism'. *Journal of the History of Ideas*. June, 1956.

Williams, B., *Problems of the Self*. Cambridge, 1973.

Wilshire, B.W., *William James and Phenomenology*. Indiana, 1968.

Wilshire, B.W., 'William James, Phenomenology, and Pragmatism: A Reply to Rosenthal'. *Transactions of the Peirce Society*. Winter, 1977.

Wittgenstein, L., *Philosophical Investigations*. Oxford, 1954.

Wittgenstein, L., *Remarks in the Philosophy of Psychology*. 2 Vols. Oxford, 1980.

Woodfield, A., *Thought and Object*. Oxford, 1980.

Index

221